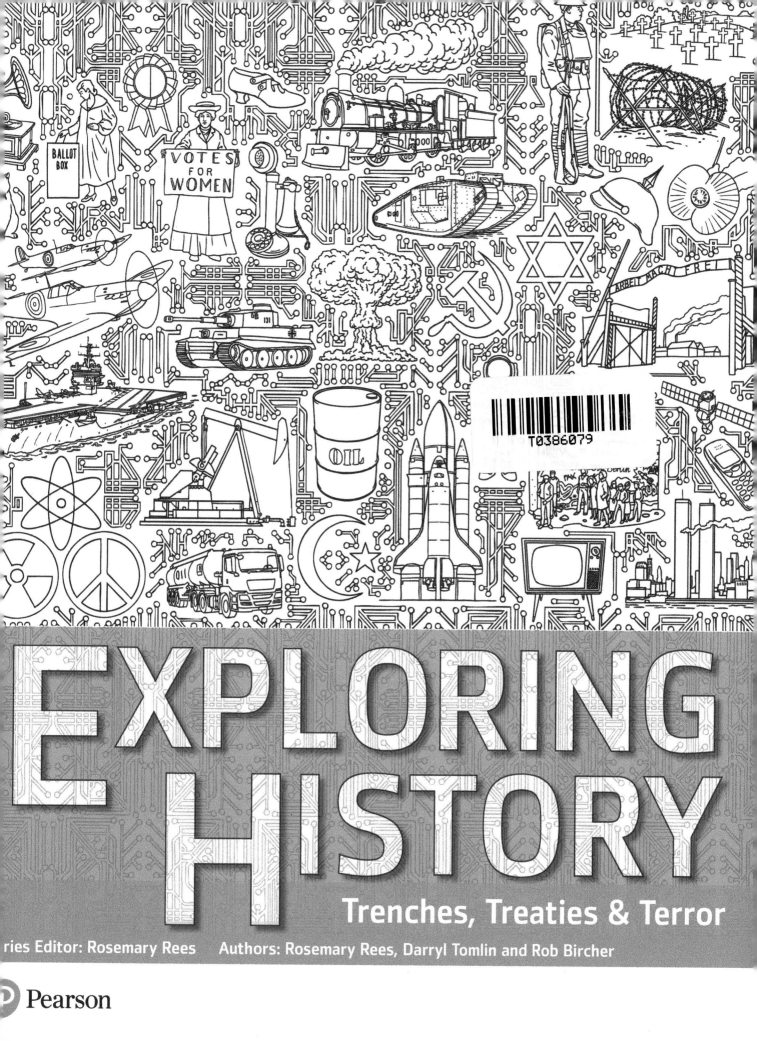

EXPLORING HISTORY

Trenches, Treaties & Terror

Series Editor: Rosemary Rees   Authors: Rosemary Rees, Darryl Tomlin and Rob Bircher

Pearson

Published by Pearson Education Limited, 80 Strand, London WC2R 0RL.

www.pearsonschoolsandfecolleges.co.uk

Text © Pearson Education Limited 2018
Series editor: Rosemary Rees
Designed by Poppy Marks, Pearson Education Limited
Typeset by Hart McLeod Ltd
Original illustrations © Pearson Education Limited 2018
Illustrated by KJA Artists Illustration Agency and Beehive Illustration
Cover design by Poppy Marks, Pearson Education Limited
Cover photo/illustration © 381Mike@kja-artists

The rights of Rosemary Rees, Rob Bircher and Darryl Tomlin to be identified as authors of this
work have been asserted by them in accordance with the Copyright, Designs and Patents Act 1988.

First published 2018

24
10 9 8 7 6

British Library Cataloguing in Publication Data
A catalogue record for this book is available from the British Library

ISBN 9781292218717

Websites
Pearson Education Limited is not responsible for the content of any external internet sites.
It is essential for tutors to preview each website before using it in class so as to ensure that the
URL is still accurate, relevant and appropriate. We suggest that tutors bookmark useful
websites and consider enabling students to access them through the school/college intranet.

Note from the publisher
Pearson has robust editorial processes, including answer and fact checks, to ensure the accuracy
of the content in this publication, and every effort is made to ensure this publication is free of
errors. We are, however, only human, and occasionally errors do occur. Pearson is not liable
for any misunderstandings that arise as a result of errors in this publication, but it is our
priority to ensure that the content is accurate. If you spot an error, please do contact us at
resourcescorrections@pearson.com so we can make sure it is corrected.

In order to ensure that the content in this book is accurate and to
the highest standard possible, Chapter 4 has been reviewed by the
Holocaust Educational Trust (www.het.org.uk).

Contents

How to use this book

This book is the third in a series of three designed to help you study history at Key Stage 3.

Book 3, *Trenches, Treaties & Terror*, looks at the period of history between 1861 and 2011 (see the timeline on pages 6–7).

The content has been carefully chosen to cover important background knowledge relevant to the Edexcel GCSE (9–1) History units. The book has depth, breadth and thematic topics to prepare you for the types of history you'll study at GCSE.

Features

As well as exciting history, the book is full of useful features to help you improve.

Enquiry questions

Every few weeks, you'll start looking at a new enquiry question. This will help you focus your learning within each chapter on a few key questions.

At the end of each enquiry, you'll find an activity that will help you to return to the enquiry question and reflect on what you have discovered.

Learning objectives

At the start of each section, you'll be set some learning objectives. These tell you what you should know and understand by the end of the section. You might cover the objectives in one or two lessons.

What do you think?

These questions give you the opportunity to show what you already know and think about what more you would like to discover about the topic.

Key terms

Where you see a word or phrase followed by an asterisk, like this: League of Nations*, you'll find a Key term box nearby that explains what the word or phrase means.

All the key terms are listed alphabetically in the Glossary at the end of the book.

Your turn!

Every few pages, you'll find a box containing activities designed to help check and embed knowledge and get you to think carefully about what you have studied. The activities may start with some simple questions, but they get more challenging as you work through them!

Checkpoints

These help you to check and reflect on your learning at the end of a section, reinforcing the knowledge and understanding you have gained and ensuring you are familiar with the basic ideas and skills.

> **What do you think?**
>
> How do wars begin?

> **Key term**
>
> **League of Nations*:**
> An international organisation that aimed to help prevent wars between countries, set up after the First World War.

Sources and interpretations

So you can really understand and explore this period of history, the book contains a lot of pictures and texts from these years, showing what people at the time said, thought or created. These are known as **sources** – you'll need to interrogate these to discover the past.

Source A: A photograph of 'flappers' in the USA in the 1920s.

Also included are extracts from the work of historians, and other reflections of the past like poems, plays and film, which show how modern people have interpreted historical events. These are known as **interpretations**.

You'll need to examine both sources and interpretations during your work on the history of this period.

> **Interpretation 2:** Written by Jesse Jackson, a campaigner for civil rights in the USA and a friend of Nelson Mandela. It was printed in the *Guardian*, a British leftwing newspaper, on 5 December 2013.
>
> Mandela was a transformational figure. To be a transformer is to plan, to have the vision to chart the course, the skills to carry it through. It is to have the courage of one's convictions, to sacrifice, to risk life and limb, to lay it all on the line. Mandela was a giant of immense and unwavering courage and moral authority. He chose reconciliation over retaliation. He changed the course of history.

Did you know?

These features contain interesting additional information that adds depth to your knowledge. Some are useful, some are just fun!

> **Did you know?**
>
> In pot-walloper boroughs, men could vote if they had a hearth big enough on which to boil a large pot of water.

What have you learned?

In the middle and at the end of each chapter you'll find pages designed to help you reflect on the chapter as a whole and think about what you have studied in a more analytical way.

There is also a **quick quiz** at the end of each chapter, ideal for checking your knowledge of the whole chapter. The answers are supplied at the end of the book.

Writing Historically

Alongside the 'What have you learned?' sections are pages to help you improve your writing skills. These include simple techniques you can use to help you write better, clearer and more focused answers to historical questions. Many of these pages embed skills you'll need for GCSE.

Pearson Progression Scale

The Pearson Progression Scale has been used to determine the difficulty of content as students progress through the course and to provide coherent differentiation. Where questions are aimed at a particular Step on the Pearson Progression Scale, we have added a small icon to indicate the Step. This gives an idea of how hard the question is – the higher the Step, the harder the question:

> **1** Look at Source B.
> **a** What message is the cartoonist giving readers of the magazine?
> **b** Is the interpretation of events in the Balkans correct? Write a short paragraph to explain your view.

We have used another icon to indicate where skills relevant to GCSE are being developed. This example indicates that the content is moving students towards being able to answer GCSE-style inference questions:

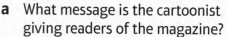

Inference questions

1861–2011 timeline

American Civil War
1861–1865

Second World W
1939–19

Franco-Prussian War
1870–1871

First World War
1914–1918

Wars

AD 1861

AD 1900

Events

1872
Ballot Act

1906
HMS Dreadnought
launched

1920
Creator of Sherlock
Holmes, Arthur Conan
Doyle, writes an article
claiming he has proof
that fairies exist!

1884
Third
Reform
Act

1912
The Titanic
sinks

1871
German states are
united into the
German Empire

1930
The Salt March is led
by Gandhi in India

1933
Hitler becomes
Chancellor of
Germany

1882
Married Women's
Property Act

1918
Representation of
the People Act: All
men over 21, and
some women over
30, given the vote

1867
Second
Reform
Act

1935
Nuremberg Laws
passed in Germany

1917
Balfour
Declaration

1936
Arab Revolt
begins

1938
Kristallnacht

1914
Franz Ferdinand
assassinated

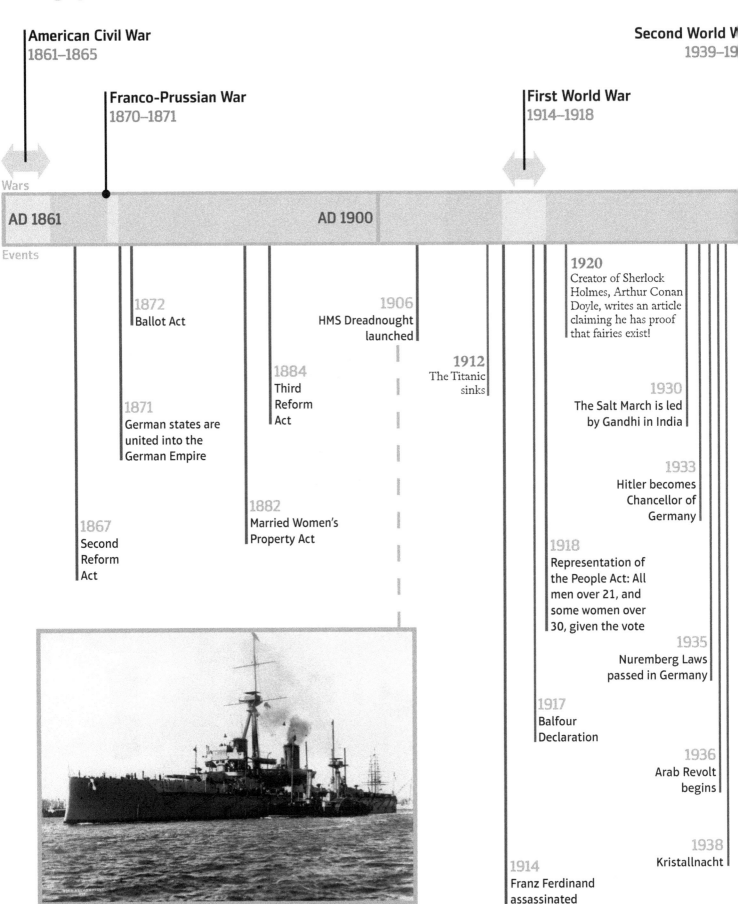

Arab–Israeli War
1948–1949

The Cold War
1945–1989

Second Gulf War/Iraq War
2003–2011

Korean War
1950–1953

Vietnam War
1955–1975

Iran–Iraq War
1980–1988

First Gulf War
1990–1991

AD 1950

AD 2000

AD 2011

1947
End of British mandate in Palestine

1969
Britain abolishes the death penalty

1967
Abortion law reform

1978
Iranian Revolution

2001
Terrorists attack the World Trade Center and other sites in the USA

1945
Two nuclear bombs dropped on Japan

1957
The Frisbee is invented

1969
Neil Armstrong becomes the first man to walk on the moon

1997
Google is used to search the internet for the first time

1956
Suez Crisis

1963
President Kennedy is assassinated in Dallas, Texas

1992
Poll tax reform

1986
Teachers in UK schools are banned from beating students when they misbehave

1955
The Montgomery Bus Boycott in America

1962
Cuban Missile Crisis

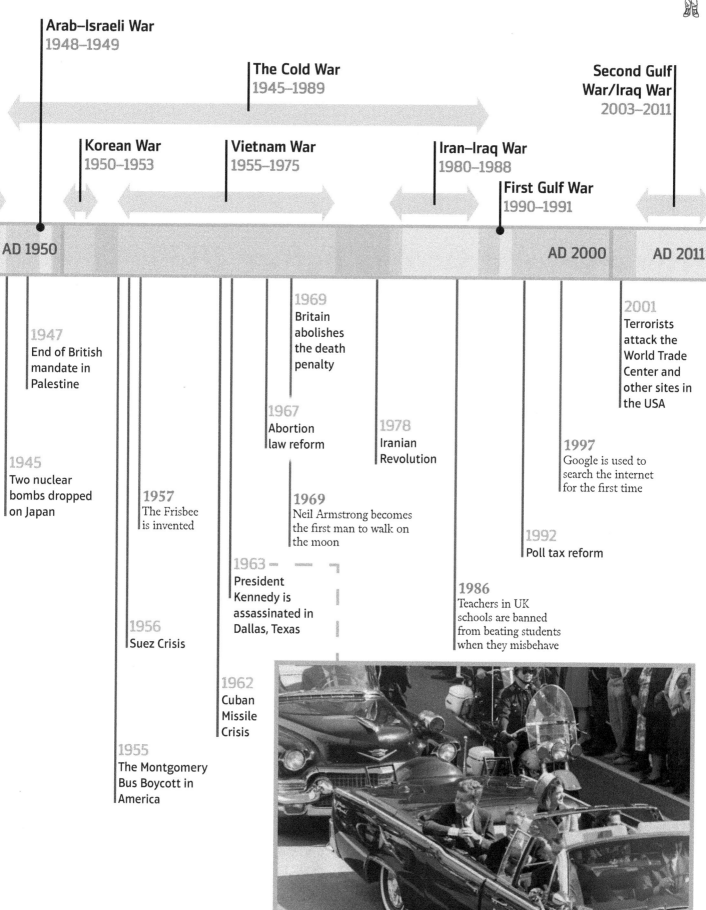

How democratic was Britain in the 19th century?

Industrialisation began in about 1750. People began migrating in large numbers from the countryside to the growing towns and cities. Manufacturing and industry became vital to Britain's prosperity. With these changes came new ideas about who should be involved in the government of Britain. In this section you will learn about:

- the pressures for change to the electoral system

- the growth of the idea of 'democracy'

- the impact of the Reform Acts of 1832, 1867 and 1884.

The electoral system before 1832

Learning objectives

- Learn about the ways in which the electoral system worked in the years before 1832 and what people at the time thought about it.
- Understand how the idea of democracy developed.

What do you think?

Who should be able to vote in general elections?

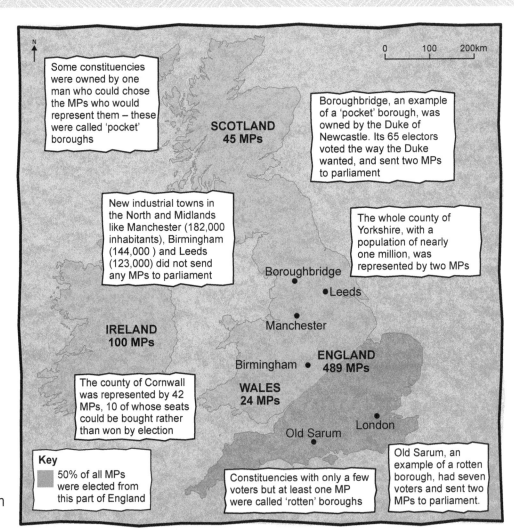

Figure 1.1: The electoral system before 1832, based on research by the historian Sir Lewis Namier.

Constituencies and the franchise

Britain was divided into two types of constituency*. Each **county** sent two Members of Parliament (MPs) to parliament. Many counties contained towns that were parliamentary **boroughs** because, in the past, they had been important. They, too, could elect two MPs. Whether a person could vote or not depended on where they lived and what they owned. In the counties, men could vote if they owned land or property worth more than £2 a year when rented out. The franchise* in boroughs varied a lot because it depended on ancient rights and customs. No women, living in either a county or a borough, were allowed to vote.

Source A: A picture painted in 1755 by William Hogarth. It is called *Chairing the Member* and shows celebrations in Oxfordshire after the election of an MP in 1754.

Key terms

Constituency*: An area represented by an MP.

Franchise*: Those who could vote in an area.

Did you know?

In pot-walloper boroughs, men could vote if they had a hearth big enough to boil a large pot of water on.

Source B: Part of a letter written by Sir Philip Francis to his wife Harriet, dated 7 July 1802. General elections were held every seven years at this time.

Yesterday morning, between 11 and 12, I was unanimously elected by one elector to represent the ancient borough of Appleby. I had nothing to do but thank the said elector for the unanimous voice with which I was chosen. On Friday morning I shall leave this triumphant scene with flying colours and a determination not to see it again in less than seven years.

Your turn!

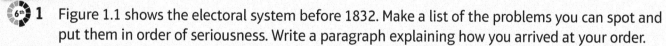

6th 1 Figure 1.1 shows the electoral system before 1832. Make a list of the problems you can spot and put them in order of seriousness. Write a paragraph explaining how you arrived at your order.

7th 2 Look carefully at Source A. William Hogarth was well known for his paintings that poked fun at society. What clues can you find in the painting that everything might not be as it seems? What point do you think he is making?

7th 3 Read Source B. Explain whether you think Sir Philip was being serious or sarcastic in this letter to his wife.

8th 4 How could Sources A and B be used together as evidence of problems with the electoral system?

Changing ideas about democracy

Source C: People queuing to vote in the 2017 British general election.

I own thousands of acres of farmland. I know about the needs of farmers and labourers. I can represent them in parliament.

I own sugar plantations in Jamaica. I know about the empire and can represent it in parliament.

Although I am very rich, there are plenty of poor people on my estates. I know all about them and can represent them in parliament.

I own several banks that lend money to different businesses. I know all about the economy and can represent factory owners and their workers in parliament.

Figure 1.2: How different interests were represented in parliament in the 18th century.

Today, Britain is a democracy run through a parliament. The constituencies contain more or less the same number of people, almost any adult can stand for election as an MP and almost all adults are entitled to vote in general elections. Voting is done in secret.

Today, most people standing for election as an MP belong to a political party, and people tend to vote for the candidate representing the political party that they agree with the most. The political party with the most MPs forms a government, led by the prime minister. The monarch and the House of Lords have very little actual power.

It wasn't always like this. Before 1832, things were very different.

- The monarch appointed ministers who formed a government. MPs could choose whether or not to support the government over different issues.

- Voters based their choice of MP on personal or local issues. Many were bribed and others were afraid to vote against the wishes of the local landowner.

- There were no organised political parties in the modern sense. There were parties called 'Whigs' and 'Tories', but MPs tended to group and regroup into Whigs or Tories according to the issues being debated.

- Voting was not secret. Voters called out the name of the person they were voting for, and this was entered in a Poll Book.

- MPs were not paid a salary. They had to own property worth at least £300 a year so they could afford to work as an MP for free.

It was not considered important that all individuals were represented in parliament. It was felt that groups like factory workers and farm labourers could be represented by rich people involved in the same areas (see Figure 1.2).

Changing ideas

Towards the end of the 18th century, new and exciting ideas about democracy were developing. In other countries, these inspired revolutions.

- In the American Revolutionary War (1775–83), colonists fought the British and won independence. Their rallying cry was 'No taxation without representation'.

- In 1789, French revolutionaries overthrew their king and later executed him. Their motto was '*Liberté, égalité, fraternité*' (liberty, equality, brotherhood).

When the same ideas spread to Britain, how would people and parliament react?

At first the government tried to suppress meetings and publications about these new ideas, but gradually MPs and those influencing them began to see the sense of making the electoral system more democratic.

Source D: From a speech made in parliament by Thomas Babington Macaulay, MP for the rotten borough of Calne, on 2 March 1831.

I support this measure [Parliamentary Reform Bill] because I am sure it is our best security against a revolution. We drive over to the side of revolution those whom we shut out from power.

Source E: A contemporary painting of what became known as the 'Peterloo Massacre'. In 1819, soldiers were ordered to break up a meeting of 60,000–80,000 people in Manchester who were demanding representation in parliament. About 15 people were killed and hundreds wounded.

Source F: From a speech made in 1830 by Henry Brougham during his election campaign and reported in a newspaper, the *Leeds Mercury*.

The great manufacturing and commercial interests of this great country should have a Representative of their own choice in Parliament. We don't live in the days of the Barons, thank God – we live in the days of Leeds, of Bradford, of Halifax and Huddersfield – we live in the days when men are industrious and desire to be free; therefore you are bound to have your rights and to choose your representatives.

Your turn!

 1 List the main differences between the current electoral system and the system before 1832. Which do you think is the most important difference? Explain your thinking.

 2 What questions would a historian have to ask about Source E before it could be used as reliable evidence of widespread pressure for reform of the electoral system?

 3 Would Source E be useful even if it wasn't reliable?

Checkpoint

1 Before 1832, how were the government and the prime minister appointed?

2 How did rich people make sure that their preferred candidates were elected?

3 How were the interests of farm labourers represented in parliament?

Towards democracy

Learning objectives

- Learn about the changes made to the electoral system in the 19th century.
- Understand the pressures for change from Chartists and from parliament.
- Understand the significance of these changes in making Britain more democratic.

The 1832 Reform Act

Enormous pressure from the public and the press resulted in parliament passing a Reform Act in June 1832. It made changes in two key areas: it reallocated seats in the House of Commons and it extended the franchise.

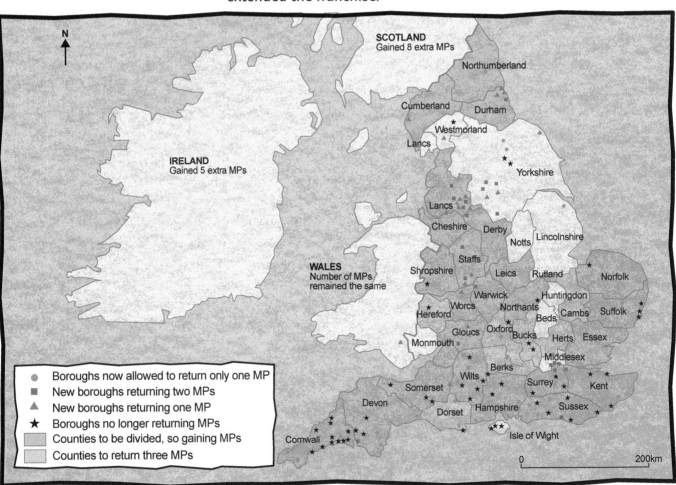

Figure 1.3: Changes made by the 1832 Reform Act to the distribution of seats in parliament.

The constituencies: where were the MPs?

- 56 boroughs lost two MPs and 30 boroughs lost one MP.

- 22 new boroughs were given two MPs and 20 new boroughs were given one MP.

- There were 64 new county MPs.

The franchise: who could vote?

- All the old borough qualifications were swept away. All men owning or renting property worth at least £10 a year could vote.

- In the counties, men could vote if they owned property worth more than 40 shillings a year, or rented land worth £50 a year.

Table 1.1: Numbers of people entitled to vote before and after the 1832 Reform Act.

England and Wales	1831	1833	Percentage increase
Counties	201,859	370,379	83
Boroughs	164,391	282,398	71
Combined	366,250	652,777	78

How democratic was Britain after 1832?

Before 1832, about one in every ten men had the vote; after 1832, it was one in every five. Most of the new voters were middle class – shop owners and owners of small businesses. The vote went only to men who owned, or had enough money to rent, property. As the ballot was not secret, bosses could still keep an eye on how their employees were voting, and had many ways of 'persuading' them to vote the way they wanted. Indeed, in the first parliament elected after 1832, 70–80 per cent of MPs represented landowners.

Before 1832, the pressure on parliament to change the electoral system came from a combination of middle- and working-class activists. In passing the 1832 Reform Act, parliament had made sure that only the 'respectable' middle class had the vote – people who could be trusted not to be part of a revolution. This left thousands of working-class people, who still couldn't vote, feeling let down and angry.

Source A: From a newspaper, the *Leeds Mercury*, 9 June 1832.

The Victory of the People is now secured, sealed and [delivered] beyond the fear of accident. The great seal of state has been attached to the new chapter of the people's rights. A mighty and ancient system of corruption and abuse will receive its death blow.

Source B: From the *Poor Man's Guardian*, a newspaper published on 27 October 1832. The newspaper was published in London during 1831–35 and cost one penny.

The [Reform Act] was never intended to do you one particle of good. The object of its promoters was not to change that 'glorious constitution', which has given you such misery, but to make it last for ever. It was an invitation to the newly enfranchised towns to join with them in keeping down the people, and thereby to quell the rising spirit of democracy in Britain.

Your turn!

 1 Explain which, in your view, were the more significant changes made by the 1832 Reform Act – those to the constituencies or those to the franchise?

 2 a Describe, in one sentence each for Source A and Source B, the opinion they hold about the Reform Act of 1832.

b How might a reader of the *Poor Man's Guardian* have argued with a reader of the *Leeds Mercury* about the Act? Write their conversation.

3 Explain how far the 1832 Reform Act made Britain more democratic.

Source C: From a speech by George Julian Harney at a Chartist meeting in Derby, reported in the *Northern Star*, a Chartist newspaper, on 9 February 1839.

We demand universal suffrage*, not only because it is our right, but because it will bring freedom to our country and give us bread, and beef and beer. We are for peace, but we must have justice – we must have our rights speedily; peacefully if we can – forcibly if we must.

The Chartists: demanding a more democratic Britain

The thousands who had been denied the vote by the 1832 Reform Act did not accept this quietly. Neither did those in the middle class who supported them. In 1838, these protesters published a People's Charter. Chartists were those who supported this charter. It had six points.

1 A vote for every man over the age of 21.

2 A secret ballot.

3 The abolition of the property qualification for MPs.

4 The payment of salaries to MPs.

5 Equal sized constituencies.

6 Annual parliaments.

Were the Chartists doomed to fail?

Many Chartists supported the use of peaceful methods of persuasion. They held meetings and marches, distributed pamphlets and held national meetings.

Source D: A contemporary print of the procession taking the second Chartist petition to parliament in 1842.

Chartists presented petitions to parliament in 1839, 1842 and 1848, demanding the six points of the charter. Each petition was signed by over a million people, but parliament rejected them all. Chartism, as a movement, had failed. Chartism failed because:

- its leadership was divided about whether to use persuasion (moral force) or violence (physical force)

- it attracted working-class support mainly when times were hard and unemployment was high, so support varied

- the power of the state was too strong, and demonstrations were easily broken up by police and soldiers. This meant parliament didn't have to listen.

What had Chartism achieved?

It's easy to see what Chartism didn't achieve: parliament never even debated the six points of the charter. However, as the first genuinely working-class movement, Chartism gave working people a sense of purpose and the knowledge that they could organise themselves on a national basis. Many believed that, united, they could make a difference.

Key term

Universal suffrage*:
Everyone being able to vote.

Parliament: making Britain more democratic

In the years after the 1832 Reform Act, there was no pressure inside parliament for reform. Many MPs believed that the reforms had gone far enough. The franchise had been extended to the 'respectable' middle-class voters, and landowners were well represented in parliament (see page 13).

However, by the 1850s and 1860s, it was becoming clear to parliament that Britain's wealth was coming from technology and industry, not from land, and that the electoral system should recognise this.

The 1867 Reform Act doubled the franchise and, after 1884, all male property-owners could vote. The 1884 act meant that about one in three men had the vote. Even so, most men (and no women) didn't have a say in how they were governed. The introduction of the secret ballot in 1872 meant that employers could no longer 'persuade' their employees to vote the way they wanted.

Timeline

1867
Second Reform Act gave the vote to those living in boroughs who occupied a house or paid more than £10 a year for lodgings

1872
Ballot Act meant all voting to be carried out in secret

1884
Third Reform Act gave the vote to men in counties on the same basis as men in boroughs

1885
Redistribution of Seats Act redrew electoral boundaries to make constituencies equal in size

Source E: The Reform League, an organisation demanding 'one man one vote', demonstrating in London on 2 July 1866. This picture was published in the *Illustrated London News* on 23 July 1866.

Your turn!

1 Why, in your view, did parliament refuse even to consider the Chartists' demands?

2 How useful would Source E be to a historian researching the reasons for the 1867 Reform Act? Explain your answer.

Checkpoint

1 Name one change made to constituencies and one change made to the franchise by the 1832 Reform Act.
2 One in how many men could vote after 1832?
3 Give two reasons why Chartism failed to make Britain more democratic.
4 Why was another reform act needed in the 1860s?

How democratic was Britain in the 19th century?

1 Draw a flow chart, starting in 1830 and ending in 1886, showing the steps by which Britain became more democratic.

2 Different people would have reacted differently to the changes in the franchise, 1830–86. In groups of three, take on the roles of (a) a wealthy landowner (b) a skilled engineer and (c) a woman and write out the conversation they could have had about these changes.

What's the truth about Victorian women?

Many rich and middle-class women filled their days with painting, sewing, singing and piano playing, visiting friends and doing charity work for the poor. Victorians believed that a respectable woman's place was in the home, supporting her husband and caring for their children. Women were to be protected from the demands of the world outside the home: that was only for men. This attitude did not, however, extend to working-class women, whose hard labour was needed to keep the economy going. In this section you will learn about:

- the ways in which Victorian women were supposed to behave, and how some refused to conform

- how women's legal status changed

- the ways in which Victorians viewed middle-class and working-class women very differently.

'The Angel in the House'

Learning objectives

- Learn about the lives of middle-class Victorian women.
- Understand the different Victorian attitudes to women.

What do you think?

What part should women play in society?

Source A: A photograph of a middle-class Victorian family having tea. It was taken in about 1855.

In 1854, a poem by Coventry Patmore was published called 'The Angel in the House'. One of the lines was 'Man must be pleased; but him to please is woman's pleasure'. In other words, the woman's role was to give pleasure to her husband. She had to create a comfortable and loving home, where her husband and children would be supported and protected from the evils of the outside world.

Source B: Part of a poem by Alfred, Lord Tennyson, published in 1847.

Man for the field and woman for the hearth:

Man for the sword and for the needle she:

Man with the head and woman with the heart:

Man to command and woman to obey;

All else confusion.

Victorian marriage: a trap or a support?

In the mid-19th century, married women were not recognised as being legally separate people from their husbands. Therefore, all the property a woman owned before her marriage became his, as did all her earnings, once she was married. The husband could do with them as he wished. The children of the marriage were his, too, and his wife had no legal rights over them. If he wanted to, a husband could refuse to let his wife see their children at all.

If a woman was prepared to accept this, then she could lead a very comfortable and sheltered life. Many, however, were not content and some of these women suffered abuse from their husbands. Gradually, largely because of pressure from women's groups, parliament saw that change had to come.

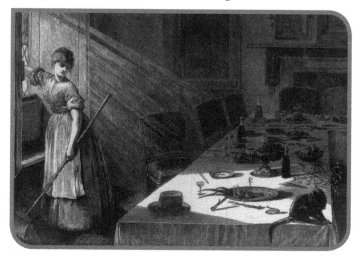

Source C: A picture called *The Morning After the Party* drawn in the 19th century.

Timeline

1857
Matrimonial Causes Act allowed divorce through the law courts instead of by the more expensive private Act of Parliament, though it still cost a lot of money

1870
Married Women's Property Act allowed a woman to keep £200 in earnings and personal property

1882
Married Women's Property Act allowed a woman to control everything she brought into a marriage and everything she earned after marriage

1884
Matrimonial Causes Act prevented a wife from being forced to live with or have sex with her husband

1886
Guardianship of Infants Act took the welfare of the children into account when deciding custody in a divorce

Did you know?

A husband could divorce his wife if she committed adultery. A wife could only divorce her husband if he committed adultery AND either bigamy, rape, sex with a man, or had deserted her for a long time.

Your turn!

1 **a** Explain how far Source A supports (i) Tennyson's poem (Source B) and (ii) the concept of the 'Angel in the House'.

   b How useful would the photograph be to a historian researching Victorian family life?

2 Read about the changes to the legal position of women shown in the timeline.

   a Which one do you think is the most important? Why?

   b Explain how likely it was that these changes would affect the woman shown in Source C.

3 Use the evidence of Sources A, B and C to show how the Victorians used two different standards in their attitudes to women.

4 Research the life of Caroline Norton (1808–77). Explain what you think drove her to lead women in campaigning for change to the legal position of women as wives and mothers.

What shall I wear?

Clothes, and particularly dresses, indicated a woman's status in Victorian society and therefore her husband's wealth. Because they had to be acceptable to her husband – the person most wives wanted to please – they also showed Victorian society's attitude to women.

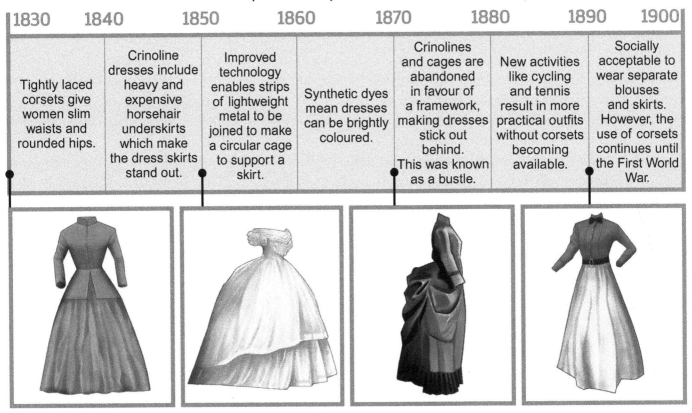

1830	1840	1850	1860	1870	1880	1890	1900

Tightly laced corsets give women slim waists and rounded hips.	Crinoline dresses include heavy and expensive horsehair underskirts which make the dress skirts stand out.	Improved technology enables strips of lightweight metal to be joined to make a circular cage to support a skirt.	Synthetic dyes mean dresses can be brightly coloured.	Crinolines and cages are abandoned in favour of a framework, making dresses stick out behind. This was known as a bustle.	New activities like cycling and tennis result in more practical outfits without corsets becoming available.	Socially acceptable to wear separate blouses and skirts. However, the use of corsets continues until the First World War.

Figure 1.4: Changing fashions in women's dresses.

Source D: From *Period Piece* by Gwen Raverat, published in 1952. Here, she remembers part of her childhood towards the end of the 19th century.

In those days, nearly everyone accepted the inconvenience of clothes as inevitable. However, the ladies never seemed at ease ... . Their dresses were always made too tight, the bodices wrinkled from the strain, and their corsets showed in a sharp ledge across the middles of their backs.

We knew it was hopeless ... but we did rebel against corsets. Margaret [Gwen's sister] says that the first time she was put into them – when she was about thirteen – she ran round and round the nursery, screaming with rage. I did not do that. I simply went away and took them off. When this was discovered, I was forcibly re-corsetted. As soon as possible, I went away and took them off again. To me, the corsets were real instruments of torture. They prevented me from breathing and dug deep holes into my softer parts on every side.

Victorians viewed tennis, which was invented in its modern form in the 1870s, as a respectable game. It was one of the few games where men and women could play together. Some changes were made to women's clothing to create sporting fashions that were acceptable to Victorian society.

However, women struggling to earn enough money to support themselves, or add to their husband's wage in order to feed and clothe a family, were not affected by fashion. Source F shows the kind of clothes worn by working-class women.

Source E: A picture called *The Tennis Match*, painted in 1888 by the artist H.H. Cauty.

Source F: A photograph of pit brow girls at the Rose Bridge Pits, Wigan, in 1865. The Mines Act (1842) prohibited girls from working underground, but they could still work on the surface.

Your turn!

 1 Read Source D. If wearing corsets caused so many problems, why did women wear them? Explain your answer.

 2 'Women's clothes in the 19th century were nothing to do with social status, only with what was practical to wear.'
How far do you agree with this statement? Remember to back up your answer with evidence.

Checkpoint

1 **(a)** What was the 'Angel in the House' view of Victorian women? **(b)** Did this apply to all Victorian women?
2 Name two things that women were allowed to do after the Married Women's Property Act (1882).
3 Name one technological advance that affected women's fashion.
4 Why didn't the rules of fashion affect working-class women?

How daring were Victorian women?

- Learn about the ways in which two Victorian women challenged society's view of how they should behave.
- Understand how changes in society and advances in technology affected women's job prospects.

Source A: In July 1863, Elizabeth Garrett Anderson applied to Aberdeen hospital for medical training. This is part of the hospital's reply, sent on 29 July.

I must decline to give you instruction in anatomy. I have a strong conviction that the entrance of ladies into dissecting rooms and anatomical theatres is undesirable in every respect, and highly unbecoming. It is not necessary for fair ladies to be brought into contact with such foul scenes. Ladies would make bad doctors at best, and they do so many things excellently that I for one should be sorry to see them trying to do this one.

To be daring doesn't always mean having the courage to attempt physical challenges, like swimming the English Channel or climbing Everest. It can mean challenging accepted views of your place in society and what you should, and should not, do. The women you will read about here did just that.

Elizabeth Garrett Anderson (1836–1917)

Elizabeth was born in Whitechapel, London. When she was four years old, her family moved to Aldeburgh, Suffolk, where her father became a successful and rich businessman. In 1859, Elizabeth met Elizabeth Blackwell, a doctor who worked in America. In that moment, her life changed forever: she decided she was going to be a doctor and work in England.

Elizabeth was not deterred by being rejected for medical training (see Source A). She found a loophole in the rules of the Society of Apothecaries, successfully sat its exams in 1865 and was able to practise medicine from her home in London. The Society immediately changed its rules, so that in future only men could sit the exams!

1866 – Opened St Mary's Dispensary in London especially for poor women, allowing women to be treated by women for the first time.

1870 – Unable to study medicine at a British university, she learned French, studied in France and gained a medical degree, qualifying as a doctor.

1870 – Appointed visiting physician to the East London Hospital for Children, she was the first woman to be appointed to a medical post in an English hospital.

1872 – St Mary's Dispensary, renamed the New Hospital for Women and Children, treated women from all over London.

1873 – Became the only female member of the British Medical Association.

1874 – Co-founded the London School of Medicine for Women. It was the only teaching hospital in Britain providing courses for women.

1883–1903 – Worked as Dean of the London School of Medicine for Women, the first woman to hold such a position.

1893 – Persuaded the British Medical Association to admit women.

1908 – Elected mayor of Aldeburgh, becoming the first female mayor in England.

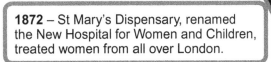

Figure 1.5: Elizabeth Garrett Anderson's career.

In spite of all her achievements, as a woman Elizabeth was not allowed to vote in general elections. She was a strong supporter of female suffrage*. In 1889, she was a member of the Committee of the National Society for Women's Suffrage, founded by her sister, Millicent Fawcett. Nevertheless, by the time of her death in 1917, no woman had the right to vote in general elections.

Gertrude Bell (1868–1926)

Gertrude was born in Washington, County Durham, where her father was a wealthy mill-owner and her grandfather a rich industrialist and MP. She graduated from the University of Oxford with a first-class degree in History – the first woman to do so. In 1892, she travelled to Persia (modern-day Iran) to stay with her uncle, who was the British minister (like an ambassador) in Tehran. This gave her a love of the Middle East and set her on the path of adventure that she was to follow throughout her life.

> **1894–1911** – Wrote and had published a number of books about her travels in the Middle East, informing the public and politicians about the people and politics of the region.

> **1899–1904** – Climbed a number of mountains, including Mont Blanc. Recorded new routes in the Bernese Alps and had a peak named after her: Gertrudspitze.

> **1907–09** – Worked on archaeological digs in the Middle East. Spoke fluent Arabic and made links with Arab tribes.

> **1914** – On the outbreak of war, her request to return to the Middle East was turned down and so she volunteered to work with the Red Cross in France.

> **1915** – Assigned to Army Intelligence Headquarters in Cairo for war service. Became the only female political officer in the British forces. Probably spied for the British.

> **1921** – Attended the Cairo Conference (the only woman to be invited) and advised on the boundaries of modern-day Iraq.

> **1921–26** – Helped install Faisal I as king of Iraq and worked in the administration of the country. Set up a library and archaeological museum in Baghdad.

Figure 1.6: Gertrude Bell's career.

Your turn!

1. Read Source A.
   a. What questions would a historian have to ask about the source before it could be used as reliable evidence of Victorian attitudes to women?
   b. We don't know whether or not Elizabeth replied to the letter from Aberdeen hospital. What do you think she would have said? Write her reply.

2. Read about the careers of Elizabeth Garrett Anderson and Gertrude Bell (Figures 1.5 and 1.6).
   a. Explain which woman you think was the most daring.
   b. Explain which woman you think did the most to change people's attitudes to women.

Did you know?

Gertrude Bell opposed women's suffrage. She believed that the majority of women in Britain lacked the education and understanding of the world to make informed political decisions.

Key term

Suffrage*: The right to vote in elections.

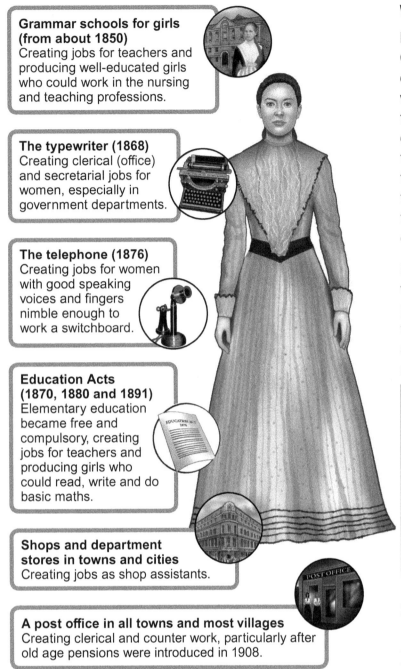

Grammar schools for girls (from about 1850)
Creating jobs for teachers and producing well-educated girls who could work in the nursing and teaching professions.

The typewriter (1868)
Creating clerical (office) and secretarial jobs for women, especially in government departments.

The telephone (1876)
Creating jobs for women with good speaking voices and fingers nimble enough to work a switchboard.

Education Acts (1870, 1880 and 1891)
Elementary education became free and compulsory, creating jobs for teachers and producing girls who could read, write and do basic maths.

Shops and department stores in towns and cities
Creating jobs as shop assistants.

A post office in all towns and most villages
Creating clerical and counter work, particularly after old age pensions were introduced in 1908.

Figure 1.7: Factors creating new jobs for women.

Working women

Elizabeth Garrett Anderson and Gertrude Bell both showed courage and determination in living the sort of lives they wanted for themselves. However, they had the backing of rich families. Many women didn't have their advantages. Nevertheless, they wanted the independence to run their own lives and it was a job and a wage that would give them this. Education, technology and a changing, growing economy gave them their chance.

Not everyone was happy about having women in the workplace. This was particularly true of office work, which in the past had usually been done by men and was now being done by women for a lower wage.

Source B: A typing class in Woolwich Polytechnic, 1906–07. Classes teaching girls and women typing and shorthand spread throughout Britain. Shorthand is a method of speed writing using symbols.

Source C: Part of a letter sent to the *Liverpool Echo* in 1911.

```
These intrepid 'typewriter pounders', instead of being allowed to
read love novels or do fancy crocheting when they are not 'pounding',
should fill in their spare time washing out the offices and dusting,
which you will no doubt agree is more suited to their sex and would
maybe give a little practice and insight into the work they will be
called upon to do should they so far lower themselves as to marry one
of the poor male clerks whose living they are doing their utmost to
take out of his hands at the present time.
```

Having fun

Women who worked as typists and telephonists, shop assistants and clerks, nurses and teachers, wanted fun in their time off. The Factory Act of 1874 limited the working week to 56.5 hours and the Bank Holidays Act (1871) created a number of fixed holidays. This created leisure time for working women to enjoy.

Cycling

The production of the safety bicycle in 1885 was a turning point for women. Unlike earlier bikes, its wheels were the same size, the saddle was comfortable and the cyclist's feet could touch the ground. Bicycles became immensely popular, especially with women. They could now travel wherever they wanted and, for the first time, travel alone. Cycling clubs, some mixed and some for women only, sprang up all over Britain. Cycling had an impact on women's fashion. Long skirts could get caught in the wheels, so women either wore shorter, divided skirts or bloomers. These were loose-fitting, knee-length trousers that many people thought were shocking.

Mountaineering

Gertrude Bell (see page 21) wasn't the only woman to enjoy mountaineering. Middle-class women (climbing was expensive) climbed with their fathers and brothers.

Source D: Three women enjoying cycling. This photograph was taken in 1895 and the photographer gave it the title *Maidens with disregard for convention*.

Checkpoint

1 How did Elizabeth Garrett Anderson open up opportunities for women?
2 Give two skills that Gertrude Bell had that made her useful to the British government.
3 List three factors that led to greater job opportunities for women by 1900.
4 Why was the invention of the safety bicycle so important for women?

Your turn!

1 Look at Figure 1.7. Explain which factor was the most important in bringing about change to women's job opportunities.

2 Read Source C. Imagine you are one of the working women about whom the letter-writer is complaining. Write a letter to the *Liverpool Echo* in reply.

3 It is 1900 and you are setting up a cycling club. Design a poster that will attract women cyclists to join.

What's the truth about Victorian women?

1 You have been asked by your local primary school to talk to Year 5 pupils about Victorian women. Working in a group, prepare a presentation.

2 Research other Victorian women who dared to be different and create a poster on one of them – for example: Ada Lovelace, Florence Nightingale, Elizabeth Fry or Josephine Butler.

What have you learned?

In this section you have learned that:

- the ways in which the electoral system worked before 1832 were not suitable for industrial Britain

- various Acts of Parliament changed the system so that, by the end of the 19th century, industrial cities were represented and one in three men had the vote

- no women could vote in general elections during the 19th century.

Inference questions

Your turn!

Below are a number of inferences. Each inference can be made from a source in this section. Find the source and the evidence in the source that leads to the inference.

1 Industrial cities should be represented in parliament.

2 Some MPs were sarcastic about the pre-1832 electoral system.

3 The authorities used violence to stop freedom of speech.

4 Chartists threatened to use violence.

5 Elections before 1832 threw society into turmoil.

6 Some MPs voted for reform because they were afraid there would be a revolution.

Making inferences

Sources provide us with information about the past, but we can get more from a source than it actually tells us directly. We can make *inferences* from a source. This means going behind the actual words of the source – reading between the lines – to find out what the source is suggesting. What is its tone? Is it funny? Serious? Sarcastic? What is the attitude of the author or artist? Is he or she, for example, sad or happy, pleased or angry? Inferences can be about the event the source is describing, or about the message the author or artist is hoping to convey. Let's look at one of the sources you will have read already – on page 9.

> One inference could be that Sir Philip was telling the truth. This is supported by the fact he is writing a private letter to his wife and so there is no clear reason for him to lie.

Source B: Part of a letter written by Sir Philip Francis to his wife Harriet, dated 7 July 1802. General elections were held every seven years at this time.

Yesterday morning, between 11 and 12, I was unanimously elected by one elector to represent the ancient borough of Appleby. I had nothing to do but thank the said elector for the unanimous voice with which I was chosen. On Friday morning I shall leave this triumphant scene with flying colours and a determination not to see it again in less than seven years.

> One inference could be that Sir Philip has been elected to represent a rotten borough. This is supported by the fact that there is only one elector.

> One inference could be that Sir Philip does not believe that his main job as an MP is to represent his constituency, Appleby. This is supported by him writing that he is determined not to see Appleby for the next seven years, which would be the length of the parliament.

Figure 1.8: Looking for inferences.

Remember that it is never enough just to say what the inference is. You will need to back it up with evidence from the source.

Writing historically

Inference questions

You are now going to look for inferences in two sources. For each inference, you must give the evidence in the source that supports the inference.

1 Look at Source D on page 14. Write down one inference you can make from this source, and two pieces of evidence that back this up. Look at the answers from two students before writing your own.

Student 1

> I can infer from Source D that Chartism was supported by a large number of people.
>
> The two pieces of evidence that tell me this are the crowds that are watching and the size of the petition.

The student has made a valid inference, but it is undeveloped. The student could have added that the crowd was London-based and so is only an indication of the interest Londoners showed in Chartism.

The supporting evidence could have been developed further, too. The fact that crowds are watching shows interest, but not necessarily support. The student is also guessing at the size of the petition: it could be a very small petition in a large container!

Student 2

> I can infer from Source D that Chartism in London was not regarded as a threat by the authorities.
>
> My inference is supported by the lack of violence in the crowd, which is large, and the fact that children are playing in the road.

The student has made a developed inference, but this would have been better if the focus had been on what could be seen in the picture, rather than making a comment on Chartism itself. The supporting evidence is not quite right because it doesn't support the inference. The fact that the crowd is peaceful and children were playing means that the authorities were right in thinking the occasion would not be threatening – but they would have had to decide that in advance of the event. Instead the student could, for example, have pointed to the militia not being present and to the fact that the procession had been allowed to take place at all.

Student 3 – you!

Write your answer. Look for an inference and make sure it is fully supported by two pieces of evidence that relate directly to the inference you have made. See if you can improve on these student answers.

2 Read Source B on page 13. Write down one inference you can make from this source, and two pieces of evidence that back this up. Look at the student answer below, and the questions following it, before writing your own.

Student 1

> The inference I would make is that the press criticised the 1832 Reform Act.
>
> The evidence I have found to support this is that the extract was published in a newspaper that was sold for a penny and that the article was very critical of the Act, saying it was never intended to help poor people.

(a) What comments would you make about this student's response? Is the inference relevant and developed? Does the evidence really support the inference, and is it detailed enough?

(b) Now write your answer.

How did women get the vote?

Everyone campaigning for the vote for women agreed on what they wanted, but they disagreed about the best way to achieve it. Parliament and the public had to be convinced of the rightness of their cause. There were people who believed women should be content with domestic matters and keep out of national affairs that were best left to men. In this section you will learn about:

- the different methods used by suffragists and suffragettes, and why some people opposed them

- the roles women played in the First World War

- the reasons why some women got the vote in 1918.

Persuasion or violence?

Learning objectives

- Learn about the different methods used by suffragists and suffragettes.
- Understand why some men and women opposed them.

What do you think?

What is the best way to bring about change?

Source A: Part of a letter written by Philippa Strachey, the secretary of the NUWSS, on 12 October 1908.

I feel that law and order are essential to all that makes life worth living, and that they are especially and particularly vital to women.

Did you know?

Millicent Fawcett (1847–1929) was the younger sister of Elizabeth Garrett Anderson (see page 20). As children, both went to a boarding school in Blackheath, London. Their father outraged the school by insisting his daughters had a hot bath every week. The school thought that was far too often.

Suffragists: using legal means to get the vote

In 1897, Millicent Fawcett linked smaller organisations into the National Union of Women's Suffrage Societies (NUWSS), known as the Suffragists. Members believed that logical argument was the way to persuade people to support votes for women. They held meetings and marches, published pamphlets and spoke to MPs. By 1914, the NUWSS had more than 400 branches throughout the country and over 100,000 members, some of whom were men.

Source B: Millicent Fawcett addressing a rally in Hyde Park, London, in July 1913.

Suffragettes: adding militancy to the campaign

Emmeline Pankhurst and her daughters, Christabel and Sylvia, founded the Women's Social and Political Union (WSPU), known as the Suffragettes, in 1903. They were impatient with the peaceful methods of the suffragists. Their aims were the same – votes for women – but their methods were very different. They organised marches and meetings, and opened shops that sold, for example, WSPU mugs, brooches and scarves, as well as distributing pamphlets urging votes for women. But they went further than this. Suffragettes heckled* speakers at public meetings, shouting 'Votes for Women', unfurling banners and, if the speakers were MPs, demanding to know when parliament would give women the vote. Alarmed at this behaviour, in 1906 the government banned women from public meetings and refused to meet women's suffrage groups. The suffragettes had to find other methods of bringing their cause to the public's attention. They chained themselves to railings, refused to pay taxes and even hid in the Houses of Parliament so they could disrupt debates.

From militancy to violence

In 1910, when a Conciliation Bill aimed at giving the vote to all men and a small number of women failed to get parliamentary approval, the suffragettes stepped up their activities. They began a more serious attack on property. They smashed the windows of shops, offices and government buildings, destroyed the contents of postboxes, used acid to burn their message into the grass of golf courses, burned down houses belonging to those who did not support them and slashed paintings in public galleries.

Source C: Suffragettes prepare to chain themselves to railings, 1909. They could make speeches to passers-by for as long as it took the police to cut them free. They were then arrested.

Source D: Part of a speech made by Emmeline Pankhurst in the Albert Hall, London, in October 1912.

Those of you who can break windows — break them. Those of you who can still further attack… property so as to make the government realise that property is in as great a danger by Women's Suffrage as it was by the Chartists of old — do so. And my last word to the government: I incite this meeting to rebellion.

Key term

Heckle*: To interrupt a public speaker with comments, questions and abuse.

Your turn!

 1 List as many differences as you can find between the suffragists and the suffragettes.

 2 Draw up a table showing the advantages and disadvantages of the different approaches of suffragists and suffragettes.

 3 Read Source D. How might Millicent Fawcett have replied to Emmeline Pankhurst? Work out a dialogue between the two women, using the information and sources on these two pages.

4 Find out what suffragettes Emily Davison in 1913 and Mary Richardson in 1914 did to bring attention to the cause of women's suffrage.

Dealing with the suffragettes

The government

Many suffragettes were arrested for their illegal actions and sent to prison. In 1909, Marion Wallace Dunlop was the first imprisoned suffragette to go on hunger strike*. Others followed suit. The government, believing that a suffragette would die in prison and afraid of public opinion if this happened, decided to take dramatic action. They authorised the force-feeding of suffragettes on hunger strike. This involved holding down the prisoner and forcing a tube into their nose or mouth and into their stomach. Food was poured down the tube. This backfired in a spectacular way. The Liberal government found that this way of dealing with suffragettes was used against them in the general election of 1910, as Source E shows.

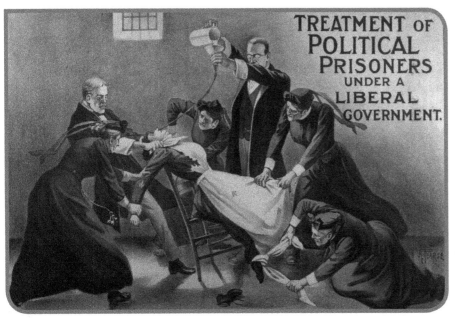

Source E: A poster published by the WSPU as part of its propaganda campaign in the election of 1910.

Source F: A postcard produced by the Anti-Suffrage Society in 1906.

Source G: A poster designed in 1912 for the National League for Opposing Woman Suffrage.

The anti-suffrage societies

Anti-suffrage groups were formed up and down the country, some only for men and some only for women. In 1910, these groups were merged into the National League for Opposing Woman Suffrage. They used suffragette tactics to persuade the public and parliament that women should not have the vote.

Key term

Hunger strike*: To refuse to eat as a protest. This could make prisoners very weak and unwell.

Conservatism versus liberalism

Those opposing female suffrage were often driven by the idea of **conservatism**. They wanted to conserve the idea of the 'Angel in the House' (see page 16), though adapted to the times. They were happy for women to vote in local elections, for example, because local councils dealt with local, domestic matters. But voting in general elections was out of the question. This should be left to men.

Those supporting female suffrage were often driven by the idea of **liberalism**. They believed in liberty and equality. They wanted equality with men as far as the franchise was concerned, but not just for its own sake. They believed that female suffrage would lead to women's issues being discussed in parliament and that women MPs would bring the qualities of the 'Angel in the House' to parliament.

Did you know?

In 1913, parliament passed an Act that said women hunger-strikers had to be released and sent home. When they had recovered their strength, they were rearrested and sent back to prison. This was nicknamed the **Cat and Mouse Act**. Can you think why?

Interpretation 1: From Bob Whitfield, *The Extension of the Franchise 1832–1931*, published in 2001.

The WSPU offended virtually all the allies on whom their success ultimately depended. Among the more sympathetic ministers in the Liberal government was Lloyd George, yet the WSPU heckled him in public meetings in exactly the same way as they directed their fire at known opponents of women's suffrage such as Asquith. They also attacked Lloyd George's country house … Instead of working to build a parliamentary coalition of suffrage supporters, the WSPU alienated [annoyed] many of the MPs who were on the side of votes for women.

Interpretation 2: From Diane Atkinson, *The Suffragettes in Pictures*, published in 1996.

The suffragettes' increasingly militant tactics earned them many enemies and put them at personal risk; and their campaign of arson, window smashing, bombing and widespread vandalism alienated public opinion. Much of the sympathy and outrage at the Government's practices of force-feeding evaporated when newspaper headlines told of suffragette terrorism. The British public felt that the suffragettes brought all the punishments upon themselves, while the Government did not want to be seen to give into extremism.

Your turn!

 1 Look at Source E. How useful would this source be to a historian researching suffragette activities?

 2 In what ways are Sources F and G **(a)** similar and **(b)** different in how they are opposing women's suffrage?

3 Read Interpretations 1 and 2 and answer the questions below.

 a What impression does each author give of the suffragette campaign?

 b What evidence is each author likely to have found that caused them to give this impression?

Checkpoint

1 When were **(a)** the NUWSS and **(b)** the WSPU founded?
2 Which suffrage organisation was led by **(a)** Emmeline Pankhurst and **(b)** Millicent Fawcett?
3 Name two legal methods used by the suffragists.
4 Name two illegal methods used by the suffragettes.
5 What was force-feeding and why was it used?

Women, war work and the franchise

Source A: A woman taking over her husband's business, sticking up posters, while he was away fighting.

Source B: A government poster published during the First World War.

Filling in for the missing men

The First World War broke out in August 1914 and everything changed. The WSPU stopped campaigning and supported the war effort. The NUWSS also supported the war effort, though some members did carry on campaigning quietly. The government made it clear that it was every man's duty to fight for king and country. It was less clear about what women should do. At first, the government simply encouraged women to take on the work of male relatives while they were away.

In 1916, the government was forced to introduce conscription* (see page 59). More and more men joined the armed forces, leaving their jobs in industry and agriculture. The economy had to be kept running to support the war effort, so the government began encouraging women to work full time.

Women joined the Women's Land Army to work with farmers. They also worked in the armed services as nurses and cooks, clerks and ambulance drivers. Women worked in gas works and breweries, for bus, train and tram companies, as window cleaners and chimney sweeps, in laboratories and dye works.

Source C: Women working as porters for the South Eastern and Chatham Railway Company.

Dangerous work: munitions*

In 1915, there was a munitions crisis: not enough shells were being produced for the army, and many that were produced were duds that didn't explode. The government started a campaign to attract women to work in munitions factories. In 1914, there were 212,000 women working in the munitions industry; by 1918, this had increased to 950,000 – 80 per cent of all weapons and shells were made by women. This was dangerous work, dealing with high explosives. An explosion in Silvertown, London in 1917, killed 73, injured 500 and destroyed over 900 houses.

Source D: An official war painting of women working in a munitions factory. It is called *For King and Country* and was painted by Edward Skinner in 1916.

Source E: In 1976, Mrs H.A. Felstead wrote to the Imperial War Museum about her experiences as a munitions worker in the First World War.

I was in domestic service and hated every minute of it when war broke out, earning £2 a month working from 6.00am to 9.00pm. So when the need came for women war workers, my chance came to get out. I started on hand cutting shell fuses. This entailed finishing off by hand the machine cut thread on the fuses that held the powder for the big shells, so had to be very accurate so that the cap fitted perfectly. We worked twelve hours a day. Believe me we were very ready for bed those days, and as for wages I thought I was very well off earning £5 a week.

Key terms

Conscription*: Forcing people to join the army, rather than relying on people volunteering.

Munitions*: Things needed for war, including shells, bullets, guns and uniforms.

Trade unions*: Organisations of workers. They aimed to defend their members' interests, for example, by negotiating better pay and conditions.

Problems with pay

At the start of the war, women were paid less than the men whose jobs they had taken over. This worried the trade unions*. Would bosses keep the women on when the men returned after the war? Or would they expect the returning men to work for the same pay as the women? Finally, it was agreed that the women would be paid the same as the men, but that the men could have their jobs back when they came home from the war.

Your turn!

 1 Imagine you are a suffragette. Write an account for your local newspaper explaining how your life has changed by 1915. Use the information in this section, including Sources A, C and E.

 2 Explain how the shell shortage in 1915 and conscription in 1916 brought about changes to women's work.

 3 What do you think were the most difficult problems faced by women doing war work? Use the information in this section in your answer, and choose three sources to back up your opinion.

Source F: A cartoon published in the magazine *Punch* in 1918.

Something lost and something gained?

The Representation of the People Act 1918

On 6 February 1918, the Representation of the People Act became law. It gave the vote to all men over the age of 21, and to women over the age of 30 who were property owners or who were married to a man who owned property. About eight million women now had the vote. However, the women who kept industry and agriculture running throughout the war were mainly single, young women and they were excluded. If all women had the vote, there would be more female than male voters and people were not sure how women would vote. It was safer to give the vote to older, usually married, women who would probably vote in the same way as their husbands.

Back to home and duty?

The war ended on 11 November 1918. The men returned home and took up their peacetime jobs again. For many women, the years after 1918 were a disappointment. They lost the freedom to earn and spend their own money.

- Thousands of women were dismissed from their jobs in factories and workshops. By 1921, there were two per cent fewer women working in industry than there had been in 1914.

- In 1918, 235,000 women were working at all levels in the civil service; in 1928, there were only 74,212. Women had been replaced by poorly qualified, inexperienced men.

- Many local authorities imposed a marriage bar. This meant that when, for example, teachers or nurses got married, they were sacked.

- By 1931, 35 per cent of all working women were in domestic service.

There were some positives.

- There was a slight increase in women entering some prestigious jobs. For example, 77 women had become barristers by 1927 and there was some increase in women becoming doctors.

Interpretation 1: From Arthur Marwick, *The Deluge: British Society and the First World War*, published in 1965.

It is difficult to see how women could have achieved so much without the unique circumstances arising from the war. The war paid women a valuable bonus: men and women joined together to praise women's contribution to the war effort, bringing a confidence in their new role to women and an acceptance of it among men, which might otherwise not be easy to create.

Interpretation 2: From Martin Pugh, *The March of the Women*, published in 2000.

Whether the war influenced the debate about votes for women is rather doubtful. It did not lead men generally to change their ideas about gender issues. The war made them see women's traditional roles as wives and mothers as even more important now that [so many young men had been killed]. The war almost certainly helped to influence the form that enfranchisement [getting the vote] took. It strengthened the feeling that the vote should not be a reward for single women so much as a recognition of married women.

- The growth of light industries in the Midlands and the South East provided further job opportunities.

- Finally, in 1928, the Equal Franchise Act gave the vote to all women.

However, the world of work once again became dominated by men. Women earned, on average, less than half that of men for doing the same work and they were often channelled into routine, less skilled work. Furthermore, the marriage bar deterred women from following careers and made them financially dependent on their husbands.

Did you know?

Crowds of thousands watched women's football matches during the war. In 1921, the Football Association banned women from using FA grounds, saying football was an unsuitable game for women. The ban was not lifted until 1971.

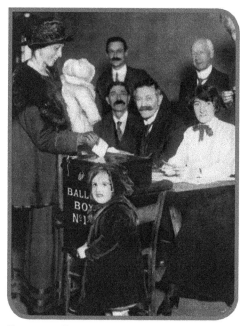

Source G: A woman voting for the first time in the general election of 1918.

Your turn!

1 Look at the changes that happened to working women, and those who wanted to work, in the years after 1918.
  a Choose the three most important changes, and explain your choice.
  b Explain whether the changes would have affected all women in the same way.

2 Read Interpretations 1 and 2.
  a On what aspects do they agree?
  b On what aspects do they disagree?
  How do you explain their disagreements?

Checkpoint

1 Name four jobs women did during the First World War (1914–18).
2 Why did the government encourage women to work in munitions after 1915?
3 What agreement was reached about women's pay for war work?
4 Who was given the vote in 1918?
5 Name two negative things and one positive thing that happened to women's work after 1918.

How did women get the vote?

1 Imagine that Millicent Fawcett and Emmeline Pankhurst were having a conversation about how women got the vote. Millicent could start by saying: 'You have to get the public on your side and WSPU militancy frightened people.' Emmeline could reply: 'Rubbish. Militancy brought women's suffrage to the attention of the public.' Working in pairs, continue the conversation.

2 'Getting the vote for women in 1918 was a waste of time. It didn't benefit them at all.' Write a paragraph explaining whether or not you agree with this statement.

How much more democratic was Britain by 1930?

The road to a Britain where parliament, and not the Crown, was the supreme governing body, and where everyone could vote, was a long one. It took centuries before all adult men and women could elect the people who made the laws they had to obey. In this section you will:

- learn how all women finally got the vote

- explore the pace of change and how it differed from century to century.

Towards democracy?

Learning objectives

- Learn about the ways in which Britain became more democratic in the years to 1930.
- Understand that the pace of change differed from century to century.

What do you think?

Should living in a democracy mean more than being able to vote in general elections?

After 1918, women were still not equal with men and millions of them still didn't have the vote. Despite giving assurances that these inequalities would be removed, the government made no attempt to do this in the early 1920s. It seemed that politicians, while agreeing with the principle of equal franchise, were either afraid of the outcome or believed they had better things to do than spend time on getting a bill through parliament that would give the vote to all women.

Source A: A photograph of 'flappers' in the USA in the 1920s.

The 'flapper' vote

Part of the problem was that some young women in the 1920s threw aside convention and behaved in a way many people thought was outrageous. They cut their hair, wore short skirts, smoked, wore make-up and listened to jazz music. They were called 'flappers' and, although the flapper movement started in the USA, hundreds of British women copied them.

Many people wondered whether women who behaved like this should be given the vote. Nevertheless, behind the scenes, pressure was put on politicians to keep their original promises.

Equal Franchise Act 1928

The Equal Franchise Act gave equal voting rights to men and women. Both men and women could vote at the age of 21. This added 5 million women to the electorate, so that women now made up 52.7 per cent of voters.

Did you know?

Many of the women who had fought for female suffrage were dead by 1928, including Emmeline Pankhurst. However, Millicent Fawcett, aged 81, attended parliament in July of that year to watch the vote being taken.

Getting democratic

Today we live in a parliamentary democracy – a country where all adults can vote for MPs who make the laws by which we all live. How did that happen?

Table 1.2: Some of the main changes to the electoral system, 1800–2000.

1800	1832	1867	1918	1928	2000
1 in 10 men has the vote			All men aged over 21 may vote		All men over the age of 18 may vote
No women may vote					All women over the age of 18 may vote
	The ballot is not secret		The ballot is secret		
Rotten boroughs sent MPs to parliament	New constituencies made: industrial towns elect MPs				

Important changes took place between 1800 and 2000 that made Britain a more democratic country. There are people who say that more must be done to make Britain even more democratic than it is today. Maybe students in the future, completing this grid with a column for 2050, will have more changes to add.

FREE AND INDEPENDENT.
The Three Leaders (together). "WANT A PILOT, MADAM?"
New Voter. "NO, THANKS."

Source B: A cartoon from the magazine *Punch*, published on 27 June 1928.

Your turn!

1 Table 1.2 shows some of the main changes that happened to the electoral system 1800–2000. Copy out and complete it, using the information in this chapter. You will need to use the internet to complete the 2000 column. You may wish to add a further row to include additional information.

2 Think about the changes that happened between 1800 and 2000 that made Britain more democratic. Write a paragraph to explain which was the most important.

3 Look at Source B.
  a What is the message behind the cartoon?
  b Did getting the vote mean that women had gained equality with men?
  Discuss your ideas in your group.

The long and winding road to democracy

The changes to the electoral system since 1800 form part of a much longer journey towards the parliamentary democracy of Britain today.

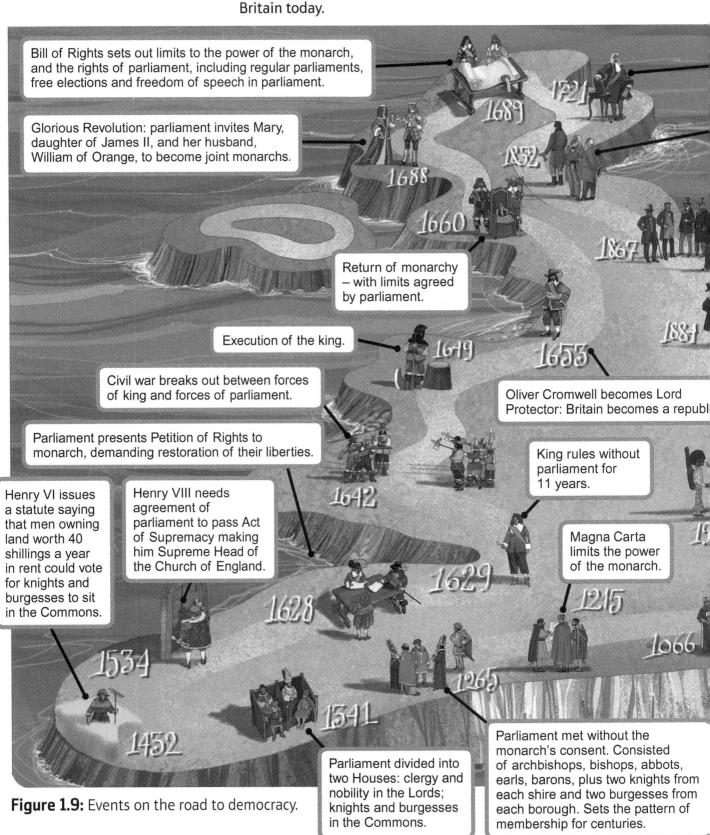

Bill of Rights sets out limits to the power of the monarch, and the rights of parliament, including regular parliaments, free elections and freedom of speech in parliament.

Glorious Revolution: parliament invites Mary, daughter of James II, and her husband, William of Orange, to become joint monarchs.

Return of monarchy – with limits agreed by parliament.

Execution of the king.

Civil war breaks out between forces of king and forces of parliament.

Oliver Cromwell becomes Lord Protector: Britain becomes a republ[ic]

Parliament presents Petition of Rights to monarch, demanding restoration of their liberties.

King rules without parliament for 11 years.

Henry VI issues a statute saying that men owning land worth 40 shillings a year in rent could vote for knights and burgesses to sit in the Commons.

Henry VIII needs agreement of parliament to pass Act of Supremacy making him Supreme Head of the Church of England.

Magna Carta limits the power of the monarch.

Parliament divided into two Houses: clergy and nobility in the Lords; knights and burgesses in the Commons.

Parliament met without the monarch's consent. Consisted of archbishops, bishops, abbots, earls, barons, plus two knights from each shire and two burgesses from each borough. Sets the pattern of membership for centuries.

Figure 1.9: Events on the road to democracy.

Robert Walpole becomes prime minister, the link between the Cabinet and the king.

Reform Act gives the vote to one in seven men and reorganises constituencies to include industrial towns.

Reform Act doubles the number of voters.

Reform Act gives men in rural areas the same voting rights as those in towns. 40 per cent of the male electorate have the vote.

Power of the House of Lords is limited. The Lords can only delay, not reject, bills.

Representation of the People Act gives the vote to all men over the age of 21 and to all women over the age of 30 who own property or are married to a man who does. The size of electorate triples from 7.7m to 21.4m.

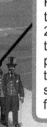

Men and women over the age of 8 given the vote.

Equal Franchise Act gives the vote on equal terms to men and women over the age of 21.

Monarchs for next 0 years rule with support of nobility and clergy, meeting in a Great Council.

Life Peerages Act allows the Crown (advised by the prime minister) to appoint respected men and women to sit in the House of Lords as peers for their lifetimes.

Your turn!

1 Look at the events on the road to democracy (Figure 1.9).

8th **a** List the three events that you think are the most important in giving control to parliament.

8th **b** List three events that you think are the most important in giving power to the people to elect their representatives.

9th **c** Write a paragraph to explain each of your choices.

2 Historians sometimes refer to a 'turning point' in history. By this, they mean an event that is so important that it brings about a huge change.

9th **a** What do you think is the most important turning point on the long and winding road to democracy? Note down three reasons why you think this.

9th **b** Now compare your choice with those of others in your class. Which event do most of your class think was the most important turning point? How many reasons can you all come up with for thinking this?

Checkpoint

1 In the Middle Ages, which two classes of people could sit in the Lords and which two could sit in the Commons?

2 Give one reason why Britain became a republic in 1653.

3 What was the importance of Robert Walpole?

4 What percentage of adult men had the vote by the end of the 19th century?

5 When did the right to vote stop being based on ownership of property?

What have you learned?

In this section, you have learned that:

- the electoral system changed dramatically between 1830 and 1928, finally giving the vote to all adult men and women

- the role of women, and attitudes to them, changed over the same period.

Change questions

Quick Quiz

1 Give two important features of the 1832 Reform Act.

2 Who was the 'Angel in the House'?

3 What did the 1882 Married Women's Property Act allow women to do?

4 Who helped to found the London School of Medicine for Women?

5 Name two of Gertrude Bell's achievements.

6 List two ways that the government tried to deal with suffragettes on hunger strike.

7 What does NUWSS stand for?

8 When was the WSPU founded?

9 List two jobs women did in the First World War that they didn't do beforehand.

10 When were all women over the age of 21 given the vote?

Focus on change

Historians are interested in change, but not all historians are interested in every sort of change. For example, a historian of fashion would not be interested in the 1867 Reform Act, and a military historian would not be interested in the actions of the WSPU for the campaign for female suffrage.

Your turn!

Three historians have different specialist subjects. They are all interested in the changes brought about by four important parliamentary reform acts, but differ in the importance they place on them.

1 Copy and complete the grid below. For each historian, put 1, 2, 3 or 4 under each reform act, where 1 is 'most important' and 4 is 'least important'.

2 Write a paragraph explaining your choices.

Historians and their interests	1832 Reform Act	1867 Reform Act	1918 Representation of the People Act	1928 Equal Franchise Act
Professor Cooper The changing role of women				
Professor Dawson The electoral system				
Professor Freeman Working-class rights				

Writing historically

We are going to explore how to answer the question: 'The 1867 Reform Act was the most important reform to the electoral system in the years 1830–1930. How far do you agree?'

Planning your answer

You need to decide upon which reforms you are going to focus. You may decide to concentrate on the four Acts you considered on the previous page. Don't just work through the reforms and add a paragraph at the end saying which you think was the most important. You need to ask yourself 'important for whom?' and 'important for how long?' This will show that you have understood the question and the historical situation.

Writing your answer

These students have drawn up their plans and have written their answers.

Student 1

The 1832 Reform Act brought great changes to the electoral system. It gave more MPs to the industrial towns and so was a great step forward. By 1867, the industrial towns needed more MPs because they were getting more and more important, and so this was done. A big change came in 1918, when women over the age of 30 were given the vote for the first time. This was equalled out in 1928 when men and women got the vote on the same basis. I think that the 1832 Reform Act was the most important because it was the first and started everyone thinking about reform.

The student has given a brief summary of the four main parliamentary reform acts. There has been no consideration of 'important for whom?' The student has simply said that all the Acts brought about great changes, with some indication as to what these changes were. The conclusion does suggest why 1832 was important, but doesn't go on to say that other Acts overtook its main clauses and so its importance was short-term.

Student 2

I disagree that the 1867 Reform Act was the most important reform to the electoral system. It did double the electorate by adding working-class men to the system, but it totally ignored women, so it wasn't particularly important for them. In many ways, it was just a development from the 1832 Reform Act, which did the basic reorganising of constituencies and the franchise. The most important reform to the system was the 1918 Reform Act because it included women for the first time. This was a tremendous achievement and historians have argued about whether it was due to women's war work or the actions of the WSPU and the NUWSS. The main point about the 1918 Act was that it took away the need to own property before men could vote.

The student has made a good attempt to think about the people for whom the Acts were important, but a little more actual data would have been helpful. The focus on the importance of women's inclusion in the electorate is a valid approach to take, although the reasons why the 1918 Act was passed are not relevant here. The final sentence touches on an important point, but doesn't go on to say that women had to own property before they could vote until the 1928 Equal Franchise Act.

Student 3 – you!

Write an answer to the question that improves on the one written by Student 2.

Why did the First World War start in 1914?

The First World War started in 1914 when tensions that had been building up between European countries since 1871 suddenly exploded into war. In this section you will learn about:

- the creation of a united Germany in 1871 and the impact this had on the balance of power* in Europe

- the ways in which tension between Germany and the other European powers, including Britain and France, built up in the years 1871 to 1914

- how the assassination of Archduke Franz Ferdinand of Austria triggered war in 1914.

The Franco-Prussian War, 1870–71

Learning objectives

- Learn about the causes of the Franco-Prussian War and the significance of its outcome.
- Understand the importance of the idea of a nation and nationalism.

What do you think?

How do wars begin?

Key term

Balance of power*: A situation where countries have roughly equal power to each other.

There was no country called Germany until 1871. There was just a collection of small states, loosely joined by language and customs. After a war with Austria in 1866, 22 of these states joined together as the North German Confederation. The most powerful of these states was Prussia.

How a telegram started a war

King Wilhelm of Prussia and his chancellor (first minister), Otto von Bismarck, desperately wanted the southern states to join with the North German Confederation to make one, united nation. War against Austria had united the northern states; maybe another war would achieve the same result with the southern states. Bismarck's chance came when King Wilhelm, while on holiday, sent him a telegram describing his friendly discussions with the French ambassador. Bismarck altered the telegram so it could be read as though the king had insulted the French ambassador. He then sent it to foreign embassies and the press.

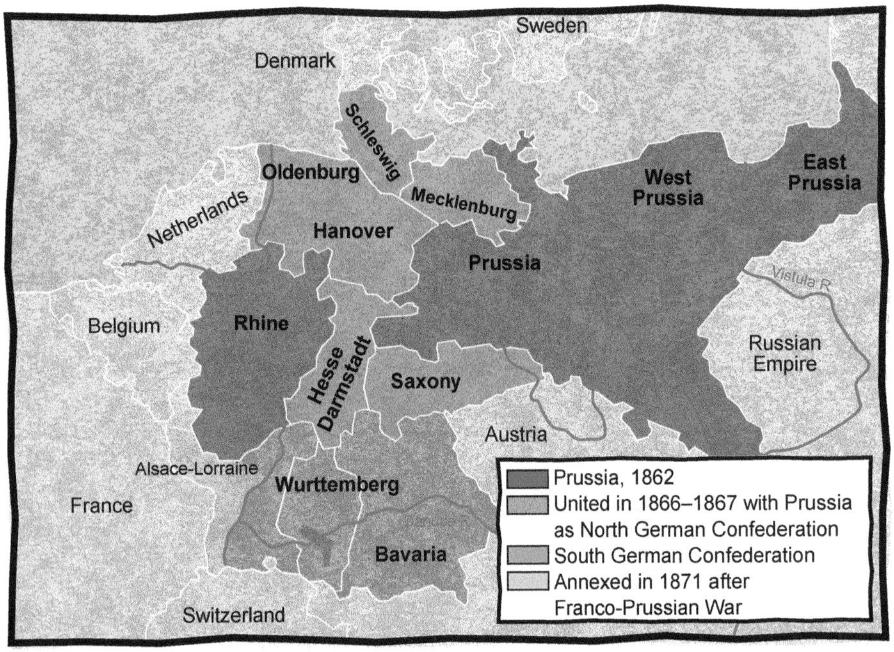

Figure 2.1: A map showing how Germany became one country.

The French government was horrified at this insult to their ambassador and to their national pride. On 19 July 1870, France declared war on Germany. The southern German states united behind Prussia and the North German Confederation. Bismarck's plan had worked.

A short, sharp war

The well-equipped German army, dominated by Prussians, mobilised* quickly and 500,000 troops marched into France on 4 August 1870. French forces, numbering 180,000 troops, were no match for them. The French army was small, slower to mobilise and not expecting an invasion.

- **The siege of Metz (19 August–27 October 1870):** French troops retreated to the fortress of Metz, where they were surrounded by the Germans. The best French troops were trapped in Metz until the end of the war.

- **The Battle of Sedan (1–2 September 1870).** This was an attempt by the French to force the Germans away from Metz. It failed. The battle started at Sedan on 1 September and, by midday, the French had suffered 17,000 casualties. By the end of the day, over 21,000 French soldiers had been taken prisoner by the Germans, including the French emperor, Napoleon III. This should have been the end of the war, but the French deposed their emperor and declared a republic. The war continued.

- **The siege of Paris (19 September 1870–28 January 1871).** The German commander, von Moltke, decided that the quickest way to end the war was to take Paris. The siege of Paris began at the end of September and lasted four months. The city surrendered on 28 January 1871.

The war was to have a huge, immediate impact on France, Germany and Europe. It also created a situation that, in the long-term, led to the First World War.

Key terms

Mobilise*: Prepare and organise troops for active service.

Kaiser*: German word for emperor. Used to describe the head of unified Germany after 1871.

Your turn!

 1 Write a short paragraph to explain **(a)** why the Franco-Prussian war broke out and **(b)** why the French lost.

 2 Look at Figure 2.2. What do you think the French would have regarded as their most important loss? Discuss this in a group.

What did France lose?

Peace treaty: French territories of Alsace-Lorraine given to Germany.

French professional army destroyed.

French army revealed as being poorly equipped, and its generals as being incompetent.

French losses

Peace treaty: France to pay Germany five billion francs over five years.

French national pride hurt and France humiliated.

France had to recognise the new German state under the leadership of Kaiser* Wilhelm I.

Figure 2.2: French losses after the Franco-Prussian War.

French resentment and German nationalism

What did Germany gain?

Following the war, the North German Confederation and the southern German states joined together to create Germany. Germany gained much from the war, as shown in Figure 2.3. This led to French resentment.

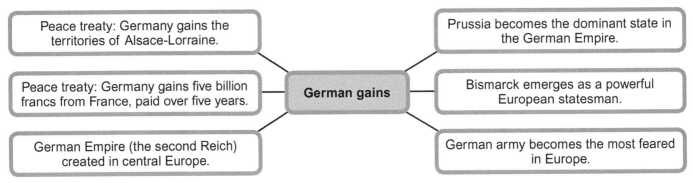

Peace treaty: Germany gains the territories of Alsace-Lorraine.

Peace treaty: Germany gains five billion francs from France, paid over five years.

German Empire (the second Reich) created in central Europe.

German gains

Prussia becomes the dominant state in the German Empire.

Bismarck emerges as a powerful European statesman.

German army becomes the most feared in Europe.

Figure 2.3: German gains after the Franco-Prussian War.

Upsetting the balance of power

A new nation had burst upon the political scene and was right in the middle of Europe. How would the great powers* of Britain, France and Russia react? What demands would this new nation make? The answers to these questions created the conditions in which a world war was possible.

German politicians were aware that the great powers might be suspicious of their new country and of Germany's ambitions. German troops might have to fight again. In 1897, Field Marshal Alfred von Schlieffen began to draw up a plan.

Source A: A painting showing German troops taking down the French flag at Fort Vanves, outside Paris, 29 January 1871.

The Schlieffen Plan

The two countries that Germany feared most were France and Russia. It was essential, Schlieffen thought, for Germany to avoid fighting Russia and France at the same time. Schlieffen developed a plan to defeat both enemies if Germany was threatened with war. The plan was to quickly attack and defeat France first, before turning to fight Russia. It required the German army to mobilise early. It was the Schlieffen Plan that Germany followed in August 1914.

Key term

Empire*: A large group of states or colonies ruled over by a single head of state.

A nation and nationalism

The idea of belonging to a single nation had been growing within the separate German states before 1871. They shared a common language and similar traditions. Pride in the German victory of 1871 spread throughout the German states. This was emphasised by the proclamation of the creation of the German Empire* (or Reich), with the king of Prussia becoming its emperor: Kaiser Wilhelm I. The proclamation was made in the Palace of Versailles outside Paris – the final humiliation for France.

Source B: A painting showing Wilhelm being proclaimed Emperor of Germany in the Hall of Mirrors in the Palace of Versailles, France, on 18 January 1871. The painting is called *The Proclamation of the German Empire* and was painted by Anton von Werner in 1885.

Your turn!

 1 Draw a concept map to show how Germany's gains and France's losses were linked.

 2 What reasons did the French have for hating and fearing the Germans in the future? Use Sources A and B in your answer.

3 What does Source B suggest about the character of the German Empire? Discuss this with a partner and back up your ideas with information from this section. Do the rest of your class agree?

 4 Write a paragraph to explain the ways in which the Franco-Prussian War brought changes to Europe.

Checkpoint

1 What was the North German Confederation?
2 Why was King Wilhelm's telegram important?
3 Name the three most important battles of the Franco-Prussian War.
4 What was the Schlieffen Plan?

Empires make enemies

Learning objectives

- Learn about the ways in which rivalries over empires created tension between the great powers.
- Understand the reasons why Germany wanted an overseas empire and how this developed into a naval race between Britain and Germany.

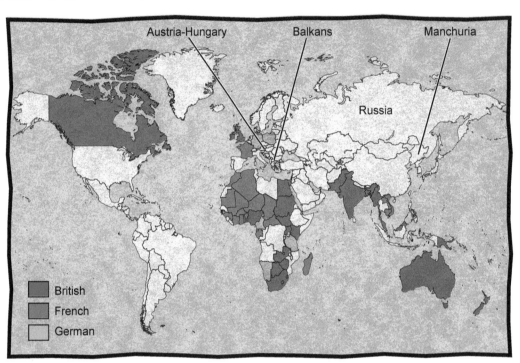

The great powers were all trying to gain and maintain colonies*. Colonies were important to them. Each colony provided raw materials for the growing industries of the great powers and markets for their manufactured goods. Colonies contributed to the wealth of the great powers and therefore to their strength and importance.

Figure 2.4: The European powers and their colonies, 1914.

Key terms

Colony*: Land settled by and under the control of people from another country.

Merchant ships*: Ships carrying goods and materials, not part of a state's navy.

The Balkans*: An area in south-east Europe that included Albania, Bosnia, Bulgaria, Herzegovina, Greece, Kosovo, Macedonia, Montenegro, Serbia and Turkey.

- **Great Britain** had a vast overseas empire, the largest in the world. Contact with its empire was by sea. Merchant ships* sailed to the different colonies, and the Royal Navy kept the sea routes open and clear of enemy shipping. Any challenge to the navy would put Britain's empire in danger.

- **France** had the second largest empire in the world. Despite troubles in some colonies, France was keen to keep all of them. Having lost the provinces of Alsace and Lorraine to Germany in 1871, France's international reputation would be further damaged if it lost colonies, too.

- **Russia** didn't have an overseas empire. However, it wanted to expand south-east into Manchuria in order to have ports that did not freeze in the winter, and into the Balkans* so that its navy would have access to the Mediterranean Sea.

- **Austria-Hungary** was a large empire in central Europe, containing people of many different nationalities, some of whom wanted independence. Its main concern was to keep its empire together.

German ambitions

The German kaiser and politicians wanted their new country to become a strong and influential world power. One way of doing this was by gaining an empire. In the years after 1871, Germany did just that – gaining as much land overseas as it could (see Figure 2.4). Germany acquired the Cameroons, South West Africa, East Africa and Togo in Africa and Kaiser-Wilhelmsland in Papua New Guinea. By 1914, Germany had the third largest empire in the world, behind Great Britain and France. Sources B and C show how Germany's new colonies were seen as a challenge by the British.

Germany's new colonies needed a strong German navy to hold and defend them, just as Britain's empire needed a strong British navy. British politicians regarded German ambitions to expand their navy as threatening the British Empire. German politicians regarded Britain as standing in the way of Germany becoming a great power.

Source A: From a speech made by the German Foreign Secretary, Bernhard von Bülow, during a debate in the German parliament on 6 December 1897.

We believe it is inadvisable, from the outset, to exclude Germany from competition with other nations in lands with a rich and promising future… We wish to throw no one into the shade, but we demand our own place in the sun… we will make every effort to protect our rights and interests… without unnecessary harshness, but without weakness either.

Source B: A contemporary British cartoon published in 1914.

Source C: A contemporary British cartoon published in *Punch* magazine in 1885.

Your turn!

  1 Write a paragraph to explain why Britain, France and Russia wanted empires.

 2 Read Source A. Explain why you think the speech would **(a)** alarm British politicians and **(b)** please German politicians.

 3 Look at Sources B and C. Both are cartoons showing the German kaiser. How far are they giving similar messages about the ambitions of Germany?

4 Work in small groups and set up a debate. One side must argue that Germany had a right to join the other European powers in possessing colonies and the other side must argue that Germany had no such right. Use all the information in this section to help make your arguments.

Whose navy was biggest and best?

Key terms

Patriotism*: Love for your own country.

Arms race*: A competition between countries for the development and production of weapons.

Britain relied on its massive navy to keep open sea routes to its empire. Britain was an island nation, and so the navy was also essential to protect it from any European threats. Britain had ruled the seas without any challenge since the Battle of Trafalgar in 1805. It had the most powerful navy in the world.

Germany builds a navy

Everything changed in 1898 when the new kaiser, Wilhelm II, announced his intention to build a powerful German navy. He believed that, if Germany was to become a world power, it had to challenge the might of the British navy.

- In 1898 and 1900, Germany passed the German Navy Laws. The first one ordered the building of 19 battleships; the second, another 38.

- The German naval chief, Admiral Tirpitz, set up the Navy League. This organisation arranged tours of shipyards and gave lectures about the growing German navy. These were intended to encourage public interest in the navy and develop a sense of patriotism* amongst German people.

Britain builds a 'Dreadnought'

Did you know?

German sailors called their own battleships the 'five-minute ships' because they believed a Dreadnought could sink them in five minutes.

British politicians were alarmed. Their response was to order the building of the most powerful battleship ever built – HMS *Dreadnought*. Launched in 1906, it was so advanced that all other battleships were instantly out of date. It gave its name to a whole new class of battleships.

Guns on rotating turrets could hit an enemy ship 18 km away

Powered by steam turbine engines

Carried a crew of 800 sailors

Could travel at 22 knots

Armour plating 28 cm thick

Figure 2.5: The British ship HMS *Dreadnought*: the most advanced warship at the time.

Source D: From a paper written by Lord Selborne, the First Lord of the Admiralty, for the British government in October 1902.

The more the… new German High Seas Fleet is examined, the clearer it becomes that it is designed for a possible conflict with the British Grand Fleet. It cannot be designed for the purpose of playing a leading part in a future war between Germany and France and Russia. A war with France and Russia can only be decided by armies on land.

Source E: From a speech made in parliament by Sir Edward Grey, the Foreign Secretary, in 1909.

There is no comparison between the importance of the German navy to Germany and the importance of our navy to us. Our navy is to us what their army is to them. To have a strong navy would increase Germany's prestige and influence, but it is not a matter of life and death to them as it is to us.

The race was on!

Germany built their own version of a Dreadnought battleship, called SMS *Rheinland*. Britain and Germany tried to outdo each other by building more and more of these powerful battleships in a dangerous naval race.

By 1914, Germany had doubled the size of its navy and was the second biggest naval power in the world after Great Britain. Britain was suspicious of Germany's motives and so began developing relationships with France and Russia. The arms race* was not just limited to ships and navies. All the European powers were building up their armies and armaments as well.

	Great Britain	Germany
1906	🚢	
1907	🚢🚢🚢	
1908	🚢🚢	🚢🚢🚢🚢
1909	🚢🚢	🚢🚢🚢
1910	🚢🚢🚢	🚢
1911	🚢🚢🚢🚢🚢	🚢🚢🚢
1912	🚢🚢🚢	🚢🚢
1913	🚢🚢🚢🚢 🚢🚢🚢	🚢🚢🚢
1914	🚢🚢🚢	🚢

Figure 2.6: The number of Dreadnought-style battleships built by Germany and Great Britain, 1906–14.

Your turn!

 1 Explain how a change in German policy led to the building of HMS *Dreadnought*.

 2 Read Sources D and E. What different reasons do they give for fearing the change in Germany's policy towards its navy? Is one reason more valid than the other? Discuss this in a group.

 3 Explain why the naval race began.

Checkpoint

1 When were the German Navy Laws and what did they order?
2 Give one reason why Germany wanted a navy.
3 When was HMS *Dreadnought* launched?
4 Give one reason why Britain was alarmed by the growth of Germany's navy.
5 What was the naval arms race?

Allies and enemies

Key term

Alliance*: An agreement between countries that benefits each of them.

European countries had different aims and ambitions (see pages 44–45), but they had some things in common. All countries wanted to keep themselves safe from attack by rivals. One way of doing this was by making alliances* with friendly countries, who would support them if they were attacked. Gradually, a European alliance system was built up (see Figure 2.7).

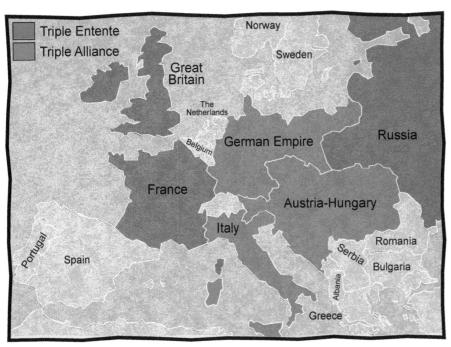

Figure 2.7: The alliance system by 1907.

Source A: From the *Times* newspaper, April 1914.

The division of the Great Powers into two well balanced groups is a two-fold check [obstacle] upon unreasonable ambitions or a sudden outbreak of race hatred. All monarchs and statesmen — and all nations — know that a war of group against group would be an enormous disaster. They are no longer answerable only to themselves [but to each other].

Threat or security?

The alliance system meant that going to war with one member of an alliance would mean going to war with all its members.

Many people believed that the system of alliances would keep Europe free from war. No one, they argued, would be crazy enough to set off a war between the countries of the Triple Entente and those of the Triple Alliance.

The German kaiser and his politicians, however, believed that Germany was being deliberately surrounded by hostile powers that were determined to stop Germany becoming a great power.

Britain and Germany were already in a race to build the most powerful navy in the world. All the great powers were building up their armies, too. Figure 2.8 shows how successful they had been by 1914.

By 1914, Europe was a dangerous place. It would only take a spark to blow Europe apart in a huge war. That spark would come from the Balkans.

Key term

Encirclement*: Being surrounded.

Interpretation 1:

From David Blackbourn, *The Fontana History of Germany 1780–1918*, published in 1997.

From the German perspective, it [the Triple Entente] amounted to encirclement*. That is hardly surprising. These powers [Britain, France and Russia] sank their differences and made agreements apparently designed to block legitimate German ambitions. Germans pointed to the French thirst for 'revenge'. A growing body of Germans saw the British as showing 'trade envy' of Germany.

Interpretation 2:

From Gordon Corrigan, *Mud, Blood and Poppycock*, published in 2003.

Ever since unification, Germany had plans for war on the continent of Europe. Every country has contingency plans and there is nothing wrong with that. Indeed, it would be surprising if they did not. The difference is that Germany, or at least many politicians and almost all the military leaders, believed that a war was inevitable and necessary.

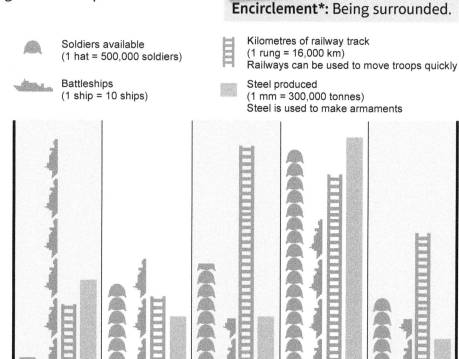

Figure 2.8: Who had what in 1914?

Your turn!

1 a Look at Figure 2.8. Working with a partner, work out which alliance – the Triple Entente or Germany and Austria-Hungary – was more powerful. Compare your decision with others in your class. Are you all agreed – and, if not, why not?

b Write a short paragraph to explain how far the data you have used supports what Source A says about the alliance system.

2 Read Interpretations 1 and 2.

a Write a sentence for each interpretation, summarising what the author is saying about Germany.

b The authors are saying different things about Germany, yet both are historians. Must one of them be wrong? Discuss this in your group.

3 'The alliance system threatened European peace.' Write a paragraph to explain how far you agree with this statement. Remember to use the information and evidence in this section to support your view.

Nationalism and nightmares

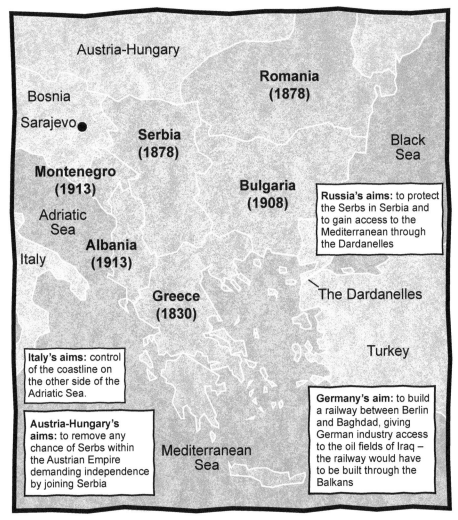

Figure 2.9: The Balkans in 1914. The figures in brackets are the dates on which the states gained their independence from Turkey.

The Balkans had once been part of the great Turkish empire – the Ottoman Empire. As the power of the empire weakened, Turkey began to lose control over the Balkan states. They began demanding their independence. Local wars broke out. This made the whole area very unstable.

For Austria-Hungary this was a nightmare. The Austro-Hungarian emperor and his politicians were afraid that the different peoples in the Austro-Hungarian Empire (see page 44), particularly the Serbs, would try to demand independence too. If this happened, the Austro-Hungarian Empire would collapse. Some of the other great powers, especially Russia, also began taking an interest in the Balkans. They hoped to increase their own power and influence in the area.

Balkan nationalism

The Balkan Wars (1912–13), where the Balkan states fought first Turkey and then each other, led to an increase in nationalism in the area.

- In 1912, Bulgaria, Greece, Montenegro and Serbia joined together to form the Balkan League.

- Serbia had grown in strength, size and influence as a result of the wars. There was a rise in Serbian nationalism. Serbia was now a direct threat to the Austro-Hungarian Empire.

The Black Hand

In 1908, Austria annexed* the provinces of Bosnia and Herzegovina, making them part of the Austro-Hungarian Empire. The provinces contained thousands of Serbs. Three years later, in 1911, a group of young Serbian army officers formed a secret society.

Key term

Annex*: Seizing an area of land and making it part of your country.

They called themselves 'Unification or Death' and their aim was to unite all Serbs in the Balkans – preferably under the leadership of Serbia. They were generally known by their symbol – the Black Hand. Membership of this secret society grew rapidly. It included Serbian army officers, along with some Serbian government officials. Their leader was Colonel Dragutin Dimitrijevic, known by his codename 'Apis'.

The Black Hand's aim to unite all the Serbs in Bosnia under Serbian rule was a direct challenge to Austria-Hungary. Black Hand members blew up bridges, planted bombs, cut telephone wires and murdered officials. Austria-Hungary was afraid that the Serbs within their empire would revolt. They also suspected that the government of Serbia was behind the Black Hand.

By 1914, the Balkans were a hotbed of hatred, suspicion, anger and aggression. It would take only a single event for the whole region to explode into war. That event happened on 28 June 1914 in Sarajevo, the capital of Bosnia.

THE BOILING POINT.

Source B: A cartoon published in the magazine *Punch* in October 1912. It shows the leaders of Britain, France, Russia, Germany and Austria-Hungary struggling to stop the Balkan 'pot' from boiling over.

Your turn!

1 Look at Source B.
  a What message is the cartoonist giving readers of the magazine?
  b Is the interpretation of events in the Balkans correct? Write a short paragraph to explain your view.

2 You have read about nationalism in this section. Write down two things that are good and two things that are bad about nationalism.

3 Work with a partner. You have both been recruited into the Black Hand. Draw up a long-term plan of action that will end with all Serbs in the Balkans being united under Serbian rule. Remember that really big objectives start off with small steps. Use Figure 2.9 and only plan things that a terrorist group could do.

Checkpoint

1 Name the countries in the Triple Alliance.
2 Name the countries in the Triple Entente.
3 What was encirclement and why did Germany fear it?
4 What was the aim of the Black Hand?
5 Why was Austria-Hungary afraid of Balkan nationalism?

Murder in Sarajevo!

Learning objectives

- Learn about the murder of Archduke Franz Ferdinand and his wife Sophie in Sarajevo on 28 June 1914.
- Understand how the murders led to the First World War.

Source A: Archduke Franz Ferdinand and his wife, Countess Sophie, arrive at Sarajevo train station.

Bosnian Serbs were causing a lot of problems for Austria-Hungary. The authorities in the empire decided the rebellious Serbs needed showing who was in charge. It was decided that Archduke Franz Ferdinand, heir to the Austro-Hungarian Empire, would pay a state visit to Bosnia. As head of the army, he would first watch army displays and then go to the capital, Sarajevo, where city officials would welcome him and his wife. The date chosen was 28 June, the national day of the Serbian people. It was also the wedding anniversary of Ferdinand and Sophie, his wife. The visit was given a lot of publicity. It was going to be a great occasion.

Enter the Black Hand

Thanks to the publicity, the Black Hand knew exactly where Ferdinand would be, and when. To kill the heir to the throne would strike a terrible blow to the empire they hated. On the morning of 28 June, six would-be assassins were in position along the route Ferdinand's official car was going to take. They were armed with bombs, pistols, ammunition and suicide pills. One of them was bound to be lucky, surely?

The route to murder: failure

The royal party travelled by train to Sarajevo. There they were met by an official welcoming party, headed by the governor of Bosnia.

The royal party were then driven in an open-top car through cheering crowds to the town hall. Lurking in the crowds were the six members of the Black Hand, intent on murder. However, when the cars passed two members, they did nothing: one couldn't get his gun out in time and the other felt sorry for Sophie and went home. Then the cars drew level with Nedeljko Cabrinovic, who immediately threw his bomb at Franz Ferdinand. The bomb bounced off the royal car and exploded under the car behind, wounding several people. The undamaged cars sped off to the town hall.

Did you know?

When Cabrinovic saw that his bomb had missed its target, he swallowed his suicide pill. But the pill was out of date and didn't work. It only made him sick. He then tried to drown himself by jumping into the Miljacka river, but it was only 10 cm deep. The police dragged Cabrinovic out and arrested him, but not before the crowd had given him a severe beating.

The route to murder: success!

Franz Ferdinand was furious. His day had been ruined. He decided to abandon plans for the rest of the day. He would go home, calling in at Sarajevo hospital to visit the wounded on his way back to the station.

The route back to the station had to be changed and the drivers took a wrong turn. They were forced to stop and reverse just next to where one of the Black Hand assassins, Gavrilo Princip, was standing. Princip could hardly believe his luck. Reacting quickly, he pulled out his pistol and fired twice into the royal car. One bullet hit Ferdinand in the throat and another hit Sophie in the stomach. With blood pouring from their wounds, they were driven at high speed to the Bosnian governor's house. Sophie was dead on arrival and Franz Ferdinand died soon after.

Riots and revenge

Anti-Serb riots broke out across the Austro-Hungarian Empire as news of the assassination spread. Some of the worst were in Sarajevo. Serbs were killed and over 1,000 of their houses, shops, offices and schools were either raided or wrecked.

Source B: A painting of the assassination of Archduke Franz Ferdinand on 28 June 1914. The picture was published in a French magazine the following month.

Did you know?

Gavrilo Princip's suicide pill didn't work either and the police arrested him. He was tried, found guilty and sent to prison for 20 years. He couldn't be hanged because he was under the age of 20 at the time of the crime. He died in prison from tuberculosis in 1918.

Source C: Anti-Serb riots in Sarajevo, 29 June 1914.

Your turn!

 1 Imagine you are in charge of the Black Hand in Sarajevo on 28 June 1914. Write a report to your boss, Apis, explaining what happened. Don't just describe events – Apis wants an explanation!

 2 You have read a narrative account of events in Sarajevo. Now rewrite the account from the point of view of Oskar Potiorek, the governor of Bosnia.

Countdown to war

The assassination of Archduke Franz Ferdinand could have resulted in just rioting. It could have led to just another Balkan war. But instead it ended in the worst war the world had ever seen, involving countries far beyond Europe, killing and injuring millions. How could this have happened?

Figure 2.10 shows how, by 4 August 1914, countries of the Triple Alliance and the Triple Entente were at war with each other. The involvement of Great Britain, with its worldwide empire, turned what could have been a European war into a world war.

Timeline

28 June
The heir to the throne of the Austro-Hungarian Empire is assassinated.

1914

5 July
Germany promises to help Austria-Hungary in any action it wants to take over the assassination. (This is known as the 'blank cheque')

23 July
Austria-Hungary blames Serbia for the assassination and sends a list of demands to Serbia.

25 July
Serbia agrees to most, but not all, of the demands.

26 July
Russia promises to help Serbia.

28 July
Austria-Hungary declares war on Serbia and shells Belgrade, Serbia's capital.

29 July
German kaiser warns Russia not to mobilise its troops. Tsar Nicholas refuses and Russian troops prepare for war.

1 August
Germany declares war on Russia and mobilises its army. French troops prepare for war.

3 August
Because of the Schlieffen Plan, Germany declares war on France and invades Belgium (to get to France).

4 August
Britain had promised to defend Belgium as a neutral country and declares war on Germany.

Figure 2.10: From assassination to world war, in 1914.

Who was to blame for starting the First World War?

Historians have argued for many years about who was to blame for starting the First World War. These are three interpretations discussing different possible arguments.

Interpretation 1: From Gordon Corrigan, *Mud, Blood and Poppycock*, published in 2003. Corrigan is a military historian.

All the evidence – and there is much – points to Imperial Germany preparing for a European war of aggression against France and Russia; and, while there were hopes that Britain might remain neutral, against her too if need be.

Interpretation 2: From an article written by historian A.J.P Taylor, *The entente that ended in slaughter*, published in the *Guardian* newspaper on 4 August 1984.

[The system of] alliances dragged the Powers into wars which did not concern them. They were supposed to make for peace, [but] they made for war. They were supposed to make the Powers secure [but] they dragged them into danger.

Interpretation 3: From historian Tony Howarth, *Twentieth Century History: the world since 1900*, published in 1979.

[There was] the nationalism of great powers who wanted to extend their boundaries and their influence to make themselves even more powerful; and the nationalism of groups of peoples who wanted to set up their own independent national homelands and states. In the early twentieth century nationalism dragged Europe down the path to disaster.

Your turn!

 1 Look at Figure 2.10. In your opinion, was there a point (or points) at which the advance to war could have been stopped? Discuss this in your group.

 2 Read the three interpretations above.
  a How do they differ as to who was to blame for starting the war?
  b How could you test each interpretation to see which was most likely to be correct?

Checkpoint

1 Who was murdered in June 1914 and who did it?
2 What did Austria-Hungary do as a result of the murder?
3 Which country backed Austria-Hungary?
4 How did **(a)** Russia and **(b)** France get involved?

Why did the First World War start in 1914?

1 Some students are arguing about what caused the First World War. This is part of their discussion:
Charlie: It's obvious. If Franz Ferdinand hadn't been assassinated, the war wouldn't have happened.
Mel: The alliance system was the cause. Europe was divided into two armed camps and something would have triggered the outbreak of war.
Chris: No – it was empires. Germany wanted one, and Britain and France wouldn't let that happen.

Beginning with the statement 'This was because…', write 2–3 sentences for each student, showing how they could have continued their argument.

2 Write a paragraph explaining why you think the First World War started in 1914. Remember to support what you are saying with evidence.

What have you learned?

In this section, you have learned:

- that events have many causes, some long term and some short term
- that nationalism can create tensions between countries and between individuals.

Causation questions

Your turn!

1 Working in a group, draw up a flow chart showing the causes of the outbreak of war in 1914.

2 Each person in your group is to choose a different cause in the flow chart you have made. Cover up one of these causes with a piece of paper. How would the flow chart be changed if that cause wasn't there? Jot down the answer and remove the piece of paper.

3 Repeat this with each event your group has chosen.

4 Now reach a conclusion, with which you all agree, about which events were necessary for war to have broken out in 1914.

5 Compare your conclusion with those of other groups. How far do you all agree?

Historians, as you have seen, can group causes in different ways. Figure 2.11 shows two of the main ways:

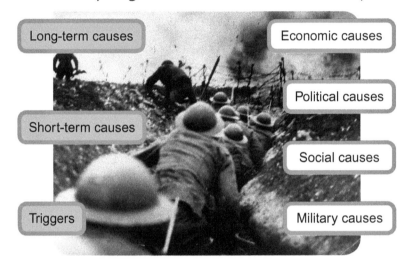

Long-term causes

Economic causes

Political causes

Short-term causes

Social causes

Triggers

Military causes

Figure 2.11: Ways of grouping the causes of the First World War.

There is another way that can be even more interesting. This is to decide which causes were necessary causes and which were contributory ones. A necessary cause is one without which the event wouldn't have happened. A contributory cause is one that contributes to the event, but isn't necessary for it to happen. For example, if you won a dance competition, it would be necessary that you had learned all the steps. This would be a necessary cause of you winning. A contributory cause might be that you had a costume that made you look great.

Quick Quiz

1 When did the Franco-Prussian War break out?

2 Which two provinces did France lose in the Franco-Prussian War?

3 When did Germany become a united country?

4 Name the German plan for preventing an war with France and Russia at the same time.

5 Give two reasons why Germany needed a navy.

6 Name the powerful battleship built by Britain and the year in which it was launched.

7 Which countries formed the Triple Entente and which formed the Triple Alliance?

8 What was the Black Hand?

9 Who was murdered in Sarajevo in June 1914?

10 By which date were all the countries of the Triple Entente at war with the countries of the Triple Alliance?

Writing historically

Causation questions

Historians often talk and write about causation. By this, they mean why things happened. It's not very often that an event has just one cause. You will have found (question 2 on page 55) that there were many reasons why the First World War broke out. Some reasons were necessary for the war to break out. Others contributed to the war, but weren't themselves necessary – take them away, and the war would still have happened at some point. This method can help you decide which causes are more important than others. Students were asked to write a paragraph in answer to the question: 'The Schlieffen Plan was the main reason why the First World War started in 1914. How far do you agree?'

Student 1

The Schlieffen Plan was the main reason why the First World War happened in 1914. The war wouldn't have happened without it because a country can't go to war without a plan. The alliance system only helped the Plan to go ahead. It wasn't, by itself, a reason why the war happened. Without the Plan, the alliance system was just a way of keeping Europe at peace because the two systems just balanced each other out. Germany wanting an empire had nothing to do with the Plan. It was understandable that a new country like Germany would want an empire like France and Britain. These two countries might have felt annoyed, but there was no need to go to war over wanting colonies. Without the Plan, there would have been no need to go to war at all.

The student is stating that the Schlieffen Plan was necessary for the First World War to happen, and that the other factors mentioned – in this case the alliance system and Germany's desire for colonies – were contributory factors only. The student is showing no understanding of the tension that was building in Europe due to, for example, the alliance system, the arms race and growing nationalism in the years before 1914. The arms race has been omitted altogether and the student has failed to appreciate the impact of the growth of the German navy on Britain, with its large overseas empire.

Student 2

The Schlieffen Plan contributed to the way the First World War started, by a German invasion of France, but it wasn't the main reason why the war broke out. The main cause of the war was Germany's desire for colonies and the threat this was to France, but mainly to Britain because Britain had the largest empire in the world and a huge navy to defend it and trade with it. Germany started building a navy as it got some colonies. This challenged the British navy and the arms race began. There would have been no arms race if Germany hadn't wanted colonies. The arms race meant that there were two armed camps in Europe because of the alliance system. It only needed the rise of nationalism in the Balkans, resulting in the assassination of Archduke Ferdinand, to set the whole thing off. Underlying everything was Germany's desire for colonies. Without that, war wouldn't have happened.

The student here has chosen Germany's desire for colonies as being the one necessary cause of the First World War. Other factors – the alliance system, the arms race and Balkans nationalism – have been selected as being contributory causes and have been linked to Germany's desire for colonies. Quite a lot of detail is missing, and there are no dates to show the linkages the student is making.

Student 3 – you!

Write an answer to the question that is better than those of Students 1 and 2. Use the work you did when working on question 2 on page 55 to help you plan your answer.

What was the First World War like?

The First World War was the most terrible war the world had ever seen. It involved armed forces from around the world, many of whom were conscripted*. The conditions in which they fought, particularly on the Western Front*, were horrendous. Civilians were drawn in, too, as their towns and cities were attacked. There were millions of casualties: dead, injured and traumatised men, women and children. This section of the book will look at:

- who fought in the war: recruitment and conscription

- trench warfare on the Western Front

- the state of Europe at the end of the war: good and bad outcomes.

Who fought, and where?

Learning objectives

- Understand why conscription had to be introduced.
- Know the main areas where the war was fought.
- Understand what trench warfare was like.

What do you think?

What made the First World War different from all previous wars?

Key terms

Conscription*: Forcing people to join the army, rather than relying on people volunteering.

Western Front*: The zone of fighting that stretched from Switzerland to the English Channel.

Did you know?

The image in Source A is of Field Marshal Lord Kitchener. He was a senior officer in the British army. He believed the war would last a long time, and so Britain would need a big army.

From volunteering to conscription

When war was declared, thousands of men volunteered to join the 247,000 regular soldiers in the British army. Recruiting offices were opened in almost every town and city. Men had to be 18 to join up and 19 to fight overseas but, desperate to join up, many lied about their age.

Source A: A poster produced by the government in 1914.

Source B: A poster produced by the government in 1915.

In the first year of the war, 1.1 million men enlisted in the British armed forces, but this was not enough. In January 1916, parliament passed an Act that introduced conscription into the British army for the first time: it became compulsory for single men aged between 18 and 41 to join up. Later in the year, this was extended to include married men.

Where did the men fight?

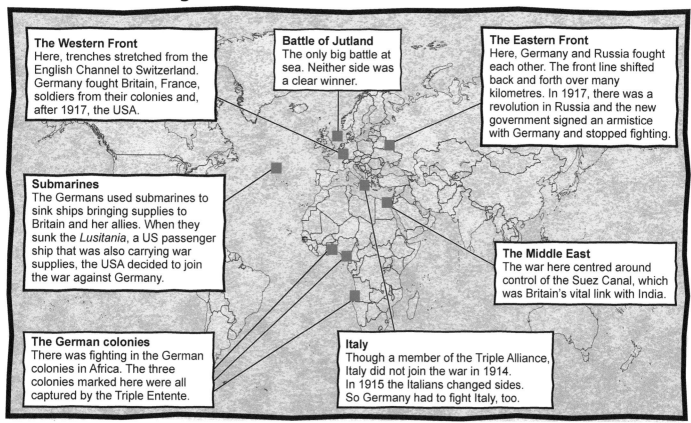

The Western Front
Here, trenches stretched from the English Channel to Switzerland. Germany fought Britain, France, soldiers from their colonies and, after 1917, the USA.

Battle of Jutland
The only big battle at sea. Neither side was a clear winner.

The Eastern Front
Here, Germany and Russia fought each other. The front line shifted back and forth over many kilometres. In 1917, there was a revolution in Russia and the new government signed an armistice with Germany and stopped fighting.

Submarines
The Germans used submarines to sink ships bringing supplies to Britain and her allies. When they sunk the *Lusitania*, a US passenger ship that was also carrying war supplies, the USA decided to join the war against Germany.

The Middle East
The war here centred around control of the Suez Canal, which was Britain's vital link with India.

The German colonies
There was fighting in the German colonies in Africa. The three colonies marked here were all captured by the Triple Entente.

Italy
Though a member of the Triple Alliance, Italy did not join the war in 1914. In 1915 the Italians changed sides. So Germany had to fight Italy, too.

Figure 2.12: The main battle areas, 1914–18.

Your turn!

1 Look at Sources A and B.
  a In what different ways is the government appealing to young men to volunteer to join the armed forces?
  b Which poster do you find most effective? Why?

2 Design your own First World War recruitment poster. What techniques are you going to use to appeal for volunteers?

3 In 1916, the British government introduced conscription. Do you think it is right that people were forced to fight? Set up a debate in your class.

4 Write a short paragraph to explain the advantages and disadvantages of 'pals' battalions.

Did you know?

Friends joined up together: whole football teams, young men from the same streets, factory floors and offices. They were trained together in **'pals' battalions***, and they fought and died together. Some villages and towns lost almost all their young men on the same day.

Key term

Battalion*: Fighting unit of up to 1,000 men.

What was it like to be in the trenches?

Learning objectives

- Find out what being in the trenches was like for soldiers.
- Understand why the Battle of the Somme was a disaster.
- Know how some people shared their feelings about the First World War in poetry.

Key term

Allied forces*: British troops and those of Britain's allies.

By December 1914, it was clear that the Schlieffen Plan (see pages 42–3) had not worked. The German advance into France had not been quick because Belgian, French and British troops had fought back more strongly than anticipated. Russia had mobilised quickly, and Germany was faced with the very thing Schlieffen had wanted to avoid: fighting France and Russia at the same time. German forces were fighting the Russians on the Eastern Front and Allied forces* on the Western Front, where both sides had dug in. Long lines of Allied and German trenches faced each other. Neither side could move forward. Thousands were killed and wounded taking and re-taking a few kilometres of mud.

Artillery fires into the enemy trenches up to 10 km (6 miles) away. Gunners target enemy fortifications and troops.

Troops from the reserve trenches could be sent forward safely through these communication trenches.

Support trench.

Reserve trench.

Aeroplanes and observation balloons were used to watch enemy troop movements and give warning of an attack.

Front-line trench.

Barbed wire was a vital part of defences. It could be metres deep and was often completely impassable.

Both sides built deep dug-outs up to 15 metres below ground. These protected troops from artillery during periods of intense shelling.

Company command post.

Front line dug-outs provide protection and shelter. A direct shell hit would still destroy them though.

Small post.

The area between the front line trenches of opposing sides was called No Man's Land. Constant shelling turned it into a mass of mud, making it even harder for troops to attack across.

Figure 2.13: A British trench system.

The fear of death and the death of friends were two of the worst things a soldier had to face. Soldiers in the trenches also had to live with poor living conditions. It was impossible to keep clean and healthy. Mud coated boots, socks and trousers; rats grew fat eating rotting bodies and clothes became covered in lice.

Source A: British soldiers photographed in a trench, 1916.

Source B: From the diary of Sergeant William Whitmore.

December 1915 Reached trenches at 5.30. Bullets and bomb fragments bursting over our heads. Slept in a dug-out, lying with legs over one another and hundreds of rats as big as rabbits crawling all over us and biting holes in bags for our rations.

Source D: From *Up to Mametz* by L. W. Griffith, published in 1931. He fought with the Allies on the Western Front.

There was always something to be done: digging, filling sandbags, carrying ammunition … strengthening the wire, resetting duckboards [wooden planks]. These duties seemed of such importance that they absorbed one's entire stock of energy.

Source C: 50 years after serving in Ypres, Edgar Norman Gladden wrote about his experiences in the war. Here, he remembers seeing a dead body for the first time.

The dead man lay amid earth and broken timber … Never before had I seen a man who had just been killed … His face and body were terribly gashed … and blood flowed from a dozen fearful wounds. The smell of blood mixed with the fumes of the shell filled me with nausea. Only a great effort saved my limbs from giving way beneath me. I could see from the sick grey faces of the men that these feelings were generally shared. A voice seemed to whisper 'Why shouldn't you be the next?'

Your turn!

1 Look at Figure 2.13. What problems can you see in trying **(a)** to attack and **(b)** to defend a trench system like this?

2 Is Figure 2.13 or Source A more useful in understanding trench systems? Why?

3 Read Sources B, C and D. They were all written by men who had been in the trenches. Which would give you the most reliable evidence of what it was like? Explain your thinking.

Did you know?

Trenches had latrines (lavatories) that were pits dug in the ground. Most soldiers hated using them. Instead, they used buckets or helmets and threw the contents into No Man's Land. For paper, they used grass or their shirt tails.

The Battle of the Somme

Source E: Men of the 2nd Battalion Cameronians (Scottish Rifles) going 'over the top' of their trenches on 1 July 1916.

The Allied infantry attack on German trenches at the Somme began on 1 July 1916. By the end of the first day, 57,470 Allied and 8,000 German soldiers were dead or wounded. Something had gone badly wrong. A week before the attack, the Allies had begun a massive bombardment*, designed to destroy the German front-line trenches. The Germans knew about Allied preparations from reports by their observer aeroplanes. Their troops simply retreated to dug-outs, and waited as the Allies shelled empty trenches. The Germans emerged unhurt and set up their machine guns when the Allied infantry attacked.

Even after the first disastrous day, the Allied commander, General Haig, saw no reason to change his tactics. Waves of men went 'over the top' into the enemy fire, marching slowly forwards. By November, 620,000 Allied and 450,000 German soldiers had been killed or wounded. The Allies advanced only around 15 km.

Source F:
From the diary of General Haig, 30 June 1916.

```
The men are in
splendid spirits.
Several have said
that they have
never been so
[well] instructed
and informed of
the nature of
the operations
before them. The
wire has never
been so well cut,
nor the artillery
preparation so
thorough.
```

Source G: Written by George Coppard, who fought at the Somme in July 1916.

```
Quite as many died on the enemy wire as on the
ground. The Germans must have been reinforcing
their wire for months. How did the planners
imagine that Tommies [British soldiers] would
get through the German wire? Who told them that
artillery fire would pound such wire to pieces,
making it possible to get through? Any Tommy
could have told them that shell fire lifts wire
up and drops it down, often in a worse tangle
than before.
```

Source H: A German soldier's eyewitness account of 1 July at the Somme.

```
Extended lines of infantry were seen moving
forward from the British trenches ... They
came on at a steady, easy pace as if to find
nothing alive in our front trenches ... When
the leading British line were within a hundred
yards, the rattle of machine gun fire broke out
... Men could be seen throwing up their arms and
collapsing, never to move again.
```

Key term

Bombardment*:
A continuous attack with shells (shelling), intended to destroy trench defences, especially barbed wire.

War poetry

There are a lot of poems about the First World War. Most were written at the time by people who fought in trenches and battlefields. Many of the poets were killed. All of the poets were telling us of their feelings about the war – and what they wanted us to know about it.

Source I: Written by Rupert Brooke in 1914. He died in 1915.

```
If I should die, think only this of me:
That there's some corner of a foreign field
That is for ever England. There shall be
In that rich dust a richer dust concealed;
A dust whom England bore, shaped, made award,
Gave, once, her flowers to love, her ways to roam,
A body of England's, breathing English air,
Washed by her rivers, blest by suns of home.
```

Source J: Part of a poem written by Siegfried Sassoon. He survived the war.

```
'Good-morning, good-morning!' the General said
When we met him last week on our way to the line.
Now the soldiers he smiled at are most of 'em dead,
And we're cursing his staff for incompetent swine.
'He's a cheery old card,' grunted Harry to Jack
As they slogged up to Arras with rifle and pack.
But he did for them both with his plan of attack.
```

Your turn!

7th / 8th 1 Read Sources F and G. Explain the differences between them.

2 Now read Source H.
  7th a How far do Sources G and H agree about what happened on the first day of the Battle of the Somme?
  8th b How useful would a historian find all three sources (F, G and H) in writing about the Battle of the Somme?

4 Read the two poems (Sources I and J).
  a What is each poem saying about the war? Write 2–3 sentences for each poem.
  7th b The poems were written by soldiers who fought in the First World War. How reliable are they as evidence of what happened?
  8th

Checkpoint

1 What were 'pals' battalions?
2 What was conscription? When and why was it introduced?
3 List three things soldiers hated about the trenches.
4 When did the Battle of the Somme start?
5 Give one reason why the first day of the Battle of the Somme was a disaster for the Allies.

The end of the war: losses and gains

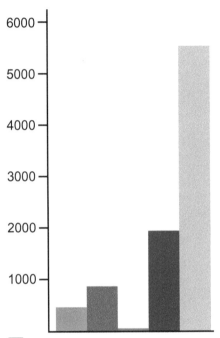

Figure 2.14: Deaths per day in major wars.

Legend:
- American Civil War (1861–5)
- Franco-Prussian War (1870–1)
- Boer War (1899–1902)
- Balkan Wars (1912–13)
- First World War (1914–18)

Losses

You can see from Figure 2.14 that the First World War was the worst war the world had seen. 616,382 British servicemen were killed. Most of those who died were men aged between 18 and 25. The loss of so many young men had terrible long-term effects. Children grew up without fathers, widows grew old without husbands and some young women remained unmarried and childless. A further 1,656,755 British servicemen were wounded and some were permanently disabled. The men who died, or were horribly injured, could have grown up to be talented doctors, engineers, poets, plumbers or policemen. Some people called them a 'lost generation'.

A land fit for heroes?

The British Prime Minister David Lloyd George promised that, after the war, Britain would become a 'land fit for heroes'. What happened?

- In the summer of 1918, Spanish Flu broke out killing 228,000 people in Britain and over 50 million worldwide – more than the number of people who died in the war – by the summer of 1919.

- Unemployment benefits for returning soldiers were limited. Many of the disabled did not qualify for an army pension. Thousands relied on their families or charities for help.

- The 1919 Housing Act ordered local authorities to build houses. 210,237 new houses were built by 1923, but this was still 800,000 short of the number that was needed.

- 40 per cent of Britain's merchant shipping had been sunk by German submarines. British overseas customers found other suppliers, affecting British industries. By 1921, over two million people were unemployed.

- Railways and coal mines were handed back to their former owners who reduced wages. In 1926 there was a general strike, led by the miners, in protest against low pay.

Source A: King George V presenting war widows with their dead husbands' medals.

What happened in Germany?

About two million German servicemen were killed or wounded during the war, resulting in family tragedies just as in Britain. The social, economic and political situation in Germany was very difficult, too.

- There were about 400,000 deaths from Spanish influenza, which hit Germany in the summer of 1918.

- There was famine in many parts of Germany: crops failed and importing food was almost impossible. A lot of European agriculture had been destroyed during the fighting, and British ships had prevented supplies reaching Germany by sea.

- Starving and desperate people rioted in Munich and Berlin. Sailors in the German navy mutinied*. Politicians feared a revolution similar to what had happened in Russia in 1917 (see page 59).

- In 1919, German politicians were forced to sign the Treaty of Versailles. Some of the most important clauses in the Treaty meant that Germany had to agree to accept full blame for starting the war. Germany also had to pay the Allies for the damage caused, reduce its army and navy, and agree to build no aeroplanes, tanks or battleships. Germany had to return Alsace-Lorraine to France. The treaty left Germany economically weak. Many blamed the government for signing the treaty.

PEACE AND FUTURE CANNON FODDER

The Tiger: "Curious! I seem to hear a child weeping!"

Source B: A cartoon published in the *Daily Herald*, a British newspaper, in 1919. The three men represent the prime ministers of Britain, France and Italy. 'The Tiger' is the nickname given to Georges Clemenceau, prime minister of France. The child crying is labeled '1940 Class'.

Key term

Mutiny*: When soldiers or sailors rebel and refuse to follow orders.

Your turn!

 1 Military historians are interested in armed conflict. Economic historians are interested in agriculture and industry. Social historians are interested in the ways people live their lives. Draw three columns, headed 'Military Historian', 'Social Historian' and 'Economic Historian'. Sort the information in these two pages as to which would interest each historian. Try to put the information in order of importance for each historian. Warning: some information may appear in more than one column!

 2 Look at Source B. The cartoonist has given his interpretation of the outcome of the Treaty of Versailles.
  a What is his interpretation?
  b What sources and information would he have used to arrive at this interpretation?

Gains

Interpretation 1: From C. Spring, *Medicine at War*, published in 1970.

High velocity bullets and shrapnel produced severe wounds. X-rays of bones became commonplace. Bone surgery developed as a highly skilled branch of surgery. Despite steel helmets, 10 percent of all injuries were to the head. Surgery to the eye, face, ear, nose and throat, and brain, and plastic surgery developed rapidly under war stimulus.

Interpretation 2: From Ian Dawson and Ian Coulson, *Medicine and Health through Time*, published in 1997.

In some ways the First World War hindered the development of surgical techniques. It stopped a great deal of medical research. In Britain, 14,000 doctors were taken away from their normal work to cope with the casualties of the war.

Interpretation 3: Part of a talk on the radio, given by the author J.B. Priestley, in July 1940.

I will tell you what we did for servicemen and their young wives at the end of the last war. We did nothing – except let them take their chance in a world where every gangster and trickster and stupid insensitive fool or rogue was let loose to do his damnedest [with them]. After the cheering and flag-waving was over, and all the medals were given out, somehow the young heroes disappeared. After a year or two there were a lot of shabby, young-oldish men who didn't seem to have been lucky in the scramble for easy jobs and quick profits.

All wars are terrible, especially for the casualties and their families. As you have seen, this has an impact on the countries at war, whether they are on the winning or losing side. However, the experience of going through a war speeded up change in many areas.

Medicine

Doctors and surgeons had to treat many badly wounded men quickly. This led them to try out new ideas and techniques. There were many medical advances in the First World War, including in blood transfusion and storage, x-rays and plastic surgery.

Industry

- Aircraft design developed during the war as aeroplanes were used for observing, and later fighting. The British government backed a new company, Imperial Airways, which developed flights to countries of the Empire. The aircraft industry grew and developed.

- Light industry developed in Britain and produced consumer goods. Unlike heavy industry (iron, steel and shipbuilding), many women worked on the new production lines.

- The Marconi Company made thousands of radios – called wirelesses – for the Allied forces. After the war, the company started selling wirelesses for people to use in their own homes.

Source C: The Bristol Aircraft Company's factory in 1918, at which point 3000 people worked there. In 1914, the company had employed 300 people.

- Chemicals were used during the war in, for example, making poison gas and high explosives. In peacetime, these techniques were used to develop photography, fertilisers and paints.

Politics and peace

You have already read (pages 34–37) how, in Britain, all men and some women got the vote in 1918. The war affected international politics, too.

The Treaty of Versailles (see page 65) set up an organisation called the League of Nations. Its main aim was to ensure that the world would not go to war again. The idea was that representatives from the countries of the world would meet to discuss and sort out problems before they ended up fighting each other. However, the USA did not want to join. Russia was not allowed to join because of the Communist revolution (see pages 71-2) and Germany was not allowed to join because of the way it had behaved in the First World War. Nevertheless, the League was a start: politicians were beginning to realise that it was better to talk than to unleash another world war.

Source D: A 1920s advertisement for electrical goods that could be used in the homes of people who could afford them.

Your turn!

Why interpretations differ

 1 Read Interpretations 1 and 2.
  a What is the difference between them?
  b How could the historians reach such different conclusions?

 2 J.B. Priestley was broadcasting when the Second World War had been going on for about ten months. In what ways might this have influenced his interpretation of the First World War in Interpretation 3?

Checkpoint

1 What was the 'lost generation'?
2 Give two things that were done to make Britain a 'land fit for heroes' after 1918.
3 Give two reasons why some returning soldiers found life difficult **(a)** in Britain and **(b)** in Germany.
4 Name three positive things that came out of the First World War.
5 Give three reasons why Germany was not happy with the Treaty of Versailles.

What was the First World War like?

Design a poster with the title 'This is what it was like in the trenches!' You won't be able to include everything, so choose what are the most important elements to you. Compare your poster with others in your class and discuss the similarities and differences in what you have chosen to include.

What have you learned?

In this section you have learned that:

- historians reach different conclusions about events

- different conclusions can arise because historians have different interests and use different sources.

Interpretation 1: From *Not for Glory*, written by P.W. Turner and R.H. Haigh in 1969.

The whole planning of the Somme campaign was ham-fisted and clumsy. The fault for the failure of most of the strategic planning must fall on Haig. Because the plan failed, Haig must be held responsible. [His strategy] proved totally ineffectual against the cold German professionalism that showed itself in the form of accurate shell, machine gun and rifle fire. Haig promised victory and failed.

Interpretation 2: From *Douglas Haig*, written by E.K.G. Sixsmith in 1976.

Haig was not deflected from his purpose. Only a man of outstanding integrity and great strength of character would have remained and done what he did. He continued to follow the strategy which he felt to be right. The events of 1918 proved it was right. It is doubtful whether anyone else could have done it so well.

Your turn!

1   Describe what the authors of Interpretations 1 and 2 think about Haig.

2   What are the details in each interpretation that support your answer to question 1?

Historians aren't only interested in events. They are interested in the people that make the events. One of these people was General Douglas Haig, the British Commander on the Western Front for most of the First World War.

General Douglas Haig

Haig strongly believed that the war would be lost or won on the Western Front. The huge casualties that his military strategy produced have made him a controversial figure. Some regard him as the butcher of the Somme, others as the man who won the war.

Haig was trained as a cavalryman and had a traditional approach to war. At first, he considered the machine gun to be an ineffective weapon, but quickly adopted them for British troops when he saw how efficient they could be. He also used tanks after he saw what they could do.

Haig has been heavily criticised for his role in the war, particularly at the Battle of the Somme (see page 62) in 1916 and, later, Passchendaele in 1917, where the British army suffered huge casualties. His policy of 'attrition', to wear down the enemy's forces, was successful, but at an enormous cost in British lives.

However, it would be wrong to condemn Haig simply because of the high numbers of soldiers killed. The nature of the war was always going to result in high casualties. Haig's tactics did have some success. The Somme may have been a disaster for the British, but it saved the fortresses of Verdun for the French. His calm response to the final German offensive of the war resulted in British victories that helped to end the war in 1918, when many thought it would last into 1919.

Writing historically

Why interpretations differ

Students were asked to use the two interpretations on the opposite page to answer the question: 'Why do Interpretations 1 and 2 give different views about General Haig? Explain your answer.'

Student 1

The two interpretations give different views about General Haig because the two historians have used different sources.

The student has given a valid reason for the differences between the interpretations, but it is very general. No explanation has been given as to what these sources might have been, nor why the historians chose differently.

Student 2

The two interpretations give different views about General Haig because the historians have given importance to different sources. For example, the first interpretation focuses on the Battle of the Somme, so the historian will have worked from sources that have to do with that battle. The second interpretation looks more generally at Haig as a general, and the historian will have used a wider range of sources to reach this view.

This is a better answer than the one given by Student 1. Here, the student explains that the historians will have chosen different sources because one is focusing on a specific battle and the other on an overall view of Haig's career.

Student 3

The interpretations may differ because they are only part of what each historian thinks about Haig. They don't actually contradict each other. Haig could have made a complete mess of the Battle of the Somme but, taking his whole career into account, could have been quite a good general overall.

Your turn!

1 Write a comment for the answer given by Student 3. Has the question been answered? Is the answer full enough? Is it complete?

2 Now write your own answer to the question. Think about combining the best from the answers of Students 2 and 3, and adding your own ideas. Look back at the section 'The Battle of the Somme', which will provide you with some useful evidence.

Quick Quiz

1 How many men had enlisted in the British army by the end of the first year of war?

2 What was conscription and when was it introduced in Britain?

3 Name two of the main battle areas during 1914–18.

4 Where were the trenches?

5 What was No Man's Land?

6 Name two features of the British trench system.

7 When did the Battle of the Somme start and who was the British commander?

8 Name the treaty that ended the First World War and the year it was signed.

9 Give one way in which the war helped the development of medicine.

10 What was set up to make sure that a world war never happened again?

How did new ideas cause conflict?

In the 20th century, millions of people fought and died in some of the most horrific wars in history. Key causes of conflict were new political ideas such as communism and fascism. This section of the book will look at:

- what communists and fascists believed in

- how their ideas caused conflict.

Workers of the world, unite!

Learning objectives

- Learn what communists believed in.
- Understand what caused the Russian Revolution, and the impact it had on the world.

What do you think?

Do you think it's right that most wealth is in the hands of a very few people?

Key term

Prolateriat*: A collective noun used by Marxists to describe the class of workers.

Source A: Extracts from *The Communist Manifesto*, by Karl Marx and Friedrich Engels, published in 1848. This summed up many of Marx's key ideas.

The world will be for the common people, and the sounds of happiness will reach the deepest springs. Ah! Come! People of every land, how can you not be roused ... Let the ruling classes tremble at a Communistic revolution. The proletarians have nothing to lose but their chains. They have a world to win.

Workers of all countries, unite!

In the late 19th century, a new political idea was created. It was called communism. The ideas of a German philosopher called Karl Marx (1818–83) formed the basis of communism, although his ideas were later built on and changed by others.

1. Communism is natural and inevitable, and will happen whether people like it or not.

2. Private property causes poverty and war. A small number of individuals shouldn't have all the wealth.

3. All private property should be confiscated by the state, and shared out amongst everyone equally.

4. Workers will become the most important people, and will take charge of the 'means of production' (i.e. factories).

5. The workers need to have a revolution, and establish communism.

6. Eventually, workers in every country will overthrow their governments and establish communism, so that national boundaries will no longer exist.

7. A 'dictatorship of the proletariat*' will need to be established. The workers will run everything and no other political parties will be allowed.

Figure 3.1: A diagram summarising some of the main ideas of communism. The red hammer and sickle shown is a communist symbol.

Russia in the early 20th century

For decades after Marx's death, only a tiny minority across the world believed communism was a good idea, or even possible. However, events in Russia changed everything.

Russia at the start of the 20th century was a country with deep problems. Russia was ruled by Tsar Nicholas II, and he believed he was God's representative on Earth. Because of this, he was extremely reluctant to share power with anyone else. However, Russia was undergoing major social and political changes that created a growing class of workers, particularly in the major cities of St Petersburg (Petrograd) and Moscow. These workers were unhappy with the social conditions of the country. In addition, a growing middle class began to call for involvement in the running of the country.

A small revolutionary political party known as the Bolsheviks went even further. Under their leader, a man known simply as 'Lenin', they began to call for a communist revolution. At this stage few people were willing to listen to such radical demands, and many Bolsheviks were either locked up by the Tsar's police or forced into exile.

In 1905, strikes and demonstrations forced the tsar to allow a kind of parliament called the Duma to be created, but as time went on he increasingly ignored it, and little changed.

In 1914, Russia was drawn into the First World War. Initially, the outbreak of the war was met by enthusiasm and patriotism. However, the war led to huge casualties and massive shortages, and the desire for change amongst many Russian people became greater than ever.

Did you know?

Tsar Nicholas, Kaiser Wilhelm of Germany, and King George V of Britain were cousins.

Source B: Cartoon published by the Union of Russian Socialists in 1900. The picture is meant to represent Russia.

Your turn!

1   Sum up what communists believe, in less than 50 words.

2   What do you think about these ideas? Summarise your view of communism in a paragraph.

3   Write a paragraph to explain why some Russian people were unhappy in the years before the First World War.

4   Look at Source B. Write down two inferences you can make from this cartoon about why groups like the socialists were unhappy with the political system in Russia.

The Russian Revolutions, February and October 1917

A series of events after 1914 shocked the world by bringing the Bolsheviks to power.

1. The war was a disaster for Russia. In February 1917, a combination of strikes and huge protesting crowds crippled Petrograd (St Petersburg).

2. Troops were brought in to restore order, but many were unwilling to open fire on the crowd. This was the first revolution in 1917.

3. In March, the authority of the tsar collapsed, and the monarchy was abolished. The Duma then formed a provisional government and tried to introduce reforms to end the unrest. However, they decided to continue the war, which made them very unpopular.

4. In October 1917, the Bolsheviks seized power in a final revolution. The Duma was closed and the Bolsheviks set about turning the largest country in the world, into the first communist state. This became known as the Union of Soviet Socialist Republics (USSR).

Figure 3.2: A summary of the events that led to the Bolshevik Revolution.

Did you know?

After falling from power, the tsar and his family were murdered by the Bolsheviks in 1918. Since then, many people have claimed to be Anastasia, one of the Tsar's daughters. These claims were all untrue: the remains of the tsar and his entire family have now been found and identified.

How did the West react to the Russian Revolution?

The capitalist* West was horrified by the establishment of communism in Russia and their withdrawal from the war. In 1918, a civil war developed in Russia between the 'Reds' (the communists) and the 'Whites' (groups who sought to overturn Bolshevik rule). The West sent troops to Russia to aid the 'Whites', but were unable to stop the complete victory of the 'Reds'. After the First World War, communist uprisings occurred in other European countries such as Germany and Hungary (see Source C). However, these uprisings failed. The USSR instead concentrated on building communism within its own country.

Stalin and the emergence of the USSR as a world power

In 1924, Josef Stalin became the leader of the USSR (Soviet Union), and set about a ruthless programme of industrialisation in which millions of Soviet citizens died. In 1934, the USSR joined the League of Nations (see page 67) and became a major world power. Many countries regarded the USSR as more of a threat than the rising power of Nazi Germany.

Source C: Extract from a speech made in Germany by the German communist Karl Liebknecht in 1919. He was later murdered by anti-communists.

> The proletariat of the world must not allow the flame of the Socialist Revolution to be extinguished. The failure of the [Russian Revolution] will be the defeat of the proletariat of the whole world. Friends, comrades, brothers arise against your rulers! Long live the Russian workers, soldiers and peasants! Long live the Revolution of the French, English, American proletariat! Long live the liberation of the workers of all countries from the infernal chasm of war, exploitation and slavery!

Your turn!

 1 Draw a timeline showing the main events that led to the Russian Revolution. Start with Russia before 1905 and finish with the victory of the Bolsheviks.

 2 Look at the events on your timeline. Colour code them into long- and short-term causes of the Russian Revolution.

 3 Explain two reasons why the Russian Revolution happened.

4 Read Source C. What can you learn from this source about the following issues?
   a How communists in other countries felt about the Russian Revolution, such as Germany.
   b Why the West might have been so concerned about communism.

5 Design a Soviet propaganda poster to encourage other countries to adopt communism. What would you include to persuade them?

Key terms

Capitalist*: An economic and political system in which money and property are controlled by private individuals. The USA is a capitalist country.

Checkpoint

1 Who was Karl Marx?
2 What was the political party called that seized control of Russia in 1917?
3 What did Russia become known as after the Russian Revolution?
4 Who was Stalin?

What is fascism?

Learning objectives

- Know what fascism is, and why it became popular in the early 20th century.
- Learn who Adolf Hitler was, and how his beliefs helped to cause the Second World War.

Did you know?

In 1927, Winston Churchill visited fascist Italy and praised Mussolini for what he had achieved. He later became one of fascism's most outspoken critics and led Britain against Mussolini and his fascist ally, Hitler.

Key terms

Dictator*: A single strong leader who can do what they want and has complete power.

Nationalist*: Believing strongly in your own country.

Militaristic*: Prioritising the armed forces over other parts of society.

Propaganda*: Communications (for example, posters and films) designed to mislead people by giving a very biased view.

In the 1920s, increasing numbers of people in Europe became drawn towards a new political idea known as fascism. Fascism emerged largely due to unhappiness with democratic governments, which were seen as ineffective, and the economic difficulties of the interwar period (1918–39). Having experienced the violence and chaos of the First World War, many people were also more willing to accept governments who used force to impose order and discipline.

Fascism is difficult to define as a political ideology. However, some of the main features are summarised in Figure 3.3.

Fascists believe that democracy doesn't work, and that countries should be run by a dictator* and a strong central government that makes all of the decisions.

No other political parties are allowed, and there are no elections. Opponents to the regime are often thrown into jail or killed.

Fascists are violently opposed to communism, seeing it as a threat to a country's way of life.

Fascists are nationalists*, and have an intense pride in their country and its culture. This also means that fascists are often racist, and are violently opposed to immigrants and people from different races.

Fascists believe economic problems can be overcome by the government, for example the government can eliminate unemployment by spending lots of money on construction, which requires lots of workers.

Fascists are strongly militaristic* and favour strong armed forces. They also believe that war is a natural way to settle differences between countries.

Fascists believe that the whole population must be motivated and united to achieve the nation's goals. Relentless propaganda* is used to try and achieve this.

Figure 3.3: A diagram summing up the main ideas of fascism. The word fascism comes from the word fasces, which is a Roman symbol made of a bundle of sticks and an axe.

In 1922, Benito Mussolini and his fascist party seized control in Italy and set about putting their ideas into action. Mussolini became the dictator of a one-party state. Criticism of Mussolini was forbidden. Massive public works projects such as building roads aimed to reduce unemployment. Many countries looked on with envy as the fascists seemed able to solve problems such as unemployment that democratic countries could not.

The rise of Adolf Hitler

Meanwhile in Germany, a failed Austrian artist and First World War veteran called Adolf Hitler watched Mussolini's triumph in Italy. He was the leader of a German fascist party known as the National Socialist German Workers' Party (NSDAP) or 'Nazi' party. For much of the 1920s, few people in Germany were interested in the ideas of Hitler and his Nazi Party. Then, in 1929, the world was plunged into a deep economic depression, which had a devastating impact on Germany. The economy collapsed and unemployment rocketed. The democratic German government seemed powerless to solve these problems.

Hitler was able to use the economic chaos of the early 1930s to present himself and his Nazi Party as the only hope to restore German pride and honour and to stop a communist takeover. By 1932, the Nazi Party had become the largest party in the German Reichstag*, winning almost 12 million votes. In 1933, Hitler was appointed chancellor (like a prime minister) of Germany by the German president, who hoped to harness Hitler's popularity while also keeping him under control. However, he set about destroying Germany's democracy from the inside, banning all political parties and throwing thousands of people who resisted him into concentration camps*. By 1934, Hitler had turned Germany, one of the largest, most powerful and civilised countries in the world, into a brutal, fascist police state* of which he was the absolute leader, or the 'Führer'.

Source A: Poster published by the Nazis in the 1930s, presenting Hitler as the only solution to Germany's problems.

Key terms

Reichstag*: The name given to the German parliament.

Concentration camps*: A prison usually for political prisoners or members of persecuted minorities. In Nazi Germany, they were usually very overcrowded, with poor facilities and a high risk of death.

Police state*: A country where the government uses the police to spy on the people and stamps out any opposition.

Your turn!

1   Describe in your own words what fascists believe.

2   Draw a table with two columns headed 'Similarities' and 'Differences'. Compare fascism and communism, and add to the table examples of ways in which they are similar and different.

3   Why do you think fascism would have appealed to many people in the 1920s and 1930s?

How did fascist ideas help to cause conflict?

Interpretation 1: Extract from A.J.P. Taylor's *The Origins of the Second World War*, 1961. Taylor was one of the first 'revisionist' historians to challenge the view that Hitler was solely responsible for the Second World War.

…Hitler never had a plan for *Lebensraum*. There was no study of the resources in the territories that were to be conquered; no definition even of what these territories were to be. There was no recruitment of a staff to carry out these plans, no survey of Germans who could be moved … When large parts of Soviet Russia were conquered, the administrators of the conquered territories found themselves running round in circles…

Interpretation 2: Extract from *BBC History Extra* magazine. Richard J. Evans, a modern historian, explains what he thinks caused the Second World War.

Hitler's beliefs are absolutely paramount as a causal factor in the Second World War. We know now through documentation that has become available over the last few years that he intended there to be a general European war really absolutely from the outset. He's telling people in private in 1932, 1933, when he's coming to power, that he's going to have a general war.

In 1924, Hitler wrote his political autobiography, *Mein Kampf*, which set out ideas that he hoped to put into practice if, or when, the Nazis came to power.

The German race, or Aryans, are the master race and are destined to rule other, weaker, races.

Germany needs living space, or *Lebensraum*, for its growing population. This should be taken from weaker races.

The peace settlement forced on Germany after the First World War is a national humiliation and must be overturned.

Communism is the mortal enemy of the Aryan people and needs to be destroyed.

Democracy doesn't work in Germany. Germans need a strong leader who will ban all other political parties and who will make decisions for them.

Figure 3.4: A diagram summing up the main ideas of Adolf Hitler and the Nazi Party.

In the 1920s, Hitler's ideas were mostly ignored. However, after 1934, with Hitler as the undisputed leader of Germany, his ideas became the basis of Germany's foreign policy, and played a major role in causing the Second World War. They led to the deaths of millions of innocent people across Europe and the Soviet Union.

Historians disagree on what caused the Second World War. Some historians believe that Hitler wanted war from the very start, whereas others argue that long-term factors were more important, and that Hitler was driven by opportunity and the weakness of other European countries and had no clear plan.

NATIONALISM

Hitler used propaganda to convince many Germans that Germany was the natural leader of Europe. The peace settlement imposed on Germany after 1918, known as the Treaty of Versailles, was destroyed piece by piece. This made Hitler very popular.

LEBENSRAUM

Hitler argued that the German people needed *Lebensraum* or 'living space'. He used this excuse both to take back territories lost in the Treaty of Versailles and also to expand into countries that had never been part of Germany, such as Czechoslovakia, Poland and Russia.

USSR

Poland

Germany

RACE

Jews were seen as inferior to the Ayran race, which meant that they were persecuted, then systematically murdered by the Nazis. It also helps to explain Hitler's invasion of the Soviet Union in 1941, which in Hitler's view was inhabited by racially inferior people.

ECONOMICS

One of Hitler's solutions to unemployment was spending huge amounts of money on the armed forces, which created jobs. However, in the long term, this made war more likely, as Germany faced economic ruin unless it took resources from other countries.

Figure 3.5: A diagram summarising how Hitler's fascist ideas helped to cause the Second World War.

Your turn!

1   Look at Figure 3.4, which shows some of Hitler's ideas as set out in *Mein Kampf*. Pick two and explain why they were likely to cause conflict, and with whom.

2   Look at Figure 3.5. Explain how Hitler's beliefs helped to cause war, giving at least two examples.

7th 3   Read Interpretations 1 and 2. Explain one difference in their arguments about what caused the Second World War.

8th 4   Why do you think Interpretations 1 and 2 are different? Try to think of at least one reason.

Checkpoint

1   List two things fascists believe in.
2   Which country in Europe became fascist first?
3   Give two reasons why Hitler was able to take control of Germany.
4   What was *Mein Kampf*?
5   What was *Lebensraum*?

How did new ideas cause conflict?

Draw two mind maps, one summarising what you have learned in this enquiry about communism and the other what you have learned about fascism/Nazism. Aim to include features specific to one ideology, e.g. *Lebensraum*, while also showing features that were factors of both.

What were the main events of the Second World War?

Before we look at the events of the Cold War, let's look at what happened during the Second World War. This will help you to understand how these events were linked.

War in Europe

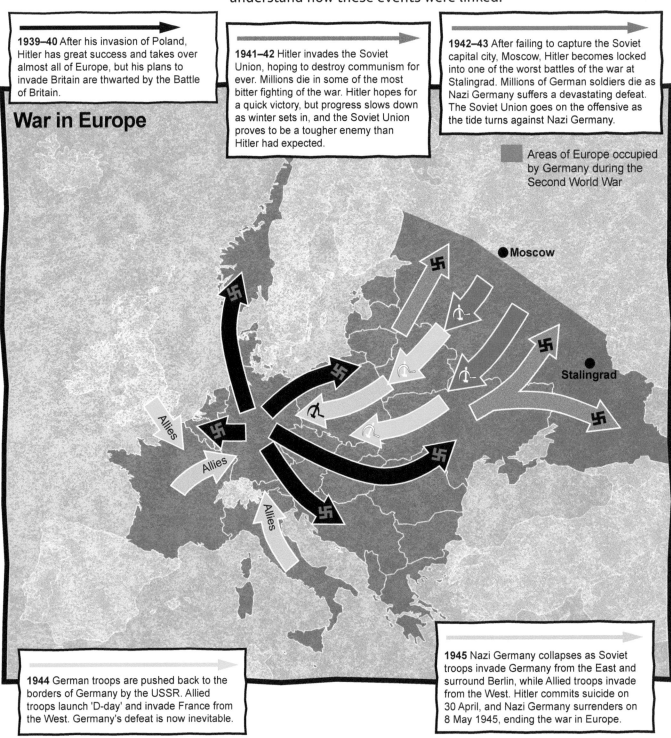

1939–40 After his invasion of Poland, Hitler has great success and takes over almost all of Europe, but his plans to invade Britain are thwarted by the Battle of Britain.

1941–42 Hitler invades the Soviet Union, hoping to destroy communism for ever. Millions die in some of the most bitter fighting of the war. Hitler hopes for a quick victory, but progress slows down as winter sets in, and the Soviet Union proves to be a tougher enemy than Hitler had expected.

1942–43 After failing to capture the Soviet capital city, Moscow, Hitler becomes locked into one of the worst battles of the war at Stalingrad. Millions of German soldiers die as Nazi Germany suffers a devastating defeat. The Soviet Union goes on the offensive as the tide turns against Nazi Germany.

Areas of Europe occupied by Germany during the Second World War

● Moscow

● Stalingrad

Allies

Allies

Allies

1944 German troops are pushed back to the borders of Germany by the USSR. Allied troops launch 'D-day' and invade France from the West. Germany's defeat is now inevitable.

1945 Nazi Germany collapses as Soviet troops invade Germany from the East and surround Berlin, while Allied troops invade from the West. Hitler commits suicide on 30 April, and Nazi Germany surrenders on 8 May 1945, ending the war in Europe.

Figure 3.6: An overview of some of the main events of the Second World War, 1939–45.

Key terms

Axis powers*: Countries who fought on the side of Nazi Germany in the Second World War. Germany's main allies were Italy and Japan.

Allied powers*: In the Second World War, the countries who joined forces to fight the Axis powers. The main allies were Britain, the USA, the USSR and China. They were helped by many groups whose countries had been occupied by the Nazis, for example French and Polish forces.

1941 Japan, looking to expand its empire, launches a surprise attack on the US fleet at Pearl Harbor, as well as Guam, Wake Island, Hong Kong, and the Philippines. The USA declares war on Japan and the other Axis powers*. The war becomes truly global.

1942–43 Japan has initial success expanding its empire in the Pacific, but is decisively defeated in a number of key battles such as the Battle of the Coral Sea (May 1942) and the Battle of Midway (4 June, 1942). As a result, Japan is forced onto the defensive.

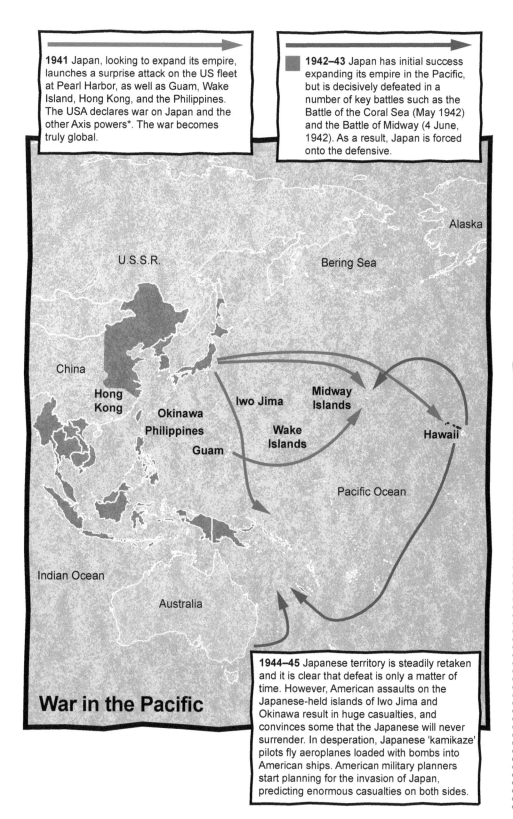

War in the Pacific

1944–45 Japanese territory is steadily retaken and it is clear that defeat is only a matter of time. However, American assaults on the Japanese-held islands of Iwo Jima and Okinawa result in huge casualties, and convinces some that the Japanese will never surrender. In desperation, Japanese 'kamikaze' pilots fly aeroplanes loaded with bombs into American ships. American military planners start planning for the invasion of Japan, predicting enormous casualties on both sides.

Your turn!

1 Draw a timeline from 1939 to 1945, and note down some of the main events that occurred during this period. You might want to indicate events in the Pacific and Europe in different colours.

2 Many historians think Hitler's decision to attack the Soviet Union was the biggest mistake he made, and led to Nazi Germany's defeat. Think back to what you have learned so far, and try to explain why Hitler attacked the USSR.

How do you fight a 'Cold War'?

Between the years 1945 and 1990, the world entered one of the most dangerous phases in its history, as the world's two nuclear-armed 'superpowers' competed for power and influence across the globe. What was the 'Cold War', and did this war ever get 'hot'? This section of the book will look at:

- what the Cold War was, and why it started

- some of the key crises of the Cold War: the Korean War, the Cuban Missile Crisis and the Vietnam War.

The nuclear age begins

On 8 May 1945, millions rejoiced as Nazi Germany surrendered and the war in Europe came to an end. However, the war in the Pacific continued, although it was clear that the Japanese were facing certain defeat. Most of the Japanese fleet had been destroyed, and Allied bombers pounded Japanese cities such as Tokyo with very little opposition. Just over two million Japanese soldiers had died fighting in the battles in the Pacific region. However, not only did Japan seem unlikely to surrender, but the fighting seemed to be reaching a new level of intensity as American soldiers approached Japan. In the battle for the Japanese island of Okinawa, at least 50,000 US soldiers died, along with at least 100,000 Japanese soldiers and civilians. Japanese soldiers fanatically defended their territory, often to the death. Japanese 'kamikaze' pilots flew suicide missions, flying aeroplanes packed with explosives directly into US ships.

American military planners tried to predict how many casualties would be caused if the USA invaded Japan, which was scheduled for 1946. Estimates ranged from 1.7 to 4 million US casualties, and up to 10 million Japanese casualties. However, the invasion never happened, as US President Truman decided to use a new and terrible weapon.

On 6 August 1945, a B-29 aircraft dropped a nuclear bomb, named 'Little Boy', over the city of Hiroshima. On 9 August, a second bomb, nicknamed 'Fat Man', was dropped over the city of Nagasaki.

Source A: A Japanese kamikaze pilot moments before hitting the USS *Missouri*, 11 April 1945.

Consequences of the attacks

The effects of the bombs were devastating. Both cities were destroyed, and an estimated 200,000 people were killed, and many more were injured. Fearing more attacks, Japan surrendered on 2 September 1945 and the Second World War finally came to an end.

For many of those who survived the blasts, the suffering was not over. Many suffered horrific radiation burns, as seen in Source C, and in the decades after the bombings many continued to die of complications caused by exposure to radiation, such as cancer.

Source B: An eyewitness account of the bombing, written by Father John Siemes, a Catholic priest living in Hiroshima.

There was an air raid alarm ... No one paid any attention and at about eight o'clock, the all-clear was sounded ... Suddenly— the time is approximately 8:14—the whole valley is filled by a garish [very bright] light which resembles the magnesium light used in photography, and I am conscious of a wave of heat. I jump to the window but I see nothing more than that brilliant yellow light. As I make for the door, it doesn't occur to me that the light might have something to do with enemy planes. On the way from the window, I hear a moderately loud explosion ... and the windows are broken in with a loud crash ... I am sprayed by fragments of glass ... I realize now that a bomb has burst.

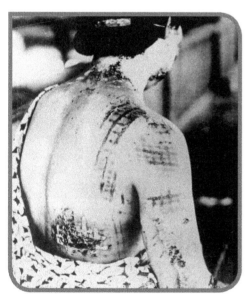

Source C: A person with burns after the bombing of Hiroshima, 1945.

Source D: Aerial photograph showing the almost complete destruction of the city of Hiroshima, which had been a bustling and crowded city before the nuclear attack.

Your turn!

1. Make a list of reasons why the USA was worried about invading Japan in 1945.

2. (7th) Look at Source A. What does this source suggest about what the fighting was like in the Pacific?

3. (7th) What can you learn from Sources B, C and D about the impact of the bombing of Hiroshima?

4. (8th) What questions would you want to ask of Sources B–D to try and understand more about the impact of the bombings?

Was the use of nuclear weapons against Japan justified?

Although the use of nuclear weapons ended the Second World War, it also sparked a debate that has continued to this day about whether using the bombs was the right decision. Much of this debate has centred on a couple of key questions.

Was Japan about to surrender?

There is no doubt that Japanese soldiers fought with a determination that had scarcely been seen in warfare before. This led some US military planners to conclude that the use of nuclear weapons would help to avoid even greater casualties resulting from a land invasion. However, there is also some evidence that Japan may have been considering surrender before the use of the nuclear bombs. Look at Sources E and F and see what you think.

Source E: Extract from the memoirs of Admiral D. Leahy, President Truman's adviser, published in 1950.

The use of this barbarous weapon was of no assistance to our war against Japan. The Japanese were already defeated.

Source F: Extract from a speech by Japanese Prime Minister Suzuki, before the use of the nuclear weapons.

I expect the 100 million people of the glorious Empire [Japan] to join themselves in a shield to protect the Emperor and the Imperial land from the invader.

Were there other reasons for dropping the bombs?

Although the primary reason for using nuclear weapons may have been to end Japan's resistance, they may also have been intended to send a message to the USSR. In July 1945, after the defeat of Nazi Germany, the Allied powers met to try and decide the future of Europe. The defeat of Germany had left the USSR in an immensely strong position, controlling half of Europe. Soviet troops were also advancing into the Far East. Truman's decision to drop two nuclear bombs on Japan may have been as much about warning the USSR about the power of the USA and stopping the USSR advance into the Far East as it was about trying to defeat the Japanese.

In addition, the USA had spent huge amounts of money developing the bomb in the closing stages of the Second World War. Using the bomb against Japan may have been the last opportunity for the USA to test the weapon on real targets before the fighting finished.

The dawn of the nuclear age

In 1949, the USSR successfully tested its own nuclear weapon, and the tension between the two 'superpowers*' reached a terrifying new level of threat. It became possible that the type of devastation inflicted upon Japan could also happen in the West, and perhaps even destroy life on Earth.

> **Source G:** From a booklet published by the Campaign for Nuclear Disarmament (CND) in 1985. CND campaigned in the decades after the Second World War to end the use of nuclear weapons.
>
> ```
> General Groves, the engineer director of the
> Manhattan Project*, was desperate to see
> the fruits of his labours before the end of
> the War. The bomb had been developed at a
> cost of $2000 million. It would have been
> difficult to justify not using it after such
> a vast financial investment. Two types of bomb
> had been developed. Nagasaki was simply an
> experiment to try out the second type.
> ```

Key terms

Superpower*: A nation that is immensely powerful and influential. Used to refer to the USA and USSR during the Cold War.

Manhattan Project*: The scientific project that developed the first atomic bombs. It was led by the USA, with support from Britain and Canada.

Your turn!

 1 What do you think – was it justified to use nuclear weapons against Japan? Draw a table with two columns, headed 'Justified' and 'Unjustified'. Look at Sources A–G, and decide which evidence belongs in each column. Remember to state your reasons why. If you think the evidence is inconclusive, you could place it in a third column headed 'Uncertain'.

 2 Review the evidence you have collected, and decide which are strong or weak pieces of evidence for either argument. To do this, consider the provenance of the sources – e.g. who wrote them, when and why?

3 Discuss your findings – which side do you find most convincing? You could then write up your table into a balanced argument, with a conclusion.

Checkpoint

1 On which two cities were nuclear bombs dropped in August 1945?
2 Give three reasons why dropping the bombs was such a controversial decision.
3 Explain why the USA might have been worried about the USSR in 1945.
4 What is a 'superpower'?
5 Explain why the possibility of a Third World War between the USA and the USSR was such a terrifying prospect.

Why did Korea become a Cold War battlefield?

By 1950, anything resembling the wartime spirit of co-operation and mutual respect that had existed between the USA and the USSR had gone, as the Cold War began.

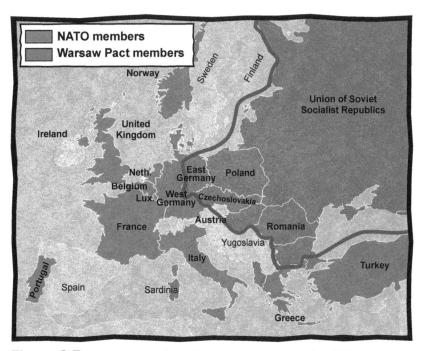

Figure 3.7: A map showing Europe during the Cold War.

What was the 'Cold War'?

After the end of the Second World War, the USA and the USSR became the world's 'superpowers' – mighty countries with huge armies and economic power, and both equipped with nuclear weapons. The USSR, after defeating Nazi Germany and liberating the countries of Eastern Europe from Nazi rule, set up communist dictatorships in these countries to ensure they stayed loyal to the USSR. People were not allowed political freedom and these countries were expected to copy the Soviet way of ruling. Winston Churchill, making a speech in 1946, declared that much of Eastern Europe was now trapped behind an 'Iron Curtain'.

The USA believed that the USSR wanted to spread communism throughout Europe, both by force and through other means such as propaganda. Therefore, the USA gave money to European countries, known as 'Marshall Aid', to show the benefits of remaining capitalist. A series of increasingly serious crises raised tensions even higher. However, it became clear to both sides that open warfare in Europe would probably lead to nuclear war.

Therefore, the Cold War came to be fought through a number of 'proxy wars*', in which US- and communist-backed forces fought each other outside of Europe. The first of these proxy wars, and the first real military conflict of the Cold War, was in Korea.

Why was there fighting in Korea?

Korea had formerly been part of the Japanese empire, but after Japan was defeated in 1945 the country was divided in half along a geographical line known as the 38th parallel. The USSR controlled the north, while the USA controlled the south. The USSR set about turning North Korea into a puppet state*, controlled by a communist dictator called Kim Il Sung, and armed the North Koreans with Soviet tanks and weapons. In the south, the USA backed a dictator called Syngman Rhee, who tried to resist communism by force.

On 25 June 1950, North Korea launched a full-scale invasion of the south. The USA saw the invasion as the first act of a co-ordinated communist takeover of the world.

In 1945, the **United Nations** (UN) had been created to try to avoid war, by providing a place for countries to discuss threats to peace. The USA asked the UN for help in defending South Korea, which was granted. 21 nations, including the USA and Britain, dispatched troops under UN command to stop the communist invasion.

These troops helped to prevent the complete defeat of the south. American UN troops under the command of General Douglas MacArthur launched a daring attack by land and sea, which took the North Koreans by surprise and forced them to retreat. The UN forces chased the communist forces north, close to the Chinese border. Had the war been won?

Source A: Extract from comments made by US President Harry S. Truman during a meeting at the White House to decide how to respond to the crisis on the Korean Peninsular, 27 June 1950.

```
The communist invasion of South Korea could
not be let pass unnoticed ... this act
was very obviously inspired by the Soviet
Union. If we let Korea down, the Soviets
will keep right on going and swallow up
one piece of Asia after another. We [have]
to make a stand some time or else let all
of Asia go by the board. If we were to let
Asia go, the Near East would collapse and
no telling would what happen in Europe.
```

Source B: A US officer points out North Korean positions to his machine gun crew, 20 November 1950.

Your turn!

1 Using Figure 3.7, describe what happened to Europe after the end of the Second World War and how this led to the Cold War.

2 Read Source A. What can you learn from this source about why the USA became involved in the Korean War?

3 Draw a concept map showing the long- and short-term reasons why the USA became involved in the Korean War.

4 Explain the term 'proxy war', and how it helps us to understand why the USA became involved in Korea.

The intervention of China

Although victory for the UN forces seemed close by the end of 1950, the war was about to take an unexpected turn as China became involved.

Source C: A propaganda poster showing the Chinese leader, Mao Tse Tung, alongside images of other famous communists – Lenin, Stalin and Marx – showing unity. In reality, relations between the USSR and communist China became very poor.

China had only recently become communist in 1949 after a long civil war. The victory of the communists, led by Mao Tse Tung, dismayed many in the West, who viewed it as yet more evidence of a communist takeover of the world. Mao saw the advance of UN forces in Korea as an attempt to invade China and overthrow communism. In response, Mao sent lots of Chinese soldiers across the border, overwhelming the UN forces and forcing them back.

Eventually, the fighting stabilised along the 38th parallel – where the war had started. An uneasy truce between the UN-led forces, North Korea and China was negotiated by the UN. Both sides agreed to a demilitarised zone along the 38th parallel, where heavily-armed soldiers were posted in case the Korean War broke out again.

The war had been extremely costly in terms of lives lost – around 40,000 US, British and UN soldiers were killed, along with 46,000 South Koreans. The numbers of North Koreans and Chinese casualties are not known, but some estimates suggest that as many as 400,000 Chinese soldiers were killed.

North Korea's invasion, June 1950

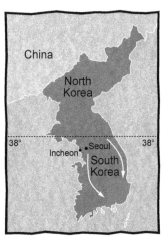

South Korea is almost defeated, September 1950

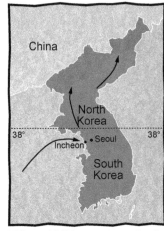

US and UN counter-attack almost wins the war

Chinese counter-attack forces both sides back to 38th parallel

Figure 3.8: Maps showing the different stages of the Korean War.

Why was the Korean War important?

The Korean War demonstrated that the Cold War could easily become 'hot' and break out into serious military clashes. UN forces had become involved in desperate, direct fighting against a major communist country – China – and the war could easily have escalated into a world war. The USA had even come close to using nuclear weapons in Korea, arguing that the weapons were pointless if they could not be used.

The long-term consequences of the war

Korea was also important as it helped to provide the blueprint for a later war in Vietnam, which was fought under similar circumstances.

However, the Vietnam War would prove to be far more controversial, and arguably more difficult to fight, as you will see later in this chapter.

The Korean War continues to cast a long shadow over the world today. At the time of writing, in early 2018, the Korean Peninsula remains divided along the 38th parallel, where the fighting stopped in 1953. Soldiers from the north and south peer across the barbed wire at each other, and both sides are still officially at war. North Korea continues to be a communist state, ruled by the grandson of Kim Il Sung. With the collapse of other communist states, such as the Soviet Union, it is increasingly isolated. Tensions remain high.

Source D: US soldiers patrol the DMZ (demilitarised zone) along the 38th parallel in 2007. The border remains one of the world's most heavily militarised areas.

> **Did you know?**
>
> In 1954, US General MacArthur (who had been relieved of his command during the Korean War), argued that he could have won the war in Korea had he been allowed to drop between 30 and 50 nuclear bombs on North Korean troops.

Your turn!

 1 Draw a flow chart showing the key events from the North Korean invasion in June 1950 until the end of the war.

 2 Note down both the short- and long-term consequences of the Korean War. What did it mean for the Cold War, and why is it still an issue in the 21st century?

 3 Imagine you were going to write a new book about the Korean War for general readers. Plan and write the blurb for the back cover of the book, aiming to give a general summary of the causes, course and consequences of the war in no more than 200 words.

Checkpoint

1 What was the 'Cold War'?

2 Give two reasons why the USA and the UN became involved in the war in Korea.

3 Why did China become involved in the Korean War?

4 How did the fighting stop?

5 Find out what is currently happening in the Korean Peninsula. Has the situation changed since this book was written?

How close did the world come to destruction over Cuba?

The small Caribbean island of Cuba, only 90 miles from the coast of Florida (USA), probably wasn't well-known to most Americans before the 1950s. Some American companies had major business interests on Cuba, while for some wealthy Americans it was an island of pleasure, where they went to gamble in its casinos. However, all that changed in the late 1950s. A civil war broke out between the capitalist, US-backed regime and a group of communists, led by the popular revolutionary, Fidel Castro. In 1959, to the horror of many Americans, the communists won. The US now had a communist country in its own 'back-yard'. To make things worse, the communist regime infuriated Americans by seizing American property in Cuba and nationalising* it.

Source A: Fidel Castro and his fellow communist revolutionaries celebrating in 1959.

Key terms

Nationalise*: To make something the property of the state.

CIA*: Central Intelligence Agency, a US government agency that gathers intelligence on other nations and uses it to influence and guide US foreign policy.

Kennedy and the Bay of Pigs affair

In January 1961, John F. Kennedy became the president of the USA. His advisers immediately put pressure on him to do something about the newly communist Cuba. Kennedy, acting on advice from the CIA*, agreed that the CIA could arm and train a force of Cubans who had fled Cuba after the communist victory. The CIA planned to land a small army in the Bay of Pigs in Cuba, to overthrow the regime.

On 17 April 1961, 1,500 Cubans landed in the Bay of Pigs. However, the invasion was a complete failure, and two days later all of the invaders had either been killed or taken prisoner.

The invasion was an embarrassing humiliation for President Kennedy, who swore not to listen unquestioningly to his advisers in the future. Fidel Castro, fearing another attempt by the USA to overthrow his new regime, turned for help to a communist ally – the Soviet Union.

The crisis begins

In September 1962, US intelligence noticed that a military build-up was starting on Cuba. Alarmed, the USA sent a U-2 spy plane to try to gain more information. The spy plane returned, and the photos it had taken were immediately passed to the White House, for they revealed something shocking. The USSR had constructed missile bases on Cuba, and they were almost ready to allow missiles to be launched.

The implications for US security were enormous. Up until this point, the USA had felt relatively secure in the knowledge that the USSR had very few missiles able to reach the USA. Soviet nuclear weapons delivered by slow bombers could easily be intercepted.

The missiles being placed on Cuba could be equipped with nuclear warheads that could destroy most of the major cities in the USA with almost no notice. The threat from the Cold War had just become far more real.

Source B: Aerial photo taken by a US spy plane showing a Soviet missile site on Cuba, November 1962.

Did you know?

Fidel Castro was Prime Minister of Cuba from 1959–1976, and President from 1976–2008. He is the longest-serving non-royal head of state in the 20th and 21st centuries.

Your turn!

1 Explain why the USA was alarmed enough by the communist victory in Cuba to want to launch the 'Bay of Pigs' invasion.

2 Give two consequences of the 'Bay of Pigs' invasion. What impact did it have on Cuba's new leader, Fidel Castro?

3 Look at Source B. What reaction do you think there was from the president and his advisers upon seeing this piece of intelligence? Explain your answer.

Kennedy's dilemma

Kennedy met with his advisers to decide what to do about the developments. Some of the advice he was given is included in Figure 3.9.

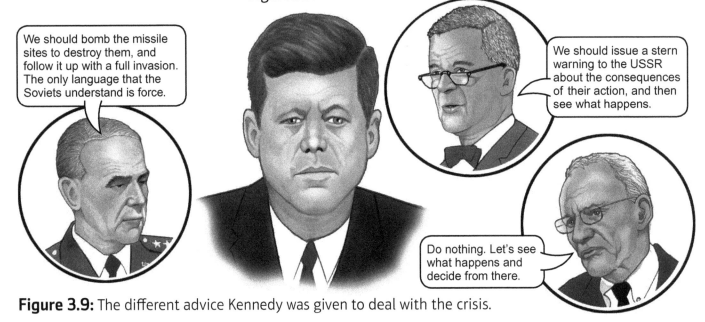

Figure 3.9: The different advice Kennedy was given to deal with the crisis.

Key term

Blockade*: When ships belonging to an enemy nation are prevented from reaching port, normally in order to damage the enemy's economy. Blockades were used to great effect by the British in the First World War.

Kennedy decided he would impose what he called a 'quarantine' zone around the island of Cuba, to prevent any more Soviet ships bringing military aid to the island. This was really a blockade*, but as a blockade was an act of war, Kennedy chose to use the more neutral term 'quarantine'. The question remained – what would the USA do if Soviet ships tried to break through the blockade?

Kennedy appeared on US television and advised the US public of the presence of the weapons in Cuba, as well as his plan for a blockade. The world was shocked. Some people began to panic-buy food and water, believing that a nuclear war was imminent.

Source C: Extract from President John F. Kennedy's address to the American people, 22 October 1962.

```
... the ... decision to station strategic weapons for first time
outside of Soviet soil — is a deliberately provocative and unjustified
change in the status quo which cannot be accepted by this country...

... I call upon Chairman Khrushchev* to halt and eliminate this
... reckless, and provocative threat to world peace and to stable
relations between our two nations. I call upon him further to
abandon this course of world domination, and to join in an historic
effort to end the perilous arms race and to transform the history of
man. He has an opportunity now to move the world back from the abyss
of destruction.

Our goal is not the victory of might, but the vindication of right.
```

What happened in the crisis?

The 'quarantine' was put in place, and the world held its breath to see what would happen next.

- On 24 October, Russian ships approached the US blockade. Tensions were high – what would the USA do if the Soviets refused to stop? However, the Soviet ships turned around before the blockade, and conflict was avoided.

- On 27 October, a US spy plane was shot down over Cuba, and its pilot was killed. US forces prepared to invade Cuba.

Just as war seemed possible once again, the USA received a note from the USSR through secret channels. The USSR offered to stop sending weapons to Cuba if the USA made a promise not to invade Cuba. However, while the USA prepared to respond to this reasonable offer, Kennedy received another, more aggressive note, in which Khrushchev said that the USSR would only remove its missiles if the USA removed its missiles from Turkey which could reach the USSR. Kennedy decided to respond to the first note, and to ignore the second. On 20 November 1962, the quarantine was lifted, and the USSR began to remove its missiles. Later, in April 1963, the USA quietly removed its missiles from Turkey.

Consequences

Nuclear war had been avoided. However, both the USA and USSR were alarmed at how close the world had come to nuclear war, and a 'hotline' was installed between the two countries to ensure that the two leaders could talk to each other directly and avoid a future crisis. Over the next few years, the USA and the USSR signed treaties that aimed to reduce the risk of nuclear war, and the threat of nuclear destruction decreased.

Did you know?

During the missile crisis, a US submarine attacked a Soviet submarine, not knowing that the Soviet submarine was equipped with a nuclear torpedo. The three commanders on the Soviet submarine voted on whether to use the torpedo. Two commanders voted for it, but it was not used as the vote had to be unanimous. Otherwise, the crisis might have turned out very differently.

Your turn!

 1 Draw a flow chart of events from the start to the end of the Cuban Missile Crisis. You might want to start with the discovery of Soviet missiles on Cuba.

 2 Try to divide your flow chart intro three sections: causes of the crisis, climax of the crisis and resolution of the crisis. When you have finished, use your chart to plan an answer to the following question:
'Write a narrative account that analyses how the 1962 Cuban Missile Crisis was resolved.'
See pages 92–3 for hints on how to structure and answer this question.

Checkpoint

1 Why was the USA so worried about communists taking power in Cuba?
2 What was the 'Bay of Pigs' incident, and why was it important?
3 Why did Fidel Castro allow Soviet missiles on Cuba?
4 Explain why Kennedy felt he had to take decisive action over the missiles.
5 What method did Kennedy decide on to deal with the crisis?

In this section, you have learned:

- how political ideas such as communism and fascism helped to cause conflict

- what caused the Cold War, and what happened in some of its key crises.

On the previous page, you were asked to plan a piece of analytical narrative answering the following question:

'Write a narrative account that analyses how the 1962 Cuban Missile Crisis was resolved.'

Structuring your analytical narrative

It helps if you can think of all historical events as having a beginning, a middle and an end. This is just the same as a novel or a film. A film wouldn't make much sense if it started in the middle of the story without setting up the plot, or explaining who the characters were, and it would be even worse if there was no 'resolution' to the film, and you left the cinema wondering how the story ended!

Below is a suggested structure for your answer to the question.

In September 1962, Soviet missiles were spotted on Cuba by a US spy plane.

Kennedy decides to create a 'quarantine' around Cuba to stop any more missiles being placed on Cuba. On 24-25 October, Soviet ships turn around instead of trying to break through the quarantine.

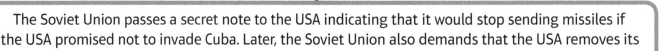

The Soviet Union passes a secret note to the USA indicating that it would stop sending missiles if the USA promised not to invade Cuba. Later, the Soviet Union also demands that the USA removes its missiles from Turkey.

Kennedy accepts the first offer in public, and the Soviet Union removes the missiles. Kennedy later quietly removes US missiles from Turkey.

The crisis ends, and the two superpowers create a direct 'hotline' to ensure that such a crisis does not happen again.

Linking your analytical narrative together

Remember that this is an **analytical** narrative – therefore, it must be a narrative that analyses the answer to a question. To do this, you will need to make sure that your answer consistently focuses on the question. Also make sure that you use linking words and phrases such as 'because', 'as a result of', 'so' and 'this led to' to show how one thing led to another.

Writing historically

Below are two examples of how students answered the question: 'Write a narrative analysing how the 1962 Cuban Missile Crisis was resolved.'

Student 1

Kennedy decided to place a 'quarantine' around Cuba. Soviet ships turned around instead of going through the quarantine. Khrushchev offered to remove his missiles from Cuba if the USA removed its missiles from Turkey.

This answer is factually accurate and has a good grasp of the events that led to the resolution to the Cuban Missile Crisis, which are tackled in chronological order. These are all important aspects of an analytical narrative. However, the answer is purely a narrative, and lacks any focus on the question. The student has not used any linking phrases to help to answer the question. Let's look at how the answer might look with some linking phrases inserted.

Student 1, with linking words and phrases added

Kennedy tried to resolve the crisis by using a 'quarantine', as many of the other options given to him by his advisers, such as bombing Cuba, would have started a war. The quarantine was a non-violent way of stopping further Soviet missiles being installed on Cuba, but also showed that the USA was prepared to take action.
The 'quarantine' meant that the USSR could not put more weapons on Cuba without starting a war. As a result, they turned their ships around rather than trying to break through the US ships.

Note how the second answer is now not purely a narrative, but focuses on the question of how the crisis was resolved. It does this through including linking phrases such as 'as a result', which show that the writer is considering the consequences of the decisions that were made.

Your turn!

Now write up the rest of the answer in your own words. Use the checklist below to make sure that your answer is as good as possible.

Analytical narrative checklist	Tick/cross
I have made a plan of the events in chronological order.	
I have divided my narrative up into three sections – beginning, middle and end.	
I have included plenty of linking words and phrases such as 'because', 'as a result of', 'due to', etc.	
My answer is focused on the question.	

How was the USA drawn into the Vietnam War?

Learning objectives

- Understand why the USA became involved in Vietnam.
- Evaluate the impact of the Vietnam War on US society.

What do you think?

Why would the USA get involved in a war so far from America?

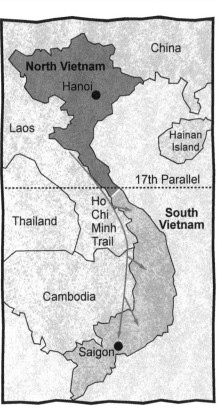

Figure 3.10: A map of Vietnam.

After the Second World War, a civil war broke out in the south-east Asian country of Vietnam between French forces and Vietnamese independence fighters. The French rulers had ruled Vietnam as part of their empire since the 19th century. The independence fighters were led by the communist Ho Chi Minh. Despite US help, in 1954 the French were defeated, and the country was temporarily divided into a communist North and anti-communist South until elections could be held. It was expected that the communists would win the elections and that Vietnam would become a unified communist state.

The USA was dismayed at the prospect of another communist state in Asia. It therefore backed the anti-communist South, which refused to conduct the elections in case the communists won. Therefore, Vietnam remained divided, like the Korean Peninsula.

By the early 1960s, Vietnam was descending into civil war again, as communist guerrillas*, with help from the North, attempted to unify Vietnam by force. The USA sent advisers and equipment, and later weapons and money, to help the South fight off the communists. In 1964, North Vietnamese torpedo boats allegedly attacked US naval vessels in what became known as the 'Gulf of Tonkin incident'. US President Johnson responded by asking the US Congress for permission to attack North Vietnam, and began bombing North Vietnamese targets.

In March 1965, as the violence spiralled out of control in Vietnam, Johnson authorised the first US combat troops to take part in the war. Soon, hundreds of thousands of US troops were stationed in Vietnam. What had been a civil war between the Vietnamese had now become a war against Vietnamese communists in which US troops fought and died.

Why was the Vietnam War so controversial?

The Vietnam War was very difficult to fight, as communist guerrilla fighters, known as the Viet Cong, or 'VC', resorted to ambush and hit and run tactics against US soldiers, before disappearing into the countryside.

Key term

Guerrilla*: A term used to describe warfare conducted by unofficial soldiers, who fight by carrying out ambushes and hit and run attacks. Guerrillas are difficult to identify as they do not wear uniforms.

The USA, facing mounting casualties from these attacks, and unwilling to withdraw from Vietnam, looked for other ways to win. US soldiers set about removing support for the guerrillas from the Vietnamese people, by forcing civilians from their villages, which were then often destroyed. The USA also tried to use its overwhelming firepower to seize victory, by pounding suspected communist positions with artillery, bombs and napalm*. As the guerrillas tended to use the jungle as cover for their ambushes, the US also sprayed the jungle with a highly toxic chemical known as Agent Orange. Agent Orange destroys vegetation but also causes health problems in people.

Source A: US soldiers on a 'search and destroy' mission in Vietnam, November 1965.

The reaction of the public

US tactics, like the use of Agent Orange, turned Vietnamese opinion against the US soldiers, while also making the war deeply unpopular in the USA. The Vietnam War was one of the first wars in which people were able to see war as it happened, on their televisions. In 1968, US troops killed 500 unarmed civilians in the village of My Lai, provoking widespread outrage and disgust. The effects of US bombing of civilians were brought home to people by images such as Source B.

Perhaps more of an issue for many were the mounting casualties amongst American soldiers, and the increasing need for reinforcements. However, it wasn't clear how the USA could ever walk away from the war without admitting defeat. Vietnam soon became one of the most important conflicts of the Cold War.

Source B: A photo taken by the photographer Nick Ut on 8 June 1972, showing a nine-year-old girl who had her clothes burned off by napalm in an air attack on suspected Viet Cong positions.

Key term

Napalm*: A type of bomb that contains flammable liquids, and which burns anything it comes into contact with.

Your turn!

 1 Draw a diagram showing the long- and short-term reasons why the USA became involved in Vietnam.

 2 Why do you think that, by the late 1960s, it would have been difficult for the USA to withdraw from Vietnam? Try to give at least two reasons.

 3 Give at least two reasons why people in the USA began to question the war in Vietnam.

Did you know?

Responding to claims that the draft was unfair, in 1969 the draft was decided by lottery on live television. Birth dates were drawn at random, live. The first date drawn was 14 September, meaning all young men of eligible age born on that date went to the top of the list to be called to fight. Numbers continued to be drawn, although those towards the end were never called for service. You can find out online whether your birth date would have made you eligible for service in Vietnam.

Why was there so much opposition to the war within the USA?

At first there had been very little opposition to the war in Vietnam. Most people either accepted it as a necessary part of the Cold War, or had little interest in events that were so far away. Only two US senators voted against sending troops to Vietnam. However, as the number of US soldiers in Vietnam increased, and the casualties mounted, opposition to the war grew. One of the major causes of opposition to the war was 'the draft'.

The draft

Since the Second World War, the USA had used a form of conscription. Men between the ages of 18 and 25 were required to register for military service. These men were then summoned to appear before a draft board of influential local people who decided who should be 'drafted' into the army and who should be turned away for reasons such as poor health and personal circumstances.

However, as the violence in Vietnam escalated, it soon became clear that the system was unfair. Young men from the middle and upper classes with rich parents were able to persuade the draft board not to accept them. In addition, university students were allowed to put off being drafted. Men who came from poorer, working-class backgrounds were far more likely to be sent to Vietnam. Also black men were more likely to be conscripted into the army than white men.

Soon, the draft became a major cause of opposition to the war. Between 1965 and 1973, 500,000 Americans became 'draft dodgers' as they either refused to fight in Vietnam or found ways to avoid the draft. Thousands of soldiers deserted from the military. Others destroyed their medals in public. One of the most famous people to refuse to fight was boxer Muhammad Ali, who had his boxing title taken away as punishment.

The USA had never seen such widespread resistance to the government before, and many were appalled at what they saw as young people's lack of patriotism.

Source C: Paul O'Brien, a student at the University of Chicago, publicly burning his draft card during a protest against the Vietnam War.

Demonstrations against the war

Demonstrations soon began to dominate the news. On 15 November 1969, 250,000 people gathered in Washington DC to call for an end to the war, in what was the largest political demonstration in US history at that point. The demonstrations were fuelled by a number of different factors.

- Many of the demonstrators were young people, who were affected by the draft. Many of these were students who were highly political.

- Almost every American family owned a television, and it was hard to ignore the violence being streamed from Vietnam.

- The civil rights movement*, which had conducted high-profile campaigns against racism and for equality for much of the 1950s and 1960s, also provided an example for the demonstrations in terms of tactics and organisation. Influential figures such as Martin Luther King spoke out against the war (see Source D).

On 4 May 1970, National Guardsmen opened fire on student protesters at Kent State University, killing four students. The resulting media publicity generated shock and outrage.

Eventually, President Nixon decided to withdraw troops from Vietnam. In 1975, Vietnam became unified under communist leadership.

The Vietnam War remains one of the most controversial aspects of recent US history: 58,200 US soldiers and an estimated 2 million Vietnamese died. The war had cost America $120 billion.

Key term

Civil rights movement*:
Refers to groups such as the National Association for the Advancement of Colored People (NAACP) and the Congress of Racial Equality (CORE), which fought for the rights of black people from the 1950s onwards.

Source D: Extract from a speech by Martin Luther King Jr criticising US involvement in the Vietnam War, 4 April 1967.

```
... the war was
doing far more than
devastating the hopes
of the poor at home
... We were taking
the black young men
who had been crippled
by our society and
sending them eight
thousand miles away to
guarantee liberties in
Southeast Asia which
they had not found in
southwest Georgia and
East Harlem.
```

Your turn!

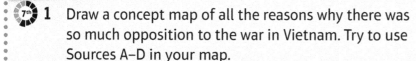

1 Draw a concept map of all the reasons why there was so much opposition to the war in Vietnam. Try to use Sources A–D in your map.

2 What do you think were the main reasons why there was so much opposition to the Vietnam War?

3 Why had there not been the same opposition to the Korean War?

4 Imagine you are a young male who had been called up to fight in Vietnam. Write a letter to the draft board explaining why you are refusing to fight.

Checkpoint

1 What led the USA to become involved in Vietnam?
2 What was 'guerrilla warfare', and why was it so difficult to fight against?
3 What methods did the USA use to fight against the VC?
4 What was 'the draft' and why was it so controversial?

What has caused conflict in the 20th century?

In this chapter, you have learned about the root causes of some of the most catastrophic events of the 20th century. In this section, you will learn about:

- how warfare changed during the 20th century

- some of the common factors that helped to cause conflict in the 20th century

- how the reasons for conflict have changed over time.

A century of war

Learning objectives

- Understand what has caused war in the 20th century.
- Know how the nature of war has changed.

Source A: A Vietnamese civilian grieving over her friend, killed by a Viet Cong mine, 1966.

Most historians agree that the 20th century was the bloodiest century in human history. The total number of deaths related to the wars of the 20th century has been estimated at 187 million people, many of them civilians. Wars have always impacted on civilians, but for hundreds of years European wars were fought in the following ways:

- A formal declaration of war was made between two states.

- The fighting took place between two 'conventional' armies, who wore uniforms and carried flags to identify themselves as the army of a particular nation. For most people the war was a distant affair.

- Fighting took place on battlefields, and often one side was decisively defeated.

- The fighting usually ended when a peace treaty was concluded between the two nations. The treaty would normally involve some kind of compensation from the defeated nation, but essentially left it intact.

However, in the 20th century, war was very different. The following are some of the major differences:

- States often attacked with no declaration of war – for example, Japan's attack on Pearl Harbor in 1941 or North Korea's invasion of the South in 1950.

- Wars did not always involve states fighting each other. Guerrilla warfare became more common – for example in Vietnam.

- Fighting increasingly involved civilian populations, for example through the bombing of cities to destroy industry and demoralise the enemy.

- Wars ending in a formal peace treaty, such as the First World War, were becoming less and less common.

- The boundary between war and peace became blurred. For example, can guerrilla wars be classed as 'wars' if there has been no formal declaration of war?

What has caused war in the period 1918–90?

One of the main reasons why the nature of war changed during this period is that the reasons for fighting also substantially changed.

Communism

 The rise of communism after 1917 caused conflict between those who wanted to spread the new ideas, and those who wanted to stop them. This can be seen in Korea and Vietnam, and was one of the root causes of the Cold War.

Fascism

 Hitler's ideas were some of the main causes of the Second World War. Hitler's attack on Poland, and his invasion of the Soviet Union, were largely a result of Hitler's racism and belief in ideas such as *Lebensraum*.

Arms races

 Throughout the 20th century, countries tried to gain power by having the strongest army or navy. The development of nuclear weapons made the danger even greater.

Tensions over the Cold War

 The Cold War created tensions between the 'superpowers', but the risk of nuclear war led to the rise of 'proxy wars' such as the wars in Korea and Vietnam.

Industrialisation of war

 Fighting the large wars of the 20th century required whole populations and economies to supply armies. This meant that the civilians who provided resources became targets.

Figure 3.11: A summary of some of the causes of conflict in the 20th century.

Your turn!

 1 Give an example of a way in which war fundamentally stayed the same across the time period and an example of how it was different. Choose examples from across the time period to make your points.

 2 Draw a continuum, with 'Change' at one end and 'Continuity' at the other. Note down examples of change and continuity about what caused war between 1918 and 1990, and what war was like. Place points on the continuum according to how much of a change you think each was.

 3 Why has the nature of war changed so much through the 20th century? Explain your answer.

Interpretation questions

How have interpretations of what caused war changed over time?

The Cold War is a good example of how views on what caused a historical event have changed over time. Below is a summary of how interpretations of the Cold War have changed.

'It was the Soviet Union's fault' – the 'Traditional Western' view

In the first few decades of the Cold War, the main view in the West was very much that the Soviet Union alone was to blame for the Cold War, due to the aggression of Stalin and his successors in the years after the Second World War.

'It was the USA's fault' – the 'Revisionist' view

From the 1960s onwards, some historians began to blame the USA for its aggressive attitude towards the USSR in the early stages of the Cold War, for example by using the nuclear bomb to 'threaten' the USSR in 1945. This view coincided with the Vietnam War, which saw many historians both within and outside the USA become more critical of the USA.

'It was no one's fault' – the 'Post-Revisionists' view

In more recent years, historians have argued that the Cold War was to a large extent unavoidable, due to the ideological differences between the USA and the USSR. A series of mistakes on both sides led the world to the brink of nuclear war.

How did views change after the collapse of the Soviet Union?

In the late 1980s, the Cold War came to an end as most communist states in Europe rejected the Soviet Union. In 1991 communism collapsed in the Soviet Union itself. The Cold War was over.

As well as bringing change and freedom for millions of people, the collapse of the Soviet Union was a gift to Western historians, who had access to evidence that had been previously unavailable, locked up inside Soviet archives. This helped to shed new light on the conflict, and allowed historians in the West to look at it from the Soviet perspective for the first time. The archives reveal that Stalin did not necessarily want world domination, but instead tried to avoid confrontation with the USA.

Source B: East German guards look on as the Berlin Wall is destroyed in 1989. This was the beginning of the end of the Cold War and for communism in Europe.

What do the historians say?

Now that you have an idea of what historians have argued about the Cold War, look at the following extracts and see if you can work out what historical 'school' the writers might belong to.

Interpretation questions

Interpretation 1: Extract from P.J. Larkin, *European History for Certificate Classes*, a student examination revision book published in 1965.

The 'Cold War' was a mixture of religious crusade in favour of one ideology or the other, and of the most ruthless power politics, striking out for advantage or expansion not only in Europe but all over the world.

Interpretation 2: Extract from *The Oxford Companion to American Military History*, written in 1999 and edited by John Whiteclay Chambers.

The United States became involved in the [Vietnam] war for a number of reasons, and these evolved and shifted over time. Primarily, every American president regarded the enemy in Vietnam … as agents of global communism … Americans compared communism to a … disease. If it took hold in one nation, U.S. policymakers expected [other] nations to fall to communism, too, as if nations were dominoes lined up on end.

Interpretation 3: Extract from *The Cold War*, a history book written by John Lewis Gaddis in 2005.

Stalin's postwar goals were security for himself, his regime, his country, and his ideology, in precisely that order. He sought to make sure that no internal challenges could ever again endanger his personal rule, and that no external threats would ever again place his country at risk. The interests of communists elsewhere in the world, admirable though those might be, would never outweigh the priorities of the Soviet state as he had determined them.

Your turn!

 1 Draw a flow chart showing how historical interpretations of the causes of the Cold War have changed over time.

2 Read Interpretations 1–3. What does each one argue about what caused the Cold War? Try to summarise the argument of each into a few bullet points.

3 Explain why historians' interpretations of what has caused the Cold War have changed over time.

What has caused conflict in the 20th century?

Draw an illustrated concept map summing up what you have learned in this chapter about conflict in the 20th century. You could also include detail on changing historical interpretations.

What have you learned?

Consequence questions →

In this section you have learned:

- the causes and consequences of some of the main events of the Cold War

- different views on why the Cold War started, and the reasons for those differences.

Quick Quiz

1. Which group came to power in Russia in 1917?

2. What was the name of the book that Hitler wrote in prison in 1924?

3. Against which two cities were nuclear bombs first used in 1945?

4. Which brutal dictator was the leader of the Soviet Union from the 1920s until his death in 1953?

5. What phrase did Churchill use in a speech in 1946 to describe how Europe had been divided in the Cold War?

6. Which 'proxy war' fought from 1950 to 1953 was the first military clash of the Cold War?

7. Over which island did the world come close to nuclear war in 1962?

8. Which south-east Asian country became the focus of an increasingly controversial war from the 1950s until 1975?

Consequences

Consequences in history are a little like the effect of throwing a rock into a pond. A small rock will generate ripples, but these will quickly disappear. However, a large rock would generate a big splash, and the ripples might radiate out for a long way.

Let's look at some of the consequences of some of the events we have covered in this chapter.

Event	Short-term consequences	Long-term consequences
The USA drops nuclear bombs on Hiroshima and Nagasaki in 1945.	The two cities are destroyed, thousands are killed, and Japan surrenders. The Second World War comes to an end.	The bombs help to start the Cold War between the USA and the USSR. The bombs also start an arms race as both countries try to build more, and more powerful, bombs.
North Korea invades South Korea in 1950.	South Korea struggles to survive and is almost defeated. The USA works with the UN to decide how to respond.	
The French are defeated by Vietnamese independence fighters.		

Your turn!

1. Copy out and complete the table above by filling in the blank spaces.

2. Try to think of some consequences of other topics, for example the Cuban Missile Crisis, and create a similar table to summarise these. Think about consequences in human terms and not just political or military ones.

Writing historically

Consequence questions

Let's look at how to answer the following question: 'Explain two consequences of the increasing US involvement in Vietnam from 1965 onwards.'

To answer this question, it would be helpful to make a plan, like the one shown in the table on the opposite page. Do this now, making sure to include specific examples as consequences.

Event	Short-term consequence	Long-term consequence
Increasing US involvement in Vietnam from 1965 onwards		

This question requires you to write about a paragraph on each consequence. You need to make sure to explain what the event led to, giving relevant, specific examples to support your points.

Below are examples of how two students tackled the question, along with feedback.

Student 1

The USA became increasingly involved in Vietnam from 1965 onwards after the Gulf of Tonkin incident. They sent lots of troops, money and supplies to help South Vietnam to resist communism. The USA used tactics such as 'search and destroy' missions to root out the communists, and also used their overwhelming firepower to try to destroy communist positions.

This student has a good grasp of what happened in Vietnam but doesn't really answer the question. The answer is too focused on describing the situation in Vietnam, when it needs to be talking about the **consequences** of US involvement.

Student 2

One consequence of increasing US involvement in the Vietnam War was a rise in opposition to the war. As one of the world's first televised wars, millions of Americans saw first-hand the brutal tactics used to fight the war in Vietnam, such as the use of napalm against civilians. This had a huge effect on US society, as some 500,000 'draft-dodgers' refused to fight, while huge numbers of people protested against the war, such as the 250,000 people who gathered in Washington DC in 1969.

This is a much better answer. It is focused on the question from the first sentence, and looks at one specific consequence – the rise in opposition to the war. It makes the links between US involvement and its consequences clear, by using specific, relevant detail.

Student 3 – you!

The question asks you to write about two consequences – see if you can think of another consequence and write that up.

Then write an answer to the following question:

'Explain two consequences of the Korean War 1950–53.'

To what extent were Jews persecuted before the Holocaust?

The murder of six million Jews during the Second World War, known as the Holocaust, was a crime worse than any other in human history. However, anti-Semitism* has long historical roots. In this section you will learn about:

- when Jews have faced persecution and prejudice before the 20th century

- why Jews were treated badly in many different countries.

Tragedy at Clifford's Tower

Key term

Anti-Semitism*: Hostility or prejudice directed against Jewish people.

Figure 4.1: A modern photo of Clifford's Tower as it appears today.

Clifford's Tower in York stands proudly over the old city and is one of its most recognisable landmarks. It was built by William the Conqueror after the Battle of Hastings, and is a reminder of an exciting past filled with kings, queens and valiant knights. However, the tower has a far darker history that tells a very different story about medieval England.

In the 12th century, York had a small but important community of Jews. After 1066, William needed cash to build his castles and cathedrals. Christians were forbidden from making a profit by lending money, but Jews were not, and so they were invited to England to become moneylenders.

In the 12th century, Jews in England were facing increasing hostility. The Crusades had whipped up religious hatred against non-Christians, and false rumours were circulating about Jews murdering children in religious rituals. Many Christians also felt bitter about being in debt to wealthy Jews. In 1170, such resentment led to open violence against Jews erupting in several cities such as Norwich, Stamford and York.

Massacre at Clifford's Tower

In March 1190, the city of York caught fire for unknown reasons. Blaming the Jews of York for the fire, an angry mob started looting the houses of prominent Jews and brutally killing some of the occupants. Terrified, the remaining Jewish families sought refuge inside Clifford's Tower, which at the time was a wooden structure under the control of King Richard I. They begged the warden to grant them sanctuary and he let them in.

The castle was surrounded by a furious mob. The siege of the castle went on for several days, and it became clear that no one was going to help the trapped Jews. The castle was set on fire. Caught between being burned to death or being murdered by the crowd outside, most of the men inside the castle made a terrible decision: they killed their wives and children before finally killing themselves.

The small number of survivors in the castle were told that they would not be killed if they converted to Christianity. Several Jews agreed and left the castle, but they were pitilessly murdered. Historians estimate about 150 people died in the massacre. After the massacre, the mob then destroyed the financial records which showed who owed money to Jewish moneylenders, which may tell us something about their real motives.

Today, most students learn about the events of the Holocaust and the dreadful persecution that Jews suffered in Nazi Germany. However, what happened at Clifford's Tower shows us that anti-Semitism existed long before the Nazis. It existed in many countries across Europe and the wider world.

Interpretation 1: A modern artist's interpretation of the burning of Clifford's Tower in 1190.

Source A: Extract from William of Newburgh's account of the massacre, written in 1190. William was the Canon of a Christian monastery in York.

The zeal [strong feeling] of the Christians against the Jews in England ... broke out fiercely. It was not [because of their] faith, but [because of their luck and] from envy of their good fortune. Bold and greedy men thought that they were doing an act pleasing to God ... [they wanted the] insolence of [those sneaky Jews to] be checked and their blaspheming tongues curbed ...

The men of York were [not worried about] fear of the ... King [Richard I] nor the vigor of the laws, nor by feelings of humanity, [when venting] their fury with the ... ruin of their ... fellow-citizens and from rooting out the whole race in their city. And as this was a very remarkable occurrence, it ought to be transmitted to [those in the future] at greater length ...

Your turn!

1 What can you learn from this section about the Jews in medieval England? Note two examples.

2 Read Source A. What can you learn from the source about **(a)** why the attack happened and **(b)** William's opinion of the attackers?

3 In Source A, William of Newburgh seems to feel it is important for people in the future to know about what happened. Why do you think he felt that? Do you agree?

Why were medieval Jews persecuted?

Key terms

Ritualistic*: Set actions performed as part of a ceremony, usually with religious importance.

Blood Libel*: Libel means to make a false and damaging claim about someone or something. 'Blood Libel' refers to the lies spread about Jews committing ritualistic murders.

Christianity was extremely powerful in medieval Europe. Jews were often treated with suspicion. Not only were they different, but Christians were taught that Jews were responsible for the crucifixion of Jesus Christ. Rumours often circulated that they practiced magic and worked with the Devil.

Negative attitudes towards Jews increased during the Crusades as Christians were promised spiritual rewards if they killed 'unbelievers'. In 1096, Crusaders on their way to fight in the Holy Land massacred 800 Jews in the German town of Worms.

Jewish money-lenders were often resented by those who owed them money. Money-lending was attractive as a trade, but it was also sometimes the only option open to Jews who were barred from other professions.

Blood Libel

In the city of Norwich in March 1144, a 12-year-old boy called William failed to return home. His body was later found tortured and mutilated. A rumour soon spread that he had been ritualistically* killed by Jews who needed the blood of a child to celebrate the Jewish festival of Passover, an accusation now known as 'Blood Libel'*. There was no evidence to support these accusations, and no one was ever convicted for William's death – but the damage was done.

Shortly after, William was declared a saint by the Catholic Church. Meanwhile, the story of his murder spread throughout Europe, where similar stories of Christian children killed in sinister rituals by Jews began to emerge. Although the story of the 'Blood Libel' was false, it survived for hundreds of years and continued to be used as a justification for attacking Jews.

Source B: An image from the Nuremberg Chronicles, published in 1493 in Germany. It shows the anti-Semitic idea of the ritualistic murder of a Christian child by Jews.

Expulsion of Jews

Some countries chose to expel Jews altogether. In 1290, Jews were forced to leave England, until the ban was finally lifted by Oliver Cromwell in 1656. From the 15th-century in Spain, a Catholic court known as the 'Spanish Inquisition', aimed to remove any anti-Catholic influences. As a result, Jews faced two options: convert to Christianity or leave Spain. Those who converted, known as 'conversos', came under intense pressure to prove their loyalty to the Catholic faith. In 1691, a trial in Majorca led to 37 conversos being burned to death. Those who chose to leave Spain often fared no better. Some ship captains charged Jews enormous sums to transport them but, once paid, threw them into the ocean. Jews were sometimes suspected of swallowing gold and jewels to hide their wealth, and so they were murdered and cut open.

Source C: Engraving showing persecution of Jews in Russia, c.1880, author unknown.

Pogroms in Eastern Europe and Russia

In the 19th century, Jews in Eastern Europe and Russia faced extreme hostility. After decades of discrimination, Jews were accused of involvement in the assassination of Tsar Alexander II in 1881. As a result, a wave of pogroms* broke out in which local people, often encouraged by government officials and newspapers, attacked Jewish citizens. Worst of all was the 1905 pogrom in Odessa, which led to the death of 2,500 Jews.

Key term

Pogrom*: Violent attacks directed against an ethnic minority, such as Jews.

Your turn!

 1   Make a rough timeline showing some of the key events mentioned in this section, such as the massacre at Clifford's Tower, the Spanish Inquisition, and pogroms in 19th-century Russia.

 2   Use your timeline to describe in your own words how Jews faced persecution in the Middle Ages and beyond. Try to describe each time period in turn. Remember to support your answer with specific details, such as the 'Blood Libel', or pogroms in Russia.

Checkpoint

1   What was 'Blood Libel'?
2   Why did money-lending become associated with Jews?
3   What happened to Jews in Spain from the 15th century?
4   What were pogroms?

Jews in 19th- and 20th-century Europe

Learning objectives

- Understand the differing experiences of Jews in this era.
- Know why anti-Semitism persisted into the modern era.

After hundreds of years of prejudice and discrimination, life for many Jews eventually improved in the 19th century. Laws that had forbidden Jews from entering certain professions, being able to vote or owning property were overturned in many countries such as Germany, France and Britain. As a result, some Jewish communities became more integrated into European societies and began to play important roles in European culture, arts and sciences. Some examples of prominent European Jews in this era are shown in Figure 4.2.

Albert Einstein (1879–1955)
Born in 19th-century Germany, Einstein went on to become one of the most influential physicists of all time.

Sigmund Freud (1856–1939)
Born in the Austro-Hungarian Empire, Freud was a leading psychiatrist, and has heavily influenced Western culture.

Rosa Luxemburg (1871–1919)
Born to a family of Polish Jews, Luxembourg was an economist, philosopher and anti-war campaigner. As leader of the German Communist Party, she tried to overthrow the German government in 1919.

Max Liebermann (1847–1935)
German-Jewish painter seen as one of the leading figures in the artistic movement known as Impressionism.

Lise Meitner (1878–1968)
Female physicist who overcame prejudice as a woman and a Jew to conduct research that led to the development of nuclear reactors and the atomic bomb.

Harry Houdini (1874–1926)
Born Erik Weisz in the Austro-Hungarian Empire, Houdini became one of the most famous escape artists of all time.

Franz Kafka (1883–1924)
Kafka is seen as one of the most influential figures in 20th century literature. He is most famous for his short story 'The Metamorphosis', in which the leading character awakes one day to find he has turned into a giant insect.

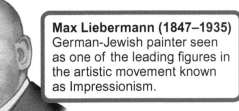
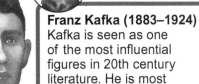

Figure 4.2: Illustration showing some of the achievements of Jewish people during the late 19th and early 20th centuries.

The rise of racial anti-Semitism

Unfortunately, many anti-Semitic stereotypes* from medieval times persisted, while new ones also emerged. Some 19th-century thinkers tried to apply Charles Darwin's new theories on evolution* to humanity. As a result, many believed there was a natural hierarchy of human races, with the white races at the top and other 'inferior' races, such as the Jews, underneath.

Such theories meant that anti-Semitic stereotypes and prejudices that had existed for centuries were now presented as scientific fact, although this 'science' is now known to be wrong.

Political anti-Semitism

These new, and old, anti-Semitic ideas were soon seized upon by new political parties in Europe. Common arguments included:

- the idea that Jews were too powerful in certain professions such as finance, law, politics, medicine, the arts, and the media

- the idea that Jews were part of a secret conspiracy to take control of the world.

Many of these ideas were contradictory – for example, Jews were accused of wanting total control of international finance, as well as controlling communist movements that wanted to destroy international finance!

However, many people believed these conspiracy theories. One such person was Adolf Hitler, who grew up in late 19th-century and early 20th-century Austria and who was heavily influenced by the anti-Semitic politicians of the day.

Source A: A card from a game made in the 1920s, illustrating a racial stereotype of a Jew as a 'shrewd' businessman. Items like this show how medieval anti-Semitism has continued through the centuries.

Your turn!

1 Why did life improve for some Jews during the 19th century?

2 Look at the individuals mentioned in Figure 4.2. Who do you think was most important, and why?

3 Give two reasons why anti-Semitism continued, or even increased, during the 19th and 20th centuries.

4 Look at Source A. What inferences can you make from this source about the kind of prejudice Jews faced during this period?

Key terms

Stereotype*: A widely held, but heavily simplified and often untrue view of someone or something – for example, that English people drink tea all day and eat fish and chips.

The theory of evolution*: Darwin theorised that evolution happens by natural selection – animals that are unable to adapt to their environment die, while those that can adapt survive and pass on their traits to the next generation.

Source B: An illustration from a 1921 French edition of *The Protocols of the Elders of Zion*. The caption says, 'The Jewish Danger'.

The Protocols of the Elders of Zion

In 1905, a book known as *The Protocols of the Elders of Zion* was published in Russia. The book claimed to include the minutes* taken from a meeting of influential Jews, in which they discussed their plan for taking over the world. The book has since been conclusively proven to be a forgery, possibly put together by Russian police agents to give them an excuse to persecute Jews. However, many people at the time believed is was real.

After 1917, the book was reprinted and translated into many different languages and its content was widely believed. Henry Ford, founder of the Ford car company, was so impressed by the book that he wrote his own anti-Semitic book entitled *The International Jew*, which repeated the false evidence in the Protocols. Adolf Hitler referred to the Protocols in many of his anti-Semitic speeches in which he demanded action against the so-called international Jewish 'conspiracy'.

Did you know?

The Protocols of the Elders of Zion was used by some German school teachers to teach children about Jews after the Nazis came to power in 1933, even though it had been proven to be a forgery in the 1920s.

Key term

Minutes*: The written notes recorded during a meeting, describing the issues discussed, as well as responses or decisions.

Jewish migration to the USA and Great Britain

Throughout the 19th century, many Jews chose to leave Europe after facing hostility. Around two million Jews arrived in the USA from Eastern Europe and Russia in the period between 1880 and 1924. Others moved to London, where 90 per cent of Jewish immigrants settled in Whitechapel, one of the poorest areas in the city. The new immigrants tried to survive as best as they could and made use of skills they had learned in their former countries, such as tailoring and shoe making.

However, Jews often faced hostility in England. Some newspapers described Whitechapel as a 'Jewish colony', while trade unions accused Jewish workers of 'stealing' jobs by being prepared to work for less. In 1905, Britain passed the 'Aliens Act', the main aim of which was to reduce the number of Jewish migrants into Britain. Records of political debates at the time reveal much about prejudice against the Jews, as shown by Source C.

Source C: An extract from a debate in the House of Commons on Jewish migration to England, 1893.

... [there are] great numbers of immigrants entering this country from the Russian Empire, of whom a large proportion are of the Jewish race ... [they have caused] ruinous competition ... out of 18,000 or 20,000 persons engaged in the [tailoring] trade, only a few hundreds are of the Anglo-Saxon race ... alien [non-British] immigration is a very serious and grave national danger ... the districts from which these unfortunate people are mainly drawn are hotbeds of disease ... their dwellings are of the most foul and loathsome character ... [which is unlike] the home-born population of this country ... their presence [is] a source of permanent danger to the health of this country ...

Source D: Photo of Jacob Rechtman's shoe shop in Cable Street, East London, circa 1900. Rechtman and his family were Jewish immigrants.

Your turn!

1 List some of the anti-Semitic claims made against Jews during this period.

7th 2 Look at Sources B and C. Explain what anti-Semitic stereotypes are revealed by each source.

8th 3 Why might Sources A–C be useful for a historian looking at prejudice against Jews?

4 Look at Source D. Write a letter from Mr Rechtman to a relative, describing where he may have emigrated from, and why. Try to imagine:
- how much his life might have improved since reaching England
- how he might feel about what English people say about Jews, such as in Source C.

Checkpoint

1 Give two examples of Jews who made a significant contribution to European society.
2 What was *The Protocols of the Elders of Zion*, and why was it so important?
3 Where did many Jews migrate to in the late 19th and early 20th centuries?

Life for Jews in Nazi Germany

Learning objectives

- Learn how and why Jews were persecuted in Nazi Germany.
- Understand the reaction to the persecution, both within and outside Germany.

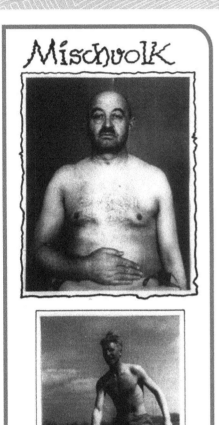

Source A: Nazi propaganda slide depicting a man of 'mixed race' compared with a racially pure 'Aryan' man, circa 1936.

Germany in the 1930s had a small but thriving Jewish population of about 500,000 people – making up less than one per cent of the German population. Most German Jews saw themselves as thoroughly German, and spoke German. During the First World War, 100,000 Jews fought for Germany and many won medals for bravery.

The period between 1918 and 1933 was a traumatic time for many Germans. After Germany lost the First World War, the country experienced one crisis after another as money became worthless, the economy collapsed, and unemployment increased. In addition, many were fearful about the growing power and influence of the Communist Party within their country. The many problems faced by ordinary Germans made them willing to believe the message of the Nazi Party that the Jews were to blame. Hitler blamed the Jews for:

- the loss of the First World War
- causing the economic crises
- being the secret force behind communism.

On 30 January 1933, Hitler became the leader of Germany, and violent anti-Semitism became government policy.

Nazi racial policy

Hitler believed that the German people were the best examples of the 'Aryan'* race. He believed Aryans were a superior race that belonged at the top of a racial hierarchy. Hitler believed that the strength of the Aryan race depended on preserving its racial purity. Other races were seen as inferior, especially the Jews. Nazis claimed that the Jews aimed to infiltrate and destroy cultures by intermarrying. Therefore, they were considered a threat who would pollute the Aryan race.

As Hitler believed that Jews were defined by their race, someone could be defined as a Jew even if they had never attended a Jewish religious service in their life. From 1935, the Nazis defined a Jew as someone who had Jewish grandparents. This even led to some Roman Catholic nuns and priests being told they were Jewish.

Nazi persecution of Jews in Germany, 1933–39

By mid-1933, Hitler was the undisputed dictator of a one-party state, which allowed him to pass laws that reflected his own prejudices.

It became clear that the decades of acceptance Jews had enjoyed in Germany would soon be over. On 1 April 1933, the Nazis ordered a boycott of all Jewish shops. Nazi thugs known as 'Stormtroopers', or the SA, stood outside Jewish shops to stop people from entering and painted anti-Semitic signs on their windows. However, the boycott was not a success, and was called off after only one day.

Source B: A photograph of SA men urging people not to shop in Jewish businesses.

Legal discrimination

On 7 April 1933, a law was passed which restricted employment in the German Civil Service to Aryans. As a result, all Jews working in the government or as teachers lost their jobs. Later, the law was extended to doctors and lawyers.

Worse was to follow. At one of the huge rallies at Nuremberg in 1935, the Nazis announced a series of measures known as the 'Nuremberg Laws'. The laws stated that:

- Jews were forbidden from having sexual relations with Aryans

- Jews were forbidden from marrying Aryans

- Jews were stripped of their rights as German citizens.

In the years 1937–38, it was declared that all Jewish property had to be registered. It was then seized and 'Aryanized' by being sold to Aryan Germans at rock-bottom prices. Jews were also now required to have a 'J' stamped on their passport.

It was becoming clear to many Jews that the situation in Germany, their homeland, was becoming increasingly dangerous.

Key term

Aryan*: In the 19th and 20th centuries, some people believed that Europeans were descended from the ancient 'Aryan' race, who were racially superior to other races. There is no real evidence for an 'Aryan' race actually existing.

Your turn!

1 Describe two features of Jewish life in Germany before Hitler came to power.

2 Explain why Nazis believed that Jews were a threat to Germany. Try to give at least two reasons.

3 Start a timeline showing the key events listed on this page. Remember to add other events you learn about to it later.

Kristallnacht

On 7 November 1938, a young Jewish man called Herschel Grynszpan shot dead a German diplomat in Paris, apparently in revenge for the treatment his family had received in Germany. On 9–10 November 1938, the Nazis used the shooting as an excuse to unleash an unprecedented wave of violence against Jews in Germany.

- Nazi thugs looted and smashed 7,000 Jewish businesses.

- Jewish cemeteries, schools and homes were ransacked.

- At least 250 synagogues* were burned or damaged.

- Dozens of Jews were murdered.

This incident has become known as 'Kristallnacht', or the 'Night of Broken Glass', due to the huge amount of shattered glass in the streets. 30,000 Jewish men were arrested by the Nazis and sent to concentration camps, where many died. The Jewish community was also ordered to pay a fine of 1 billion Reichsmark ($400,000,000) to pay for the damages.

Source C: The aftermath of *Kristallnacht*, 9–10 November 1938.

Interpretation 1: Extract from *The Third Reich – A New History* by Michael Burleigh, a history book published in 2001.

```
… the pogrom [Kristallnacht] was not only murderous, but an
opportunity for mindless and resentful mobs to loot and vandalise the
homes of their social superiors, [broadly fitting the] socio-economic
profile of the German-Jewish community. They destroyed anything not
easily removed … It was also an opportunity for fit young men to
chase, punch and kick often elderly victims, including women, while
children were terrorised with guns. In some places, Jews were publicly
humiliated by being forced to walk over their prayer shawls, to read
Mein Kampf aloud …
```

The situation for Jewish refugees

Although it wasn't an easy decision to make, many Jews now tried to leave Nazi Germany. By 1938, 150,000 Jews had fled. They were forced to leave almost all their property behind.

Fleeing Nazi Germany could be very difficult, as many countries around the world refused to take Jewish refugees. In May 1939, the steamship *St Louis*, carrying 937 refugees, was refused entry to Cuba and then the USA. The Jewish passengers were finally accepted by European countries, where some later became victims of the Nazis.

There were some genuine examples of compassion towards the Jews. After observing the horrors of *Kristallnacht*, British volunteers negotiated with the UK government to arrange for trainloads of Jewish children to be rescued from Nazi Germany and settled in Britain in an operation known as the 'Kindertransport'. Between November 1938 and September 1939, around 10,000 Jewish children were moved. However, in September 1939 the Second World War started and it became almost impossible for Jews to leave Nazi Germany.

Source D: A Jewish child refugee arrives in England in 1938, as part of the 'Kindertransport'.

Your turn!

 1 Read Interpretation 1. What can you learn about why people took part in the *Kristallnacht* pogrom?

 2 Many historians see *Kristallnacht* as a turning point in persecution of the Jews in Germany. Why do think this is?

3 Some historians divide people's involvement in the persecution of the Jews into the following categories:
- 'Perpetrators' (those who were actively involved in discrimination/violence).
- 'Bystanders' (those who did not actively take part, but their lack of opposition may have made things worse for the Jews).

Can you think of any examples of people/countries that might belong in each category?

Checkpoint

1 About how many Jews lived in Germany in 1930?
2 Give two examples of Nazi ideas on race.
3 Describe the ways in which Jews were discriminated against in the years 1933–38.
4 What was 'Kristallnacht'?
5 Why was it so difficult for Jews to leave Nazi Germany?

To what extent were Jews persecuted before the Holocaust?

Look back over this chapter and make a large diagram giving details on how, when, where and why Jews were discriminated against in this period. You could do this as a concept map, or you could annotate a simple map of Europe.

What have you learned?

Source utility questions →

In this section, you have learned:

- what life was like for Jewish people in Europe before the Second World War
- how and why Jewish people have faced persecution.

Source A: A ceramic holder for spare coins in the shape of an Orthodox Jewish man, made in Britain in the 19th century. The figure is part of the Katz Ehrenthal collection, which consists of 900 anti-Semitic objects made in the 19th and 20th centuries, and collected by Peter Ehrenthal, a Romanian Holocaust survivor.

As a historian, you will often be confronted with questions that ask you to consider how far a source is reliable, and to what extent the source is useful for a specific enquiry. Students sometimes confuse the two, but in fact they are quite different. Let's look at one example opposite.

Source A is a crude piece of anti-Semitic art and is typical of similar objects created across Europe in the 19th and early 20th centuries. The figure is a racist stereotype of an Orthodox Jew. The outstretched arms of the figure, combined with gold coins instead of eyes, and the fact that the object is meant to be used as a holder for spare coins, are all meant to reinforce the anti-Semitic idea that Jews are greedy money-grabbers.

If we were to ask the question, *'How reliable is this source as evidence of the role of Jews in 19th-century Europe?'* the answer would have to be: it's not at all reliable. As you've learned, the Jewish experience at that time was extremely diverse. Jewish people made vital contributions to science, art and literature, amongst other fields. Yes, there were Jewish money lenders, and there were Jews involved in finance and banking, but clearly the image is a gross, and unfair, exaggeration.

However, if we were to change the question, we might get a different answer. For example:

'How useful is this source as evidence about anti-Semitism in 19th-century Europe?'

Our answer to this would have to be that it's very useful, as it tells us a lot about the stereotypes that Jewish people commonly faced in this era, as well as the discrimination directed against them.

Bear in mind that no source is useless. It just depends what you are using the source for!

Your turn!

1 What was the purpose of the object shown in Source A?

2 Draw up a list of enquiry questions that Source A could help to answer.

Writing historically

Source utility questions

You are now going to look at the difference between the reliability and utility (usefulness) of a source. Below are some sample student answers to the question about Source A on page 116. Try to identify what makes a good answer before you have a go at your own.

How useful is Source A as evidence about anti-Semitism in 19th-century Europe?

Student 1

Source A is not reliable as evidence about Jews in 19th-century Europe. It's racist and shows a horrible caricature of a money lender. It's not useful as it's incredibly biased. I know that at the time there was a lot of anti-Semitism towards Jews. I think the source is really unfair to Jews and isn't at all reliable.

This answer is confusing reliability with usefulness. While we can all agree that the source is unpleasant, and it is incredibly biased, this isn't what you are being asked to assess in the question. Instead, the student needs to think about what they know about anti-Semitic stereotypes in 19th-century Europe and use that to evaluate the source.

Student 2

Source A is not useful as evidence about anti-Semitism in the 19th century. It is just an object and doesn't tell us anything about the persecution that Jews faced. I know that in the 19th century thousands of Jews were forced to leave Russia due to the anti-Semitic pogroms that were taking place there. I also know that Jews faced discrimination in other countries such as France and Germany, where they were accused of being a shadowy group that wanted to control the world. Overall, the source is not useful as it would be much better to have a diary of a Jewish person, or a photo of a pogrom.

This answer is more focused on the question, and does use a lot of specific knowledge, but it's a very negative evaluation of the source. Instead, it would be better to focus on what it is that makes the source useful, rather than why it isn't useful.

Student 3

Source A is useful as evidence about anti-Semitism in the 19th century, as it gives us an insight into the everyday discrimination that Jews faced at this time. Even a relatively innocent object like something to store your change in is used to discriminate against Jews, by showing them as greedy money-lenders. I know from my own knowledge that this was a common stereotype about Jews dating back to medieval times, and this source shows that. The fact that it is typical of 900 similar objects just goes to show how much discrimination Jews had to suffer in this period.

The source is less useful for telling us about other types of anti-Semitism, for example the reasons for the pogroms in Russia at the time. It also doesn't tell us how Jews felt about this kind of discrimination. However, on balance, it's a useful source that gives us a good insight into 19th-century anti-Semitism.

This answer is much better. It answers the question by considering how the source is useful to tell us about anti-Semitism at the time and uses some knowledge to put the source into context. It also considers the limitations of the source, but without arguing that the source is useless. In general, it's always worth approaching sources in this way.

Your turn!

Write an answer to the following question, using Source C on page 111.
How useful is Source C as evidence about why Jews were discriminated against in the 19th century?

How were the Nazis able to implement the 'Final Solution'?

With the outbreak of the Second World War, measures against Jews in Nazi-occupied Europe escalated from discrimination and persecution to attempts to destroy the entire Jewish race. This is now known as the Holocaust. In this section, you will learn about:

- the story of Leon Greenman and his family
- what happened in Europe that made the Holocaust possible.

The story of Leon Greenman and his family

Learning objectives

- Understand how the Holocaust started.
- Know the impact the Holocaust had on one family.

What do you think?

Why do you think many Jews were still living in Europe at the outbreak of war?

Source A: A photograph of Leon and Else Greenman with their son Barney, June 1942.

Leon Greenman lived in Rotterdam in the Netherlands with his wife Esther ('Else)'. Both Leon and Else were Anglo-Dutch Jews who had been born in London, but they decided to settle in Rotterdam to look after Else's grandmother. Leon divided his time between Rotterdam and London, where he owned a hairdressing business.

In 1938, the news was dominated by talk of war, and Leon considered taking his family out of the Netherlands. However, he was reassured by the British embassy that, as he and his wife were British, they would be evacuated in the event of a war. Therefore, Leon decided to remain in Rotterdam.

In September 1939, Hitler invaded Poland and Britain declared war on Germany. However, there was no fighting in the Netherlands, and in April 1940 Else gave birth to a son, Barnett Greenman. They called him Barney.

A few weeks later, the Nazis began their invasion of Western Europe. The Netherlands soon surrendered. The British embassy staff fled, and no evacuation was organised for Leon and his family. Leon was concerned but was convinced that he and his family would be protected, as they were British citizens. He gave his British passports and all his savings to some friends for safekeeping. Leon's friends, terrified of being accused of helping Jews, burned the documents.

Soon, the Nazis began introducing the same racial laws in the Netherlands that they had already used against the Jews in Germany. In April 1942, the Nazi authorities ordered all Jews, including Leon and his family, to wear yellow stars on their clothes to mark them out publicly as being Jewish.

The Greenmans are deported

In October 1942, Leon, his wife, his son, and Else's grandmother, were sent to the Westerbork transit camp in the Netherlands. In January 1943, the Greenmans, along with 700 other people in the camp, were told that they were going to be moved east to work in a labour camp in Poland. Leon protested that he and his family were British subjects, but without any documents he was unable to prove this. Instead, the family was packed onto a train and sent east. The journey lasted for 36 hours, during which Leon's son Barney was ill.

Source B: A photograph of Leon Greenman late in life.

On 21 January 1943, the train arrived at its destination – a series of camps known as Auschwitz-Birkenau. After leaving the train, the 700 people were sorted into two lines. About 50 people, including Leon, were chosen to work as slave labour. The rest, including Else, Barney and Else's grandmother, were loaded onto trucks. Leon could see them clearly as they drove away, as Else and Barney were wearing bright red capes that Else had made from a pair of curtains.

This was the last time Leon saw his family, who were immediately taken away and murdered in gas chambers*.

Leon spent the next two years enduring horrific conditions in several camps, until he was finally liberated by the US Army. After months in hospital, Leon eventually discovered that almost his entire family, as well as all his Jewish friends from Rotterdam, had been murdered. Out of the 700 people with whom Leon had travelled to Auschwitz-Birkenau, only one other person survived.

Did you know?

After the war, Leon never remarried. Instead, he devoted the rest of his life to educating people about the Holocaust and Auschwitz. In 1998 Leon was awarded the OBE for his services to Holocaust education, and he died in 2008, at the age of 97.

Key term

Gas chamber*: In Nazi death camps like Auschwitz-Birkenau, prisoners were often killed by being put in sealed rooms, which were then filled with poisonous gas.

Your turn!

1 Discuss your reaction to Leon's story with a partner. What questions are you left with?

2 With a partner, list the different factors that led to the drastic change in the status of Leon and his family in the Netherlands, before his deportation to Auschwitz.

3 Write a paragraph to explain what you think the key turning points were that led to Leon's family being murdered.

How did the Holocaust begin?

Source A: Extract from the minutes of the Wannsee Conference, 20 January 1942, in which Reinhard Heydrich talks about the implementation of the 'Final Solution':

... during the course of the Final Solution, the Jews will be deployed ... in large labor columns, separated by gender, [where] able-bodied Jews will be brought to those regions to build roads, whereby a large number will doubtlessly be lost through natural reduction. Any final remnant that survives will doubtless consist of the elements most capable of resistance.

Leon's story gives us a small glimpse into the tragedy that was the Holocaust. Between 1939 and 1945, several key events helped to allow the Holocaust to happen.

1939–41: War begins

Between September 1939 and May 1940, German troops took control of most of Europe. Millions more Jews found themselves under Nazi control. Many Jews in occupied countries were deported to German-occupied Poland. There they were forced into **ghettos** – walled-off areas of cities in which Jews were made to live in terrible conditions. In the largest of these, the Warsaw Ghetto, at least 400,000 Jews were packed into an area of 1.3 square miles. Many died of disease and starvation, while the Nazis decided on a long-term plan.

1941–45: The Holocaust begins

In June 1941, Hitler invaded the Soviet Union, and the war entered an even more brutal phase. Behind the invading Nazi armies followed the 'Einsatzgruppen' – SS* killing squads who were given the task of murdering Soviet officials and Jewish men, women and children. By 1943, more than a million people had been shot or gassed by the Einsatzgruppen.

But many Jews still remained in Nazi-occupied Europe. In 1941, SS General Reinhard Heydrich was told to make plans for a 'complete solution to the Jewish question'. At some point in the next six months, Hitler authorised the mass murder of all Jews in Europe. In January 1942, Nazi officials met at the Wannsee Conference, near Berlin. Aware of the criminal nature of what they were discussing, they didn't directly mention murder, instead calling it the 'Final Solution' of the 'Jewish problem'. In the meeting, details were worked out that would lead to the final stage of the Holocaust.

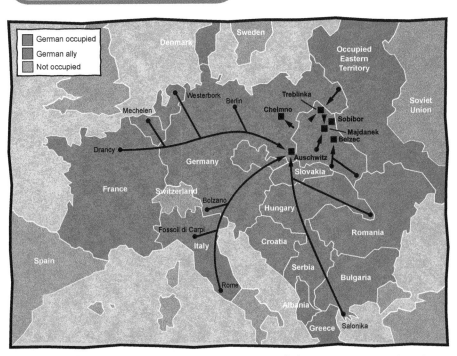

Figure 4.2: A map showing the locations of the main extermination camps, and the deportations to them.

The development of extermination camps

The Nazis looked for more 'efficient' ways to carry out the murders. Extermination camps were built throughout Poland. Largest of all was the camp at Auschwitz-Birkenau known as Auschwitz II, which was built specifically to enable the mass murder of Jews. Experiments in late 1941 led to the use of the toxic pesticide Zyklon B to gas prisoners in purpose-built gas chambers in the camps at Auschwitz and Majdanek. Figure 4.3 shows how Auschwitz II functioned.

It is thought that around 2,700,000 Jews were murdered in the extermination camps. In total, six million Jews were murdered in the Holocaust – two out of every three Jewish people living in Europe before the war.

There is no doubt that hundreds of thousands of people, either directly or indirectly, helped the Holocaust to happen. In 1963, political theorist Hannah Arendt used the phrase 'the Banality of Evil'. She argued that those who planned, built and ran camps such as Auschwitz were not necessarily fanatics, or naturally evil, but were instead ordinary people who arranged the mass murder of millions of innocent men, women and children without thinking too much about the consequences. Not all historians agree with this theory, as there are numerous examples of calculated cruelty to challenge this idea.

Key term

SS*: Short for *Schutzstaffel* (protection squad), the SS were elite Nazi troops. Some operated within the army, others as police. They were heavily involved in running concentration and extermination camps during the Holocaust.

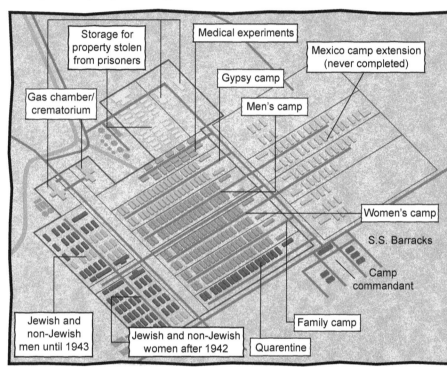

Storage for property stolen from prisoners | Medical experiments | Mexico camp extension (never completed) | Gypsy camp | Gas chamber/crematorium | Men's camp | Women's camp | S.S. Barracks | Camp commandant | Jewish and non-Jewish men until 1943 | Jewish and non-Jewish women after 1942 | Quarantine | Family camp

Figure 4.3: A diagram of Auschwitz II, the main extermination camp at Auschwitz-Birkenau, where one million Jews were murdered.

Your turn!

7th 1 Make a flow chart plotting the main stages that led to the Holocaust from 1939–45. Add detail on what happened in each stage.

8th 2 Explain why the start of the Second World War led to a radical change in Nazi policy toward Jews.

3 Do you agree with Hannah Arendt's theory of the 'Banality of Evil'? What do you think explains how 'average' humans can be involved in such inhumane acts?

Checkpoint

1 Why did the outbreak of war help to speed up measures against the Jews?
2 What were 'ghettos'?
3 What was the purpose of the Wannsee Conference?
4 Describe what measures were taken to implement the Holocaust from 1941–45.

Jewish resistance against the Nazis

Source A: Photograph of Mordechai Anielewicz, leader of the Jewish Fighting Organisation.

Resisting the Nazi regime was almost impossible for most of the victims of the Holocaust, many of whom were children or the elderly. However, many people bravely tried to stand up to the Nazis.

The Warsaw Ghetto Uprising, 1943

In 1942, the majority of the people in the Warsaw Ghetto were deported to extermination camps. Rumours spread that the remaining people in the ghetto would soon be deported and killed too. This led to groups of mostly young Jewish men within the ghetto forming a resistance group called the 'Jewish Fighting Organisation', who armed themselves with smuggled firearms and homemade weapons. Their leader was Mordechai Anielewicz, who was 23 years old.

On 19 April 1943, the Nazis made their final attempt to clear the ghetto. They were met by determined and ferocious armed resistance, in what has become known as the 'Warsaw Ghetto Uprising'.

Resistance fighters barricaded themselves inside houses and attacked German soldiers. The Nazis used experienced German troops armed with flamethrowers to clear the buildings, which they burned one by one to root out the resistance fighters.

Source B: Extract from a leaflet attributed to the Jewish Fighting Organisation, January 1943.

```
Jews in your masses, the hour is
near. You must be prepared to
resist, not to give yourselves up
like sheep to slaughter … Now our
slogan must be: Let everyone be
ready to die like a man! … Know
that escape is not to be found by
walking to your death passively,
like sheep to the slaughter. It
is to be found in something much
greater: in war! … Let every mother
be a lioness defending her young! …
Let every house become a fortress
for us! Not even one more Jew is
to find his end in Treblinka [an
extermination camp]!
```

Source C: German soldiers burn buildings down to defeat the Warsaw Ghetto Uprising, 1943.

Despite the hopeless odds, the Jewish fighters managed to hold out for an entire month, until they were killed or forced to surrender. 7,000 Jews were killed, including Anielewicz. The remainder were sent to the extermination camps. Although the uprising ultimately failed, it was remarkable in being the first popular uprising against the Nazi regime anywhere in Europe. It inspired other groups to fight back.

Jewish partisans

Some Jews managed to escape from the camps and ghettos. They usually hid in thickly wooded areas. Some formed resistance groups known as 'partisans' that organised attacks on German forces. One group near Vilna in Lithuania derailed hundreds of trains and killed 3,000 German soldiers. However, life as a partisan was incredibly dangerous: those who were captured faced execution and many were tortured for information.

Resistance in extermination camps

Resistance in extermination camps was difficult. The Nazis tried to hide from prisoners that they were about to be killed until the last minute, to prevent them panicking and resisting. However, this didn't stop some heroic examples of resistance.

In Auschwitz II, members of the Sonderkommando* learned that they were to be killed to hide the evidence of what they had been doing. On 7 October 1944, they staged an uprising in which they killed three guards and blew up the crematorium* using dynamite. Several hundred prisoners managed to escape in the chaos, although most were recaptured.

In 1943, inmates at Sobibor extermination camp killed 11 guards and set the camp on fire. Around 300 inmates managed to escape across a minefield and, although most were recaptured, 50 of them survived the war.

Source D: Photo of armed Jewish partisans near Vilna, Lithuania. An estimated 30,000 Jews fought in partisan groups and around ten per cent of them were women.

Key term

Sonderkommando*: Jewish prisoners who were forced to help the Nazis to operate the gas chambers.

Crematorium*: A place where bodies are burned (cremated).

Your turn!

1. Look at Sources A, B and D. What can you learn from these sources about Jewish resistance to the Nazis?

2. What makes Source B useful as evidence about why the Warsaw Ghetto Uprising happened?

3. How useful are Sources B and C as evidence about the effectiveness of Jewish resistance? Do they have any limitations?

Did you know?

Some Germans did try to help Jews. For example, during the Second World War, a German businessman called Oskar Schindler saved hundreds of Jews who worked in his factory from being sent to concentration camps.

123

Jewish participation in the war against Hitler

Although some Jews heroically resisted the Holocaust from within Nazi-occupied Europe, their efforts ultimately failed. They were outarmed, outnumbered, and must have known they had no hope of winning. However, outside the borders of German-occupied Europe, Jews played a role in fighting, and ultimately defeating, Nazi Germany.

Source E: Medal citation for Staff Sergeant Isadore Jachman, a Jewish soldier serving in the US Army in Belgium. Jachman was killed in this incident and posthumously received the Medal of Honor, the USA's highest award for bravery.

On 4 January 1945, when his company was pinned down by enemy [fire] … 2 hostile tanks attacked [his] unit, inflicting heavy casualties. S/Sgt. Jachman … left his place of cover and with total disregard for his own safety dashed across open ground … and seizing a bazooka from a fallen comrade advanced on the tanks … Firing the weapon alone, he damaged one and forced both to retire. S/Sgt. Jachman's heroic action, in which he suffered fatal wounds, [stopped] the entire enemy attack, reflecting the highest credit upon himself.

The Soviet Union

Some of the most brutal fighting of the Second World War took place on the Eastern Front. Around seven million Soviet civilians were killed, including 1.3 million Jews. In addition, around three million Soviet prisoners of war were starved to death or otherwise killed by the Nazis, who regarded them as racially inferior. However, Hitler's armies were eventually pushed back and defeated by the Soviet Army. 500,000 Jews fought in the Soviet Army, of whom 120,000 were killed. 160,000 Soviet Jewish soldiers received awards for their bravery, while 150 were designated 'Heroes of the Soviet Union', the greatest honour in the Soviet Army.

Polish Jews

Around 100,000 Jews had fought for the Polish Army against Hitler early in the war. About 30,000 of them were killed resisting the Nazi invasion. Many others escaped and joined the 'Free Polish' armed forces in Britain where they continued the struggle against Nazi Germany.

Jewish participation in the Allied Armies

Around 550,000 Jewish soldiers fought in the US Army, and many took leading front-line roles in helping to liberate Europe through the D-Day campaigns and onwards, such as Staff Sergeant Jachman (see Source E).

During the 'Battle of Britain', when Britain was desperate for pilots, 34 Polish Jewish pilots joined the Royal Air Force (RAF). Around 30,000 Jews also fought in the British Army. Jews from Palestine (which was under British control at the time) fought in their own units, such as the Jewish Brigade. They also helped to deal with the enormous numbers of Jewish refugees who had been displaced during the Second World War.

Many Jews, far from being passive victims, played an important role in the downfall of Nazi Germany.

Survivors of the Holocaust

For those Jews who survived the Holocaust, the future looked bleak. Tens of thousands of refugees entered displaced person's camps and tried to find their family members. Many, such as Leon Greenman, had lost their entire families, and started new lives in countries such as Britain and the USA. Others tried to return home, only to find that their homes were now occupied by strangers. Many Jews decided that there was no future for them in Europe, and instead travelled to Palestine, which was considered by many Jews to be the historic home of the Jewish people. Britain attempted to control the flow of refugees, as violence broke out between Jewish nationalists, the British Army and Arabs who felt that Palestine belonged to them. However, in 1948 the Jewish people proclaimed the creation of the state of Israel as a permanent Jewish homeland.

Source F: A photograph of the *SS Pan Crescent*, packed with Jewish refugees trying to reach Palestine. The ship was not allowed to dock in Palestine. The passengers were instead sent back to Europe.

Your turn!

 Study Sources A–F in this section. Which two sources do you think would be the most useful to challenge the idea that Jews were 'passive victims of their own fate' in the Second World War? Explain your choice, using your chosen sources and your own knowledge.

Checkpoint

1 What happened in the Warsaw Ghetto Uprising?
2 What were 'partisans', and what did they do?
3 Give an example of a rebellion within an extermination camp.
4 What kind of contributions did Jewish soldiers in the Allied armies make in the war against Hitler?
5 Why did many Jewish refugees try to travel to Palestine after the war?

Why did the Holocaust happen?

Learning objectives

- Know some of the long- and short-term reasons why the Holocaust happened.
- Analyse different historical interpretations of the causes of the Holocaust.

Why did the Holocaust happen? Why were the Jews persecuted in this way? These are some of the most difficult questions to answer. Below are some possible explanations.

The role of Hitler

Hitler frequently made speeches about his deep hatred of the Jews. Hitler encouraged the attitudes and ideas that made the Holocaust possible. It is impossible to imagine that the Holocaust would have happened without his approval.

However, there is little recorded evidence of a specific order from Hitler directing the Holocaust to begin. This does not mean such an order did not exist. The Nazis were careful to cover their tracks, and frequently used code words such as the 'Final Solution'.

The Holocaust could not have happened without the direct and indirect support of thousands of people. Therefore, responsibility must go beyond Hitler.

Source A: A photo of Hitler examining plans.

'Working towards the Führer' – the role of Nazi officials

In 1993, historian and expert on Nazi Germany Ian Kershaw offered a new view on how Nazi Germany worked. He argued that Hitler was a lazy dictator who did not manage every aspect of the Nazi state. Instead, he left it to his subordinates to work out the best 'solution' to his problems. Knowing that Hitler often preferred the most radical solutions to problems, different groups within the Nazi government competed amongst themselves to present ideas that would please Hitler. This concept is known as 'working towards the Führer'.

This does help to explain certain aspects of the Holocaust. For example, the head of the SS, Heinrich Himmler, was given almost total freedom to rule occupied Soviet territory, leading to mass murder. In addition, the Wannsee Conference saw Nazi officials meeting to discuss how logistically to carry out the Führer's wishes to resolve the 'Jewish question'. The development of increasingly brutal methods, such as the building of the extermination camps, could represent Nazi officials using 'radical' methods to implement Hitler's wishes in the way he would most approve of.

The outbreak of the Second World War

The outbreak of the Second World War certainly accelerated the Holocaust. Before 1939, Nazi policy had been aimed at removing Jews from public life and forcing them to leave Germany. However, in the long term, the war had the dual effect of:

- making it impossible for Jews to leave Nazi Germany, due to the closure of sea and land routes

- ensuring millions more Jews fell under Nazi control as the Nazis occupied most of Europe.

The war also led to the first organised mass murder of Jews, who were rounded up and shot during the invasions of the Soviet Union.

Attempts to resolve the 'problem' escalated from attempts to shoot, starve and work Jews to death to the construction of an efficient extermination camp system capable of the mass murder of an entire people.

Who or what else was responsible?

It's easy solely to blame Hitler and the Nazis for the Holocaust. However, there were thousands of other people who either made the Holocaust possible or did nothing to stop it. You've also learned that anti-Semitism existed long before the Nazis.

- Although many people did not directly kill the Jews, they did make the Holocaust possible by following orders: for example, driving trains to and from the concentration camps.

- Deeply rooted anti-Semitism was also a factor. In some places such as Latvia, Nazi troops stood aside while violently anti-Semitic locals murdered their Jewish neighbours.

- Some people enthusiastically supported Hitler. This support helped the Nazis gain power. Even though they may not have taken part in the Holocaust directly, those who voted for the Nazis helped make the Holocaust happen.

> **Did you know?**
>
> Few people appear to have been punished by the Nazis for refusing to take part in persecuting the Jews.
> The Church spoke against the Nazi's programme to kill disabled people, and the programme was suspended. If more people had spoken out in defence of the Jews, would fewer have died?

Source B: Photo of Jews from Eastern Europe awaiting deportation.

Your turn!

1 a Draw an arrow across a page with the label 'Most responsible' at one end and 'Least responsible' at the other. Look at all the different people mentioned in this section and decide where they belong along the line.

   b Annotate the diagram with reasons for your answers. For example, consider how much responsibility the Auschwitz train drivers should take.

2 Make a hierarchy showing what you think were the five most important causes of the Holocaust. Arrange them in order and write a paragraph to explain your choices.

Interpretations of the Holocaust

Interpretation questions

Extreme Intentionalist

Hitler always had an intention to carry out the Holocaust. He was making threats to murder the Jews since the 1920s. The actual killing was the end point of years of secret planning.

Moderate Intentionalist

I agree that Hitler made the decision to kill the Jews before the Holocaust began, but I would argue it was a bit later – perhaps in the late 1930s.

Extreme Functionalist

I think you're both wrong. I doubt any such decision was made. If it was, why were the Nazis trying to get the Jews to leave right up until the outbreak of war? I think groups such as the SS took the initiative to make the Holocaust happen themselves.

Moderate Functionalist

I don't think the decision was made until later in the war – probably 1941. The war changed the situation completely and the Nazis reacted to it. However, I think the Nazi leaders did make plans, but it was individuals such as Himmler and Heydrich who carried them out using their own initiative.

Figure 4.4: Illustration showing the debate amongst historians over the Holocaust.

Since 1945 and the fall of Nazi Germany, the Holocaust has become one of the most contested areas of historical research. This is partly because the Nazis tried to hide what they were doing and destroyed much of the evidence, meaning many aspects are far from clear. In addition, new evidence has come to light that has changed our understanding, such as the opening of Soviet archives since the end of the Cold War.

Some of the key questions that have concerned historians include the following:

- How much of a direct role did Hitler play? Did he plan the Holocaust personally, or were his wishes carried out by his followers?

- At what point was the decision made to murder Europe's Jews? Was it a plan the Nazis had from the start, or was it something that developed over time?

- Was the Holocaust a 'top down' event, in which Nazi officials gave orders and local groups carried them out, or was it a 'bottom up' event in which individual groups such as the SS drove the killings?

Since the 1980s, historical debate on the Holocaust has been dominated by a significant disagreement between two 'schools of thought': Intentionalists and Functionalists. Figure 4.4 summarises their arguments.

Compromise

In more recent years, historians such as Ian Kershaw have combined elements of both arguments. Most argue that, while there was probably no clear plan to instigate the Holocaust until around 1941, Hitler's violent anti-Semitism was vital in making it happen. The argument follows that Hitler made his wishes clear and left his subordinates to carry out his wishes in the way they saw fit. Almost all historians today accept this view.

Recent historians also increasingly focus on other aspects of the Holocaust, such as the role of resistance, and to what extent economic factors played a part in the Holocaust – for example, the desire of some people to profit from the persecution of Jews.

The Holocaust in history

Due to its uniquely horrific nature, the Holocaust continues to be one of the most intensely researched and debated areas of history. Soon, the Holocaust will pass beyond living memory as the last of its survivors die. However, it looks likely that the historical debate over the Holocaust will continue for many years to come.

Interpretation 1: From an article written by historian Lucy Dawidowicz, published in 1981.

The murder of the Jews was Hitler's most consistent policy, in whose execution he persisted relentlessly, and obsessiveness with the Jews may even have cost him his war for the Thousand Year Reich.

Interpretation 2: From 'Hitler's role in the Final Solution', an article by historian Ian Kershaw, published in 2008.

Nazi activists at different levels of the regime were adept in [good at] knowing how to 'work towards the Fuhrer' without having to wait for a precise Fuhrer order. It seems unlikely that Hitler ever gave one single, explicit order for the 'Final Solution' … he needed do no more than provide … authorization at the appropriate time to Himmler and Heydrich to go ahead with the various escalatory stages [steps] that culminated [ended] in the murder of Europe's Jews.

Your turn!

1. Which of the historical 'schools of thought' do you find most convincing, and why?

7th 2. Read Interpretations 1 and 2. Sum up the main difference in their arguments about what caused the Holocaust.

8th 3. Explain why these two historians might have different interpretations of the same event.

4. Look at Interpretations 1 and 2.
   a. Make a list of any knowledge you could use to support or challenge the claims made in either interpretation.
   9th b. Write a paragraph to explain which interpretation you find more convincing, and why.

Checkpoint

1. When did the Second World War come to an end?
2. What do 'Intentionalist' historians believe caused the Holocaust?
3. What do 'Functionalist' historians believe caused the Holocaust?

How were the Nazis able to implement the 'Final Solution'?

Make a timeline or flowchart showing the most important stages from 1939–45 that led to the Holocaust. Make sure to include important moments such as the outbreak of war, the invasion of the Soviet Union, and the Wannsee Conference.

What have you learned?

Why interpretations differ

In this section, you have learned:

- how and why the Nazis were able to murder millions of Jews during the Holocaust.

Interpretation 1: From *The Third Reich – A New History* by Michael Burleigh, published 2001. Burleigh's book is a general history of Nazi Germany that looks at many different aspects. Below is an extract from a chapter on the Holocaust.

> The mass murder of the Jews evolved, not in a simple, linear way, but as a result of blockages and stoppages, options denied and opportunities seized upon, rather as a deadly virus bypasses the human immune system, until the whole continent [became aware of its] … presence. The enterprise was so vast and detailed in execution … that it is difficult to convey its terrible scope …

Interpretation 2: From *KL: A History of the Nazi Concentration Camps* by Nikolaus Wachsmann, published 2015. Wachmann's book uses primary sources to investigate the experience of individuals in the concentration camp system. In the extract below, Wachsmann describes the arrival of a trainload of Jews at Auschwitz in 1942.

> The shock of arrival at Auschwitz was overwhelming … everything seemed to happen at once. The doors flung open, and SS men and some inmates in striped uniforms hurried the Jews off the trains … they screamed and pushed those who hesitated. There were kicks and blows … In great haste, the 2,500 or so Jews … spilled onto the platform, clutching each other and their belongings; left behind were the bodies of old people and children who had been crushed to death during the journey.

Historians' different interpretations

You've learned in this section that there is an ongoing historical debate over how and why the Holocaust happened. However, the Holocaust is a wide-ranging subject. As a result, the aspects of the Holocaust focused upon by different historians often differ widely. Read the two interpretations and see if you can identify the difference in their focus.

Clearly, these two historians have a very different focus. As Burleigh's book is a general history of Nazi Germany, he offers more of an overview of the Holocaust, in which he focuses on how and why it happened on a Europe-wide level. However, Wachsmann's book, which is 829 pages long, is focused solely on the concentration camp system. The length of this book, combined with its use of primary sources, means that we get much more of a 'bottom up' view of the Holocaust, and how it affected individual people.

Do you think one view is more 'correct'? Which would you rather read? Why?

Quick Quiz

1 In what ways did Jews contribute to European society before 1933?

2 What was '*The Protocols of the Elders of Zion*'?

3 What was '*Kristallnacht*'?

4 What was the 'Kindertransport'?

5 What happened in September 1939 that is considered a turning point in the treatment of the Jews?

Writing historically

Why interpretations differ

We are going to explore how to answer the following question on Interpretations 1 and 2 on page 130:
Explain why Interpretations 1 and 2 have different views on the Holocaust.

Planning your answer

To plan your answer, you could use a table like the one below. Make a copy of this table and fill it in for Interpretations 1 and 2.

	Interpretation 1	Interpretation 2
What is the focus of the historian?		
Key quote to support focus		
Summarise the difference		

Writing your answer

Remember, for this kind of question you need to provide valid reasons why the interpretations are different and try to avoid generalisations. Here are some extracts from sample answers to the question, written by different students.

Student 1

Interpretations 1 and 2 are different because they are written by different people. They are also written in different years. Interpretation 1 likens the Holocaust to 'a deadly virus', while Interpretation 2 talks about Jews arriving at Auschwitz. Interpretation 2 is about concentration camps, so the historian hasn't researched why the Holocaust happened.

This answer identifies some simple differences between the two interpretations, such as the date they were written. It also spots some surface differences between the two interpretations. However, it doesn't really explain **why** the interpretations are different, and instead provides simple points of comparison between the two interpretations.

Student 2

Interpretations 1 and 2 are different because they focus on different aspects of the Holocaust. Burleigh focuses on the 'big picture' and the political reasons why the Holocaust happened. In contrast, Wachsmann in Interpretation 2 is focused on what it was like for those who were affected by the Holocaust. He describes what it was like for Jews arriving at Auschwitz, which helps to give us a first-hand impression of the reality of life in the extermination camp system.

This answer is better, as it answers the question on why the interpretations are different. It gives a valid reason, by exploring the differences in focus of the two historians.

Student 3 – you!

Now use your table to answer the question. Try to explain other reasons why the interpretations are different. You might want to focus on one of the following.

• the purpose of the book and what it is trying to get across.
• the kind of sources they may have used.

What are the long-term causes of conflict in the Middle East?

Western media portrays the Middle East as a region gripped by conflict. However, the stories often ignore the role of the West in the causes of conflict there. In this section you will learn about:

- why Arabs in the Middle East supported Britain against the Ottoman Empire

- the consequences of the First World War for the Middle East

- the reasons for conflict between Arabs and Jews in Palestine.

Independence in the Middle East?

Learning objectives

- Understand which countries are in the Middle East now.
- Learn about the Ottoman Empire and why Arabs wanted independence.
- Consider why Britain went back on its promises about Arab independence.

What do you think?

What five words would you use to describe 'the Middle East'?

The two cartoons in Sources A and B were published at least 100 years apart, but they have the same idea in common. The idea is that foreign countries want to control the region known as the Middle East.

This political cartoon is from the 19th century. The lion represents the British Empire, the bear is the Russian Empire and the turkey is Turkey – the Ottoman Empire.

This political cartoon is from the 21st century.

Sources A and B: Two cartoons about foreign countries using their powerful positions in the world to interfere with the Middle East.

What and where is the Middle East?

The term 'Middle East' comes from the age of the European empires, as the region is between the east of Europe and the Far East. These empires are also important for understanding the causes of conflict in the Middle East. The Middle East is where farming, cities and writing all began, thousands of years ago. Three world religions began here, too: Judaism, Christianity and Islam. With such an ancient and rich history, it is not surprising that the Middle East is a complex region, with many different cultures, beliefs and ethnic groups.

Did you know?

The people who live in the Middle East often call their region ash-Sharq al-Awsat, which means 'the Middle East' in Arabic. However, other names that don't come from Western colonial times are also important. One is *Jezeera Al-Arab*, meaning the island of Arabs' to refer to the Arabian peninsular.

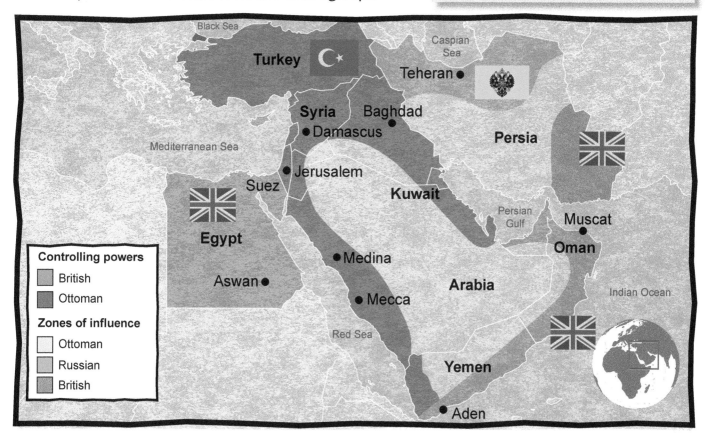

Figure 5.1: The Middle East at the start of the 20th century. The Ottoman Empire controlled most of the Middle East, although other empires were involved, too.

Your turn!

1. Study Sources A and B. What are the similarities between the two cartoons? Try to identify at least two. What are the differences? Again, try to spot at least two.

2. Study Figure 5.1. Which of the following modern-day countries were part of the Ottoman Empire at the start of the 20th century: Egypt, Iran, Iraq, Kuwait, Lebanon, Oman, Russia, Syria, Turkey, Yemen. Write your answers as a list.

3. Look again at the cartoons in Sources A and B. Describe the expressions of the middle characters in both cartoons: Turkey and the Middle East. Suggest a speech bubble for each of these two middle characters that expresses their thoughts and feelings.

The Arabs under Ottoman rule

By the start of the 20th century, over 20 million people lived in the Ottoman Empire. It was a multi-ethnic empire, with Turks, Greeks, Arabs*, Kurds, Armenians and many other ethnic minorities. Half the people in the Ottoman Empire were Turkish, and Turks were in charge.

In some areas of the empire, Ottoman control was not very strong. This was true for much of Arabia (see Figure 5.1). Away from the coasts, much of Arabia was desert. Small groups of nomadic* Arabs lived there, such as the Bedouin. The Ottomans used force to make some nomadic groups settle in one place, but many remained free and independent.

The rulers of the Ottoman Empire saw themselves as the leaders and protectors of the Muslim world. The Ottoman Empire was a caliphate*. Many Arab Muslims respected the leaders of the caliphate and, in turn, the Ottomans trusted Arabs to run the local government in Arab regions.

Bédouins en groupe avec chameaux

Source C: A group of Bedouin Arabs with their camels. These Bedouin were from Lebanon.

Key terms

Arabs*: People originally from the Middle East or North Africa, whose language is Arabic.

Nomadic*: Moving around from place to place rather than living in one place only.

Caliphate*: A state ruled by a caliph, a person considered to be a successor to the prophet Mohammed and a leader of the entire Muslim community.

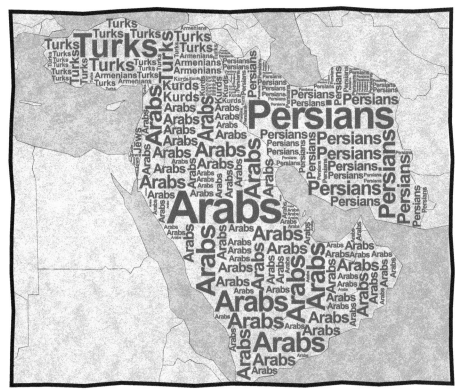

Figure 5.2: The Middle East contains many different ethnic groups. This map shows a basic picture – the reality is much more complicated!

The First World War

In November 1914, the Ottoman Empire joined the First World War on the side of Germany. This worried Britain, as its trade and communications relied on the Suez Canal*, especially the supply of oil from Persia (modern-day Iran). The Ottoman Empire could use their control over the Middle East to block this vital route, seriously damaging Britain's military strength in the war.

A revolution in Turkey in 1908 had led to attempts to develop industry and break free from religious traditions. However, these reforms were not popular in other parts of the Ottoman Empire and led to an increased desire for independence among Arabs.

The British promised the Arabs independence if they helped them defeat the Ottomans in the Middle East. As a result, there was an Arab revolt against Ottoman rule and Arab forces helped the British to fight the Ottoman Empire.

Sykes-Picot Agreement

Towards the end of the First World War, it looked certain that the Ottoman Empire would fall apart. Britain and France saw an opportunity to get control over the Middle East.

On 19 May 1916, a secret agreement was made to divide the Middle East between Britain and France. The deal was put together by a British man called Màrk Sykes and a Frenchman called François Georges-Picot. This went against British promises to help the Arabs to become independent. Instead, Britain wanted to add parts of the Middle East to its empire.

Source D: A British man called Thomas Edward Lawrence was involved in the Arab revolt against the Ottomans. He helped Bedouin Arabs with military strategy. In Britain he was called 'Lawrence of Arabia'.

Key term

Suez Canal*: Canal that connects the Mediterranean Sea to the Red Sea, meaning that ships going from west to east do not have to travel all the way around Africa. It opened in 1869, took 10 years to construct and is 100 miles long.

Did you know?

The Sykes-Picot Agreement was supposed to stay secret but, in 1917, the new leader of Russia, Vladimir Lenin, revealed the agreement to the world. This was very embarrassing for France and Britain. Lenin described the countries as 'colonial thieves'.

Your turn!

 1 Explain why Arabs wanted independence from the Ottoman Empire in 1914.

 2 Give two reasons why Britain wanted to defeat the Ottoman Empire in the First World War.

 3 'Britain was wrong not to help the Arabs become independent after the Ottoman Empire had been defeated.' Using one piece of evidence from the chapter so far, write a sentence agreeing with this statement. Then try writing a sentence that disagrees with the statement.

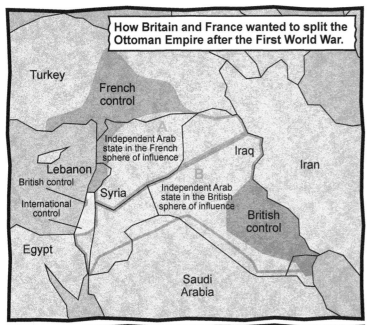

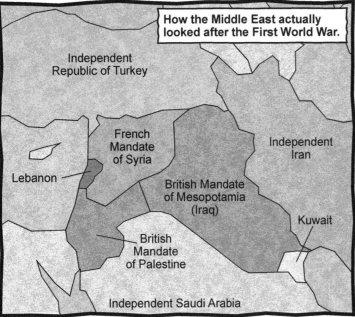

Figure 5.3: The top map shows the Sykes-Picot Agreement. The bottom map shows the mandates set up for the Middle East after the end of the First World War.

Mandates after the First World War

After the First World War, many countries criticised the colonial empires of countries like Britain, France, Turkey and Germany. The USA wanted all countries to have 'self-determination': to be independent and free. This meant a change to the plans of Britain and France to divide up the Middle East between them. Instead of controlling areas of the Middle East, Britain and France had **mandates** in the Middle East.

What is a mandate?

The idea was that some areas that had been part of the Ottoman Empire were not yet ready to be independent countries. Instead, they needed other countries to help them develop until they were ready for independence. The task of helping the new countries to develop was called a mandate.

The mandates were set up by the League of Nations*. Britain and France agreed to take on mandates. They wanted to control this area of the Middle East to protect their own interests, such as securing oil supplies and vital communication and supply routes.

Which countries had mandates and for where?

- Britain had the mandate for Palestine. This lasted from 1920 until 1948.

- France had the mandate for Syria: this also included Lebanon. This lasted from 1923 until 1946.

- Britain had the mandate for Iraq. This lasted from 1921 until 1932.

Consequences for Arab independence

Arab leaders had hoped to create an Arab state across the whole Middle East. The mandate system did not unite Arab areas of the Middle East. Instead, it split up the region and kept Arabs living in Palestine, Iraq and Syria under foreign control.

The Balfour Declaration

On 2 November 1917, Britain said Jewish people should have a 'national home' in Palestine. This was called the Balfour Declaration, because it was made by foreign secretary Arthur Balfour. For centuries, Jews had not had a country of their own. Their ancestors had lived in Palestine. The Balfour Declaration gave support to Jews who wanted to build lives in Palestine.

One reason the British government may have made the Balfour Declaration was to impress influential Jewish people living in the USA, so they would encourage greater US involvement in the First World War on Britain's side. But there were major problems with the Balfour Declaration. Palestine was not an empty country: people already lived there and most of them were not Jews, but Arabs.

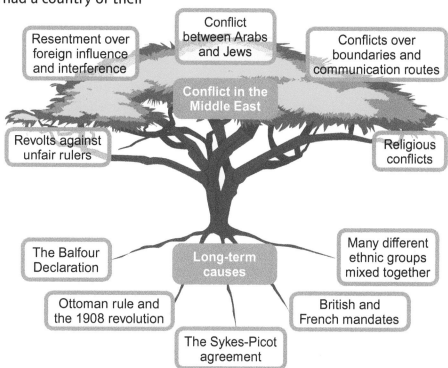

Figure 5.4: Many of the conflicts in the Middle East have long-term causes.

Your turn!

1 Study Figure 5.3. Describe two differences and two similarities between the Sykes-Picot Agreement map and the map of the British and French mandates.

2 Explain how the Sykes-Picot Agreement and the mandates in Palestine, Syria and Iraq went against the ideas of Arab independence.

3 Write a letter from Lawrence of Arabia (see page 135) to his Bedouin friends, explaining why the British decided not to keep their promises about Arab independence.

4 Study Figure 5.4. Work out which long-term causes you think link best to which conflicts in the Middle East. Some types of conflict may have more than one cause.

5 Pick two pairs of cause and conflict from question 4 and explain the link between each of them. Do this in full sentences. These could start like this: *British and French mandates led to resentment over foreign interference because …*

Checkpoint

1 Name three countries in the Middle East.

2 Why did Britain and France want to keep the Sykes-Picot Agreement secret?

3 What did the Balfour Declaration declare?

4 Why were people who hoped for Arab independence disappointed by what happened in the Middle East at the end of the First World War?

5 What is a mandate?

What caused the Arab–Israeli War?

Learning objectives

- Understand the reasons why Jewish immigration led to war in 1948.
- Explore the consequences of the Arab–Israeli War for conflict in the Middle East.

Key term

United Nations* (UN): An international organisation set up in 1945 to try to solve international problems and to build peace around the world.

Did you know?

Great Britain had 20,000 British troops in Palestine in 1939. By 1947, there were 100,000.

After the Balfour Declaration (see page 137), Jewish migration to Palestine increased. By 1922, the Jewish population of Palestine had increased to 85,000. After the Nazis came to power in Germany in 1933, 60,000 German Jews were allowed to emigrate from Europe to Palestine officially, but many others tried to make the trip illegally. By 1936, Jews made up 28 per cent of the population there.

Britain controlled Palestine because of its mandate. It tried to limit the numbers of immigrants because local Arab populations resented so many Jews arriving and taking over land to live on.

The Arab Revolt of 1936–39

By 1936, Arab people in Palestine had had enough. They demanded independence from Britain. There were strikes and political protests and violence against the British. Britain used its soldiers and police to put down the revolt by force. Around 5,000 Arabs were killed in fighting against the British, or were executed.

In 1939, the British put tight restrictions on any more Jewish immigration to Palestine. Jews trying to escape from Nazi Germany to Palestine were sometimes sent back to Germany. This continued even after the world learned about the Holocaust (see Chapter 4).

Source A: This photo from 1947 is of a ship called the *Exodus*. It was carrying 4,500 Jews from Europe, many of them survivors of the Holocaust. The British refused to let the *Exodus* land in Palestine and all its passengers were sent back to Europe.

Jewish terrorism

In Palestine, Jewish groups attacked British policemen and soldiers because the British would not allow the Jews to have Palestine as their own state. Many Jews felt that, after the Holocaust, Jews had to have a state of their own to keep them safe. But the British could not do this without risking a civil war in Palestine between Jews and Arabs.

A major terrorist attack happened on 22 July 1946. Jewish terrorists planted bombs in the British military headquarters, in the King David Hotel in Jerusalem. When the bombs exploded, 91 people were killed.

The end of the British mandate

In 1947, the British decided to give up their mandate in Palestine because of the increasing cost and the loss of British lives there. The United Nations* agreed to take on Palestine's mandate on 15 May 1948. However, when this was announced, fighting began between Jews and Arabs.

The United Nation's plan

In November 1947, the UN agreed a plan to divide Palestine into a Jewish state and an Arab state. The UN gave areas to the Jews where many Jews already lived and owned land, and did the same for Arab areas. Jerusalem was made an international zone as it was so important to everyone.

Responses to the UN's plan

- Palestinian Arabs refused to have anything to do with the UN's plan. This was partly because Jews would get more of Palestine (56%) than the Arabs (43%) despite being only 32% of the population. Mainly, though, Palestinian Arabs did not think that a Jewish state should be created out of their country at all.

- Palestinian Jews did accept the plan, but were unhappy that Jerusalem would not be part of their state and that not all areas of Jewish settlement in Palestine were in the Jewish state.

Fighting escalated into a civil war. There were massacres on each side. Thousands of Palestinians left the country to escape the war. The British did little to stop the violence.

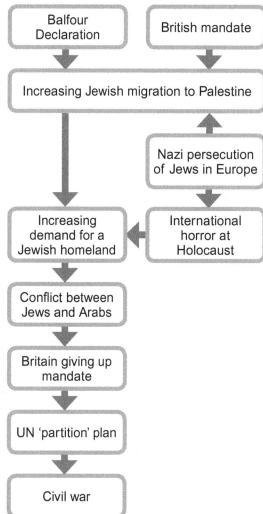

Figure 5.5: Causes and consequences in the run-up to the Arab–Israeli War (1948–49).

Consequence questions

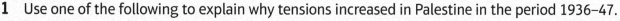

Your turn!

1 Use one of the following to explain why tensions increased in Palestine in the period 1936–47.
   a British controls on Jewish immigration.
   b The Holocaust.
   c The UN's plan to 'partition' Palestine.

2 Study Figure 5.5. Identify three causes and three consequences of conflict between Jews and Arabs from the diagram. Are any both cause and consequence? Explain how that can happen.

3 Use Figure 5.5 and these two pages to write an answer to the question: explain two consequences of the introduction of the British mandate in Palestine in 1920.

The Arab–Israeli War (1948–49)

On 14 May 1948, Jews in Palestine declared the creation of a new independent state called Israel. David Ben-Gurion became Israel's first prime minister. He had been important in the fight for a Jewish homeland for many decades.

Source B: This photograph from July 1948 shows Israeli soldiers in a jeep holding an Iraqi flag, captured from Iraqi soldiers after the Israelis took control of the town of Nazareth.

However, Arabs did not accept the new state of Israel. On 15 May, the five Arab countries surrounding Palestine joined together with Palestinian Arabs in attacking Israel. This conflict is called the Arab–Israeli War.

An Egyptian army attacked from the south; Lebanese, Syrian, Iraqi and Jordanian troops attacked from the north and east. It seemed impossible that Israel could survive. By July 1948, however, the Israelis were pushing the attackers back. By October, the Israelis were capturing new areas. In July 1949, the Arab–Israeli War ended. Israel had won.

How did Israel win the Arab–Israeli War?

There are three important reasons why Israel won the war.

1 The Arab forces were not well trained and did not have a clear plan. The Israeli troops were experienced because of their struggle with the British. Their leader, David Ben-Gurion, had a strong plan that everyone followed.

2 The Israelis were one country against five, but they did have support from the USA, with its large Jewish population. Money from the USA bought 30,000 rifles, 4,500 machine guns, 84 aircraft and millions of rounds of ammunition.

3 The UN ordered ceasefires at different points in the war. The Israelis used the ceasefires to get new weapons and develop new plans. The Israelis also broke the ceasefires several times so they could attack by surprise.

Consequences of the Arab–Israeli War

Palestinian Arabs refer to 1948 as 'al-Nakba', which means 'the catastrophe'.

- By the end of the war, 10,000 Arabs had died and 700,000 Palestinian Arabs had become refugees. Around 600,000 of the refugees settled in huge refugee camps in neighbouring Arab countries.

- Israel gained territory meant for the UN's Arab state (which the Arabs rejected). Jordan and Egypt also gained territory.

To this day, Palestinian Arabs say they should have the right to return to their old land, which they say Israel forced them to leave. Some of the Arab countries where they are living have never given them citizenship, because they agree with them that their home is in Palestine.

For Israel, the outcome of the war was a triumph. Israelis celebrate 1948 as the 'Year of Liberation'.

- Although 6,000 Israelis died in the war, Israel survived.

- Not only had Israel defended the territory given to them by the UN, it had also gained half the area of the proposed Arab state.

Israel's neighbours did not accept Israel even after its victory. They still wanted to destroy the state and return the land to Arabs. Israelis therefore made sure their small state was very well protected.

Source C: This photo, taken in 2000, shows a Palestinian Arab holding evidence that he owned a house in what is now Israel, which he left in 1948.

Your turn!

 1 Choose one of the following factors and explain how it led to the Arab–Israeli War in 1948.
   a Jewish immigration.
   b The creation of Israel (May 1948).
   c British involvement in Palestine.

2 Explain why the man in Source C may have kept the key to a house he had not seen in 50 years.

 3 Write two paragraphs to explain **(a)** why Arab armies invaded in June 1948 **(b)** why Israel won the war.

Checkpoint

1 Describe two features of Palestine in the 1930s.
2 What does the Arabic phrase 'al-Nakba' mean?
3 Name the countries that attacked Israel in the Arab–Israeli War (1948–49).
4 Explain two consequences of the Arab–Israeli War for Israel.

What are the long-term causes of conflict in the Middle East?

Write notes for a blog post explaining ways in which Britain contributed to conflict in the Middle East. Then get into a group, compare your notes and use them to write the blog post.

After that, each write comments about the post, reflecting different views.

How did the Cold War cause conflict in the Middle East?

In the last section you saw how colonial powers like Britain contributed to conflict in the Middle East. In this section you will learn about Middle Eastern conflict during the Cold War*, including:

- why a conflict over the Suez Canal led to Britain being branded a loser and Egypt a winner

- how the USA became involved in a brutal war between Iran and Iraq

- the influence of the superpowers – the USA and USSR – on conflict in the Middle East.

What caused the Suez Crisis?

Learning objectives

- Investigate the different causes of the Suez Crisis (1956).
- Decide which of the different causes were most important.

What do you think?

Why might the Middle East have become involved in the Cold War?

Nasser demanded that British troops leave Egypt.

- Nasser threatened to make links with Britain's enemy, the USSR, who would then have some control of the Suez Canal.
- Britain agreed to pull its forces out of Egypt by 1956.

▼

Nasser decided to build a huge dam across the River Nile at Aswan.

- This would control flooding of the Nile and produce hydroelectric power for the Egyptian people. Nasser asked the USA and Britain to help pay for the dam.
- Britain and the USA initially agreed.

▼

Nasser wanted to bring all Arabs together.

- He wanted all Arabs to be proud of their heritage and unite against their enemies. He began to act as the leader of the Arab world.
- The other Arab states were impressed by Nasser. They hoped that Nasser would lead an attack to destroy Israel and return Palestine to the Arabs.

Figure 5.6: Nasser's aims and motives.

The Suez Canal (see page 135) runs through Egypt. In 1882, Britain occupied Egypt to make sure no one ever closed the canal to British shipping. When Egypt became independent in 1922, Britain kept its troops in Egypt to defend the canal. In the 1950s, Britain had 70,000 soldiers in Egypt.

The leader of Egypt from 1954 was President Nasser. Nasser had three main aims.

1 Remove British troops from Egypt.

2 Use Egypt's resources to improve the lives of his people.

3 Bring all Arabs together.

Nasser began to buy weapons, aircraft and tanks to prepare Egypt for conflict with Israel. After the British and Americans refused to sell to him, Nasser bought a huge amount of Soviet weapons from Czechoslovakia in 1955. (Czechoslovakia was a communist country dominated by the USSR.) When Britain, the USA and the United Nations found out about this, they refused to lend Nasser the money he needed to build the Aswan Dam* (Figure 5.7).

Key terms

Cold War*: A war where countries threaten and spy on each other, but they do not fight each other directly.

Aswan Dam*: A dam across the River Nile in Egypt, which protects the country from flooding, provides water for irrigation and generates hydroelectricity.

Nationalising the Suez Canal

After Britain, the USA and the UN refused to lend Nasser money for the Aswan Dam, Nasser responded by announcing that the Suez Canal would be nationalised. Instead of the canal being run by a British-French owned company (the Suez Canal Company), with laws preventing it ever being closed, Egypt would take full control of it. The money from charging ships to use the canal would pay for building the Aswan Dam. Egypt would decide which countries could use the canal. This delighted Arabs throughout the Middle East as it showed an Arab leader standing up to foreign powers.

Source A: Part of a speech made by President Nasser on 26 July 1956, announcing that the Suez Canal would be nationalised. The income he is talking about is money earned by charging ships to use the Suez Canal each year.

> This Canal is an Egyptian canal. The income of the Suez Canal Company in 1955 reached… 100 million US dollars. Of this sum, we, who have lost 120,000 persons, who have died in digging the Canal, take only … three million dollars. This is the Suez Canal Company, which was dug for the sake of Egypt and its benefit! Do you know how much assistance America and Britain were going to offer us over 5 years? 70 million dollars. Do you know who takes the 100 million dollars, the Company's income, every year? They take them of course … This money is ours. This Canal is the property of Egypt.

Source B: President Nasser announcing the nationalisation of the Suez Canal to a crowd of 250,000 people.

Your turn!

1   Use Source A and your maths knowledge to answer the following three questions.
    a   What did Nasser say that digging the canal had cost Egypt?
    b   What percentage of the income from the canal did Egypt receive?
    c   What percentage of the Company's income over five years was Egypt to receive in aid?

7th 2   Why did Nasser decide to nationalise the Suez Canal? Use Source A and information in this section to back up your answer. (Hint: think about Nasser's three aims.)

8th 3   What do you think was the main reason for nationalising the canal? Explain your answer.

Israel attacked through the Sinai Desert on 29 October and Egypt fought back.

↓

Britain and France ordered both sides to stop fighting. When Nasser refused, Britain and France invaded on 5 November to 'keep the peace'. Their real aim was to take back control of the Canal.

↓

Nasser sank ships filled with concrete in the Suez Canal to stop British and French forces using it in their attacks. This closed the canal.

↓

The UN ordered a ceasefire.

↓

The USA and the USSR strongly criticised Britain and France. The USA even threatened to stop lending Britain money. Britain had no choice – it could not afford to lose US loans.

↓

All British troops stationed in Egypt withdrew by 22 December 1956.

Figure 5.7: Events of the Suez crisis.

The Suez Crisis (1956)

The British prime minister in 1956 was Anthony Eden. He was determined to stop Nasser from taking control of the Suez Canal. Eden made a secret plan with David Ben-Gurion, Israel's prime minister, and Guy Mollet, prime minister of France. All three were worried about Nasser's new military power, his popularity with other Arab countries and his growing links to the USSR. Ben-Gurion was also worried that Nasser was building up to attack Israel. They all had strong reasons for wanting to get rid of him.

Source C: From an article in the Soviet newspaper *Pravda*, published on 2 November 1956.

```
Defying the United Nation's Charter and
international law, the Anglo [British]-French
imperialists [empire-seekers] have attacked
the independent Egyptian Republic. They are
trying to seize the Suez Canal and to occupy
Egypt. The Israeli attack on Egypt [on 29
October] was just the first step in the plot
by England, France and Israel to spread their
control to all Arab states.
```

Source D: Nasser sunk 47 ships to block the Suez Canal. This photo is from November 1956.

Source E: (left) Because the Suez Canal was blocked, oil tankers did not reach the UK and petrol began to run out.

The Suez Crisis: winners and losers

Nasser
Other Arab countries saw him as a hero and a leader of all Arabs. He had complete control of the Suez Canal and its income. His three aims were secure.

Other Arab countries
They saw that the USSR would help them if it meant the USA and its allies were damaged. Arab nationalism increased, and the region began to oppose the West more.

Israel
Although Egypt would not let Israel use the Suez Canal, the Israeli armed forces had easily beaten the Egyptian forces. An attack from Egypt looked unlikely. The UN also created a stronger border between Egypt and Israel, protecting Israel.

WINNERS

LOSERS

Britain
Prime Minister Eden resigned in 1957, mainly because of the crisis. Britain had gone against the USA and had been humiliated. The USA was now the chief global power, not the British Empire. Britain's influence in the Middle East was finished.

Figure 5.8: Winners and losers of the Suez Crisis.

Source F: This Soviet cartoon was published in 1956. It criticises Britain and France for causing the Suez Crisis, and mocks them for their failure to achieve their aims.

Your turn!

1 Who caused the Suez Crisis? Was it:
  a President Nasser of Egypt, for nationalising the Suez Canal
  b Prime Minister Eden of Britain, for trying to take back control of Egypt and the Suez Canal
  c Prime Minister Ben-Gurion of Israel, for invading Egypt?
  Write a paragraph for each leader, explaining why they were each to blame in different ways.

2 Draw a spider diagram of the causes of the Suez Crisis. Which is the most important, in your view? Write a sentence that justifies your decision.

3 Study Sources C and F. Explain why the USSR was critical of Britain and France.

Checkpoint

1 Describe two features of Nasser's leadership of Egypt.
2 How did Cold War rivalries help Nasser get weapons for his army?
3 Why was Israel worried about Nasser's growing links with the USSR?
4 When and why did Nasser announce the nationalisation of the Suez Canal?

What caused the Iran–Iraq War?

Learning objectives

- Investigate the different causes of the Iran–Iraq War (1980–88).
- Develop a causal argument about the Iran–Iraq War.

The Iran–Iraq War (1980–88) shares causes of conflict you have already seen, and adds some new ones.

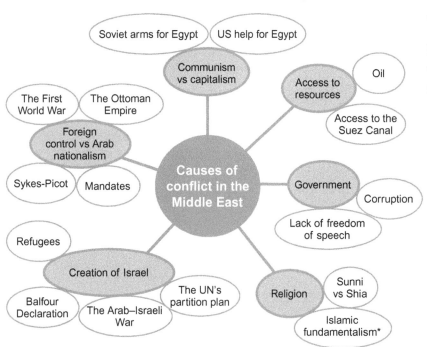

Figure 5.9: Some of the causes of conflict in the Middle East, with examples from this chapter so far.

The Iranian Revolution

By the end of the 1970s, many Iranians were very unhappy with their leader, the shah.

- Oil had made the shah and his family very rich, but many Iranians remained very poor. There was a lot of corruption and unfairness.

- Iran was modernising, but this was putting religious traditions under threat. This upset many Iranians.

- The shah supported the USA against the USSR. This upset Iranians who hated the USA because it gave money to Israel. It also upset Iranian communists who wanted a fairer society.

In 1978–79, there was a revolution that overthrew the shah and replaced him with an Islamic Republic. The new leader was a Shia* religious scholar (an ayatollah) called Ruhollah Khomeini. The revolution brought in strict religious laws. Western influences came under attack. Iran's leaders did not want to be controlled by either the USA or the USSR. They wanted a fairer society throughout the Middle East, but based on Islam, not on communism or Western democracy. The new Islamic Republic tried to encourage other countries in the Middle East to overthrow their leaders and become Islamic Republics, too.

Key terms

Islamic fundamentalism*: A movement where some Muslims want to live similarly to how the prophet Muhammad lived. They follow the teachings of the Islamic holy texts literally and want to protect religious traditions.

Shia* and Sunni*: Branches of Islam. Shias share many beliefs and practices with Sunni Muslims, but there are also differences that have led to conflict between Sunni and Shia.

Did you know?

There are approximately 1.8 billion Muslims in the world: 24 per cent of the world's population. The vast majority of these are Sunni* Muslims: perhaps 85 per cent.

Saddam Hussein's aims

The leader of Iraq in 1980 was Saddam Hussein. He was from the Sunni tradition of Islam and Iraq's Shia population was not treated well under his leadership. Hussein wanted to become the leader of the Arab world, and this meant he was critical of the USA and Israel.

The Iranian Revolution was a direct threat to Hussein for two main reasons:

1 Iran wanted countries like Iraq to become Islamic Republics by overthrowing their leaders. Ayatollah Khomeini said he wanted to see this happen in Iraq.

2 Iraq's Shia population had close links to Iran, because Iran was mainly a Shia country. Hussein worried that Iraqi Shias would be keen to start a revolution because of his harsh rule.

The Iran–Iraq War

Hussein thought that the best strategy for dealing with Iran was to attack immediately while the new government of Iran was still getting to grips with running the country. Hussein promised his country that they would beat Iran very quickly. However, his strategy turned out to be an enormous mistake.

Timeline

September 1980
Iraq's surprise attack fails to defeat Iran. Instead, it brings Iranians together. Hundreds of thousands volunteer to defend Iran and its revolution.

1984: The 'tanker war'
The USA becomes involved as Iran attacks tankers carrying Iraqi oil through the Persian Gulf.

June 1982
Iran attacks Iraq. Khomeini says Iran will not stop until Iraq is an Islamic Republic. However, the war turns into a stalemate, with neither side strong enough to defeat the other.

1988
Following an Iraqi attack into Iran, Iran agrees to a United Nations ceasefire, ending the war.

Figure 5.10: Timeline of the Iran–Iraq War.

Source A: This photo was taken in February 1986 in Teheran, Iran. It shows volunteers at a rally before they leave to fight against Iraq. The banners support Shia Islam and the volunteers chanted anti-USA slogans.

Your turn!

1 Explain why one (or more) of the following was an important reason for the Iranian Revolution: **(a)** religion **(b)** the USA. Write your answer in full sentences.

2 Explain why the Iranian Revolution was a threat to Saddam Hussein's leadership of Iraq.

3 Study Figure 5.9. Come up with one way in which each of these causes of conflict in the Middle East were involved in the conflict between Iran and Iraq. You could answer this as a spider diagram of your own, with 'Causes of conflict in the Iran–Iraq War' in the middle.

Why did the war last so long?

The war became a stalemate* because:

- Iraq did not have enough troops to successfully invade Iran, but it did have the military technology to stop Iranian attacks

- Iran had huge numbers of fighters, but their weapons were old.

Many of the volunteers for the Iranian attacks were very young men (and even boys) who believed that, if they died, they would become martyrs*.

The Iran–Iraq war and the Cold War

The USA had been an ally of the shah of Iran, but the Iranian Revolution was hostile to the USA. The Iranians had US weapons left over from the shah's time, but the USA would not supply the Iranians with spare parts to repair the weapons or ammunition. The USSR did not support Iran either. It did not want to see Iran encouraging Islamic revolutions in Muslim parts of the USSR.

The USA supported Iraq in the Iran–Iraq War. It did not send weapons, but it sent information and supplies that could be used for military purposes. The USA supported Iraq mainly because of oil. The USA worried that, if Iran won the war, it might go on to lead revolutions in Kuwait and Saudi Arabia, which supplied the USA and its allies with much of their oil. Without reliable sources of oil, Western economies would grind to a halt.

The USSR had been a close ally of Iraq since the 1950s. It did not want to lose Iraq to the West, so it increased its support to Iraq further as well.

The 'tanker war'

Both Iran and Iraq blew up oil tankers in the Persian Gulf in order to damage each other's economies. The attacks on tankers brought other countries into the war. Kuwait asked for international protection after its tankers were destroyed by Iran. Both the USA and the USSR used their navies to protect Kuwaiti tankers. The USA also attacked Iranian oil platforms in revenge for attacks on Kuwaiti tankers.

Source B: This photo from October 1987 shows four US warships and a US helicopter escorting two Kuwaiti oil tankers through the Persian Gulf.

Consequences of the war

- Between half a million and one million people died in the war.

- After eight years of war, the borders of each country did not change at all.

- The war turned the Iranian Revolution into something many Iranians would die to defend.

- The many failures of the Iraqi army meant Hussein's importance in the Arab world was reduced.

- The USA started supporting Iraq. The USSR did not want to lose Iraq to the USA, so it increased its support for its old ally too.

Why was the war so brutal?

- Iran had very little military technology and so it used what it did have – huge numbers of volunteers – to try and swamp the better-equipped Iraqis. This created brutal battlefields.

- Hussein did not trust his people. Brutal methods were used to make his conscripted Iraqi troops fight. He launched attacks against Iraqi civilians who he thought might support Iran.

- Hussein used chemical weapons, even though their use was banned by international law. Reports suggest that 20,000 Iranian troops were killed by nerve gas. Hussein also used chemical weapons against Kurdish Iraqis – his own people. 5,000 people – mostly women and children – were killed in an attack on the Iraqi town of Halabja in 1988.

- When the war became a stalemate, artillery and air raids were used to attack civilian cities in both countries, with thousands of casualties. Iraq had a modern Soviet-supplied air force. The Iranians used missile attacks instead.

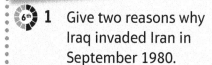

Your turn!

6th 1 Give two reasons why Iraq invaded Iran in September 1980.

8th 2 'The Cold War was the main reason why the Iran–Iraq War was so brutal.' Write one sentence that supports this statement and one sentence that argues against it. Back up both sentences with evidence.

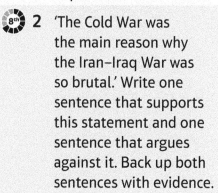

Checkpoint

1 What happened at the town of Halabja in 1988 and who was to blame?

2 Explain why the USA and USSR got involved in the Iran–Iraq War.

3 Describe two features of the Iran–Iraq War that help explain why it was so brutal.

4 Identify three consequences of the Iran–Iraq War.

How did the Cold War cause conflict in the Middle East?

Working as a group, put together a slideshow presentation about the superpowers and the Middle East. Your presentation should include slides that:

- introduce the Cold War and the two superpowers (the main differences between them)

- introduce the Middle East as a region and identify Egypt, Iran and Iraq

- explain how superpower involvement contributed to the Suez Crisis

- explain how superpower involvement contributed to the Iran–Iraq War

- conclude with a discussion of how important the Cold War was as a cause of these conflicts.

In this section, you have learned:

- about the long-term causes of conflict in the Middle East
- about the Cold War and its impact on conflict in the Middle East.

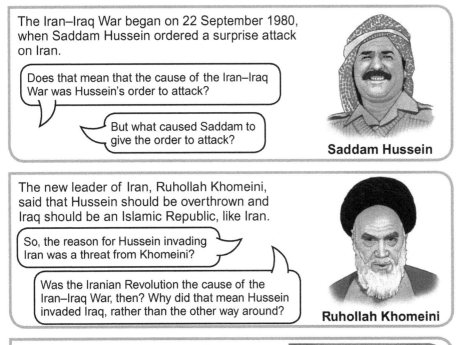

The Iran–Iraq War began on 22 September 1980, when Saddam Hussein ordered a surprise attack on Iran.

Does that mean that the cause of the Iran–Iraq War was Hussein's order to attack?

But what caused Saddam to give the order to attack?

Saddam Hussein

The new leader of Iran, Ruhollah Khomeini, said that Hussein should be overthrown and Iraq should be an Islamic Republic, like Iran.

So, the reason for Hussein invading Iran was a threat from Khomeini?

Was the Iranian Revolution the cause of the Iran–Iraq War, then? Why did that mean Hussein invaded Iraq, rather than the other way around?

Ruhollah Khomeini

The Iranian Revolution (1978–79) had overthrown Iran's shah so Iran could be ruled under Islamic law. Khomeini thought all Middle Eastern countries should do the same.

But what caused Khomeini to say Hussein should be overthrown?

That's a good question!

As historians, we know that something as big and important as a war is likely to have several different causes. We also know that a war is not going to just finish and have no further impacts – it is going to have significant consequences.

Figure 5.11 looks at the causes of the Iran–Iraq War (1980–88).

You could probably add several more causes as well. Figure 5.12 sets out the different causes covered by this chapter.

So, when a question asks you how far you agree that something was the most important cause of something like a war, how should you tackle it?

Figure 5.11: What caused the Iran–Iraq War?

The Cold War

Leadership of Khomeini

Conflict between Sunni and Shia Muslims

Causes of the Iran–Iraq War

Leadership of Saddam Hussein

The Iranian Revolution

Access to oil

Figure 5.12: Causes of the Iran–Iraq War considered in this chapter.

Writing historically

How far do you agree?

Deciding how far you agree with something involves evaluation – that means weighing up the importance or value of different factors. A good way to set out an evaluation answer is to write a paragraph about each side of the argument, with a conclusion to finish that says how far you agree.

'The main cause of the Iran–Iraq War was Saddam Hussein's leadership.' How far do you agree?

To answer this question, you would need to:

- consider evidence that agrees with this statement: for example, what started the war was Hussein's decision to launch a surprise attack

- consider evidence that disagrees with this statement: for example, that Khomeini wanted Iraq to overthrow Hussein and become an Islamic Republic

- make an overall judgement at the end of your answer. That means, based on your evidence, saying how far you agree with the statement.

There is no single right answer to this kind of 'how far do you agree?' question. What is important is using evidence to back up your judgement.

Writing your answer

Here are some extracts from the conclusions to two different student's answers:

Student 1

I agree that Hussein's leadership was the main cause of the Iran–Iraq War because, if he hadn't ordered the invasion of Iran in 1980, the war wouldn't have happened.

This answer says how far Student 1 agrees with the statement that the main cause of the war was Hussein's leadership. However, it doesn't fully explain why.

Student 2

Although Hussein's leadership was important, I do not think that it was the main reason for the war. There were other causes. It was very important that a lot of Shia Muslims lived in Iraq, because they had been persecuted under Hussein and now he was worried that they would rise up against him. Iran's leader, Khomeini, had encouraged Shias in Iraq to do this because he wanted to see an Islamic Republic in Iraq, just like the one he had encouraged in the Iranian Revolution – where most people were Shia. In my opinion, without the Iranian Revolution and the threats from Khomeini about encouraging an uprising, Hussein would not have led a war against Iran in 1980.

This answer is better because it says clearly what Student 2's judgement is and then backs up this judgement with reasons.

Your turn!

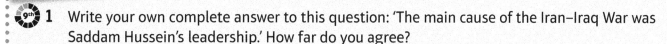

1 Write your own complete answer to this question: 'The main cause of the Iran–Iraq War was Saddam Hussein's leadership.' How far do you agree?

2 Try writing a complete answer to this question: 'The main cause of the Suez Crisis was the Cold War.' How far do you agree?

Why is the Middle East in the news so much?

The Middle East is a very important region for the West. That is perhaps one reason why it is in our news so often, compared to other regions experiencing conflict around the world. The West also feel under threat from terrorism inspired by Middle Eastern conflict. In this section you will learn about:

- the reasons why the USA led a war in Kuwait and its consequences

- the reasons why Middle Eastern terrorists attacked the USA on 11 September 2001

- how the West's 'War on Terror' resulted in conflict in the Middle East.

What caused the First Gulf War?

Learning objectives

- To investigate the causes of the First Gulf War (1990–91).
- To understand the events of the First Gulf War.

What do you think?

What sorts of news stories do you associate with news about the Middle East?

The invasion of Kuwait

On 2 August 1990, Iraq invaded Kuwait, its small, oil-rich neighbour. 120,000 Iraqi soldiers and 2,000 tanks swept through Kuwait, taking its 20,000 troops by surprise. The invasion was ordered by Saddam Hussein, the leader of Iraq. Having taken control of Kuwait, the Iraqis gathered on the border of Kuwait and Saudi Arabia. Many feared Iraq was planning to attack Saudi Arabia next.

Did you know?

Toilet paper and school books were two of many items that were banned from being exported to Iraq under the UN economic sanctions, as well as a ban on other countries buying Iraqi oil.

Source A: In this photograph from February 1991, a soldier from the United Nations force scans the Kuwaiti desert for Iraqi troops. In the background, Kuwaiti oil wells are on fire.

Kuwait and Saudi Arabia asked for help from the USA and other Western powers. At first, the United Nations used economic sanctions* against Iraq to try to make it leave Kuwait.

The sanctions failed to force Iraq to leave Kuwait. In November 1990, the UN demanded that Iraq leave Kuwait by 15 January 1991 or military force would be used against them. Hussein refused. The UN organised a force of 956,000 soldiers from 39 different countries. On 16 January, the UN forces attacked, in what became known as the First Gulf War. They were led by the USA, which contributed nearly three-quarters of the troops. The UN force also included soldiers from Arab countries – Saudi Arabia, Syria and Egypt.

Hussein promised the 'mother of all battles' between his forces and the US-led coalition*. He also ordered missile attacks on Israel. Although two Israelis were killed and hundreds injured, Israel did not retaliate (fight back). Hussein was hoping to pull Israel into the war – if Israel started fighting Iraq, Arab countries would probably pull out of the coalition, because they would not want to be allies with Israel.

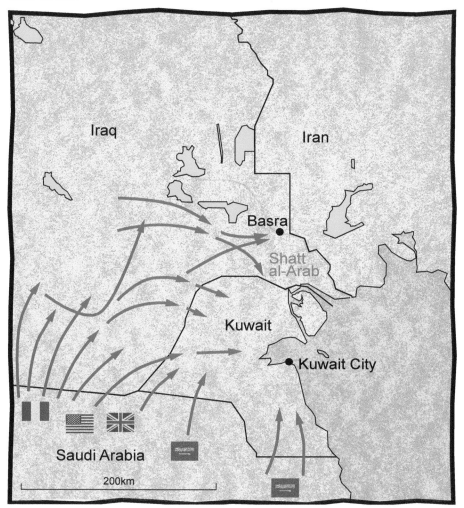

Figure 5.13: This map shows the US-led coalition's attack on Iraqi forces in Kuwait in January-February 1991.

Key terms

Sanction*: A type of punishment. Sanctions (such as bans on exports to other countries) are used internationally to punish countries that break international laws.

Coalition*: A group that gets together to achieve a particular aim.

Did you know?

The First Gulf War lasted 42 days. It cost $61 billion, of which $36 billion came from Middle Eastern countries. 30,000 Iraqi soldiers died in the war, and 22,000 were captured as prisoners of war.

Your turn!

1 The First Gulf War was won very quickly by the USA and its allies. Explain why you think this was.

2 Explain why Saddam Hussein hoped that Israel would join the fight against him.

3 'It is surprising that Egypt joined a coalition led by the USA to attack another Arab country in the First Gulf War.' Use your historical knowledge to write a sentence supporting this statement.

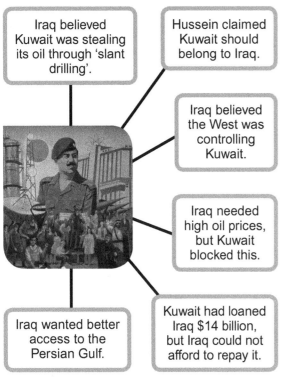

Iraq believed Kuwait was stealing its oil through 'slant drilling'.

Hussein claimed Kuwait should belong to Iraq.

Iraq believed the West was controlling Kuwait.

Iraq needed high oil prices, but Kuwait blocked this.

Iraq wanted better access to the Persian Gulf.

Kuwait had loaned Iraq $14 billion, but Iraq could not afford to repay it.

Figure 5.14: Reasons for Saddam Hussein's invasion of Kuwait in August 1990.

Why did Hussein order the invasion of Kuwait?

The reasons for Hussein's invasion were linked to the history of Iraq and the Middle East.

- Under the Ottoman Empire, Kuwait had been a district of Iraq – before the British took control in 1899. Hussein claimed this meant Kuwait belonged to Iraq: the Kuwaiti state was just a Western creation.

- The Iran–Iraq War was an economic disaster for Iraq. It needed oil prices to stay high so it could earn as much money as possible, but Kuwait would not agree to this. Kuwait released more and more oil onto the market, lowering prices.

- During the 'tanker war' (see page 148), Kuwait loaned Iraq $14 billion to help it fight Iran. Hussein did not think Iraq should have to repay it, because Iraq had defended Kuwait from Iran.

- Hussein believed Kuwait was stealing oil from the Iraqi side of a large oil field on their border by using 'slant drilling' technology: drilling at an angle under the border rather than straight down.

- Iraq only had access to the Persian Gulf through the Shatt al-Arab waterway, on the border with Iran. Control over Kuwait would give Iraqi ships better and much more secure access to the sea.

Why did the USA and its allies fight Iraq?

There was very strong international criticism of Iraq's invasion of Kuwait from almost all nations. The USSR and China stopped selling weapons to Iraq. Internationally, everyone agreed the invasion was wrong and must end. Other reasons countries fought Iraq are listed below.

- To defend Saudi Arabia. Gathering his troops on the Kuwaiti border with Saudi Arabia suggested that Hussein was planning to attack Saudi Arabia and gain control of all oil in the region. The USA and its key allies, like Japan, needed oil supplies to be secure.

- Neighbouring Arab countries had become concerned about Hussein's stockpiling of weapons since the end of the Iran–Iraq War, including long-range rockets and a 'super cannon'. Joining an attack on Iraq was a good opportunity to reduce Hussein's military threat.

- The Cold War had ended (the USSR split apart in December 1991). As the only superpower, the USA hoped that it could now lead coalitions of other countries to ensure world peace.

Consequences

- Iraq lost the First Gulf War. It came to an end on 28 February 1991.

- President George H.W. Bush decided not to go after Hussein by invading Iraq, as he did not think other countries in the Middle East would be happy about the USA intervening in this way.

- Persecuted Shia and Kurdish Iraqis rose up against Hussein. They thought the USA would help them, but it didn't. Hussein crushed their uprisings.

- The UN insisted that weapons inspectors be allowed to enter Iraq to find out if Hussein still had chemical weapons. Hussein made this very difficult, eventually banning the inspectors from making more visits. This would eventually lead to the Second Gulf War (see page 157).

Source B: From a speech to the American people made by US President George H.W. Bush on 8 August 1990. This was when the president announced he was sending troops to Saudi Arabia.

America does not seek conflict, nor do we seek to chart [organise] the destiny of other nations. But America will stand by her friends. Our mission is entirely defensive. Hopefully, our troops will not be needed long. They will not initiate [start] hostilities, but they will defend themselves, the Kingdom of Saudi Arabia, and other friends in the Persian Gulf.

Source C: From a speech to the British people by British Prime Minister John Major on 28 February 1991: the day the war ended.

The war has been won. Now we have to set about making the peace. This peace must keep Kuwait safe and other countries in the Persian Gulf area safe as well. Also, it must deal with the other problems of the region, above all that of the Palestinians. We should be clear that our quarrel has been with the Iraqi leadership not the Iraqi people, who are themselves victims of the war which Saddam Hussein dragged them into.

Your turn!

1 Write a paragraph (or more) setting out the reasons for the First Gulf War. To extend your answer, decide which reason you think was most important and explain why.

2 Study Source B. What can you infer from this source about the reasons for the USA's intervention in Kuwait?

3 Study Source C. Who did Prime Minister Major blame for Iraq's invasion of Kuwait? Do you agree that this was the main reason or were other factors important?

4 'The USA was right not to try and remove Hussein from power in 1991.' How far do you agree? Write your answer in full sentences and try to back up your point(s) with evidence.

Checkpoint

1 Which country was invaded to start the First Gulf War?

2 State one reason why the USA got involved in the First Gulf War.

3 Name one Middle Eastern country that joined the UN's force against Iraq.

4 What were UN weapons inspectors sent to Iraq to look for after the end of the First Gulf War?

What caused the 'War on Terror'?

Learning objectives

- Understand why Islamic extremists attacked the USA in September 2001.
- Explore reasons for Western intervention against the Taliban and in the Second Gulf War.
- Review the causes of conflict in the Middle East in the 20th century.

Source A: On 11 September 2001, Islamic extremists attacked New York City's World Trade Center.

Reasons for the September 11 attacks

On 11 September 2001 (written as 9/11 in the USA), 19 members of the terrorist group al-Qaeda, attacked targets in the USA by hijacking aeroplanes and flying them into important buildings: the World Trade Center in New York City and the Pentagon in Washington DC. Another aeroplane crashed before it reached its target. Nearly 3,000 people were killed in the attacks.

A year after the attack, the leader of al-Qaeda, Osama bin Laden, published a 'letter to America' on the internet stating his reasons for the attacks on the USA. These reasons included:

- US support for Israel. This led, bin Laden argued, to the oppression of the Palestinian people.

- US forces had invaded Arab territory and occupied Arab countries with their military bases.

- US sanctions against Iraq had caused great suffering to the Iraqi people.

- US support for governments in the Middle East that oppressed al-Qaeda and which would not allow government according to Islamic religious laws.

Source B: From Osama bin Laden's 'letter to America', which was published in Arabic on the internet in November 2002. Here bin Laden gives his reasons for attacks on American civilians.

> The American people are the ones who pay the taxes which fund the planes that bomb us in Afghanistan, the tanks that strike and destroy our homes in Palestine, the armies which occupy our lands in the Arabian Gulf, and the fleets which ensure the sanctions in Iraq. These tax dollars are given to Israel for it to continue to attack us and penetrate our lands. So the American people are the ones who fund the attacks against us.

The 'War on Terror'

The US President, George W. Bush (the son of President George H.W. Bush), launched a 'War on Terror' to attack extremist* terrorist networks around the world and any country that supported these terrorists. The main target was al-Qaeda forces in Afghanistan, who were supported by the extremist Islamic Taliban group who controlled most of Afghanistan. In October 2001, a US-led coalition invaded Afghanistan and defeated the Taliban by mid-November. However, Osama bin Laden escaped.

Did you know?

Osama bin Laden was eventually tracked down in Pakistan and killed by US Special Forces on 2 May 2011.

The Second Gulf War

President Bush also linked Iraq to the 'War on Terror'. Saddam Hussein was accused of supporting extremist terrorists. Hussein was also resisting the UN weapon inspections. The US and UK governments claimed that Iraq was developing weapons of mass destruction (WMDs)*. More economic sanctions were imposed on Iraq to force Hussein to give in to weapons inspections, but these did not work, despite causing considerable suffering to the Iraqi people.

On 20 March 2003, the USA , the UK and their allies invaded Iraq and started the Second Gulf War. Three weeks later, Hussein's leadership ended. However, victory in the Second Gulf War had unanticipated consequences.

Source C: From a speech made by US President Barack Obama on 2 May 2011, announcing that Osama bin Laden had been killed.

> The death of bin Laden marks the most significant achievement to date in our nation's effort to defeat al Qaeda... The United States is not — and never will be — at war with Islam. Our war is not against Islam. Bin Laden was not a Muslim leader; he was a mass murderer of Muslims. Indeed, al Qaeda has slaughtered scores of Muslims in many countries, including our own. So his demise should be welcomed by all who believe in peace and human dignity.

Your turn!

 1. Osama bin Laden was from Saudi Arabia, not Palestine. Why do you think he made the situation in Palestine his number one reason for the attacks on the USA?

2. Study Source B. Explain in your own words bin Laden's justification for attacking American civilians.

 3. Study Source C. Suggest why President Obama stressed that the USA's war against terrorism was not a war against Islam and Muslims. Use evidence from Source C to back up your answer.

 4. 'The "War on Terror" was a success.' To what extent do you agree with this statement? Suggest two points you would make in answer to this question.

Key terms

Extremist*: Someone with political opinions and aims that most people would see as unacceptable. For example, Islamic extremists have opinions and aims that most Muslims would find unacceptable.

Weapons of mass destruction*: Nuclear, chemical or biological weapons that can kill very large numbers of people.

The Second Gulf War succeeded in removing Saddam Hussein from power, but it increased conflict in the Middle East. Terrorism by Islamic extremists also increased, despite President Bush's hopes that ending Hussein's regime would make the world safer.

Consequences of the Second Gulf War

Public opinion in the West was often very critical of the USA and UK for intervening in Iraq because no weapons of mass destruction were ever found in Iraq, and because the consequences of the war were so terrible. When the UK considered intervening in the Syrian Civil War in 2013, the British parliament voted against joining the US in strikes.

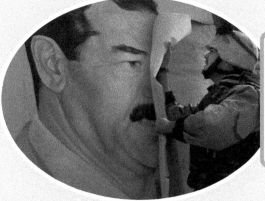

Iraq had been created by the British Empire and the country included three main groups: Sunnis, Shias and Kurds. Hussein's regime was Sunni, and he kept the country together by persecuting Shias and Kurds. Without his brutal regime, the three groups came into conflict with each other over the future of the country.

Iran grew much more powerful in the Middle East. Iran funded and encouraged Shia groups in their struggle to take power in Iraq. This was the opposite of what the USA had wanted, as Iran remained very hostile to the USA.

US involvement in the Second Gulf War did not end in 2003. In fact, it dragged on until 2011. The invasion had got rid of Hussein's army and police force. With little law and order, rival Shia and Sunni militia* groups fought each other for power in a civil war. The USA and its closest allies stayed to try and help build up the new government, police force and army. Over 4,000 US troops died in the war and 32,000 were wounded.

Figure 5.15: Consequences of the Second Gulf War.

Key term

Militia*: A group of people trained as soldiers, but not part of a regular army.

The extremist group ISIS took part in the civil war in Iraq. With no strong government to stop them, ISIS took over many Sunni areas after 2006 and declared the Islamic State of Iraq. They fought Iraqi Shias and the US troops in Iraq and became very powerful.

Resentment against the USA increased, causing more people to support anti-Western extremist groups. Many people in the Middle East believed the USA had invaded Iraq because it hated Arabs and hated Islam, and because it wanted to control the region's oil. They did not believe the USA had been trying to make the region safer.

The civil war was extremely violent. Estimates suggest that more than 100,000 Iraqi civilians were killed by the violence, while 500,000 died from war-related causes – for example, not having access to health care.

Your turn!

1 Explain two reasons for the Second Gulf War.

2 Using your knowledge of the consequences of the Second Gulf War, complete these sentence starters:
   a After Saddam Hussein's regime ended, conflict continued because …
   b ISIS became more powerful after the Second Gulf War because …
   c Iran became more powerful in the Middle East after the Second Gulf War because …

3 'Going to war with terrorists only makes things worse.' How far do you agree? Consider at least two different points in your answer, and back them up with evidence. Conclude your answer by explaining whether you agree with the statement or not.

What are the causes of conflict in the Middle East?

Causation questions

News stories about the Middle East are focused on stories about civil wars, terrorism, violence and destruction (as this chapter has, too). This can give the impression that conflict in the Middle East is inevitable, or that there is just something about the Middle East that means there is always fighting there. As historians, we should dig deeper than this when searching for the causes of conflict.

There are three resources on these pages: the quotes from teenagers in Figure 5.16, Figure 5.17 and the timeline. Use all three to help you complete the activity on the next page.

The Middle East has so much conflict because people there are divided into different groups that dislike each other, for example Arabs and Jews or Sunni Muslims and Shia Muslims.

The Middle East has always been such an important region for resources and for communications. Countries have always fought to control the Middle East, and always will.

The West is to blame for the conflict in the Middle East. They have always tried to take our resources from us and deny us our independence. The West is frightened of the power that Arab countries would have if we all joined together.

Unfortunately, the Middle East has often been caught up in global conflicts that have increased tensions in the region. For example, the Holocaust during the Second World War meant international support for the creation of the state of Israel, leading to conflict between Arab nations and Israel.

Figure 5.16: Different views about causes of conflict in the Middle East.

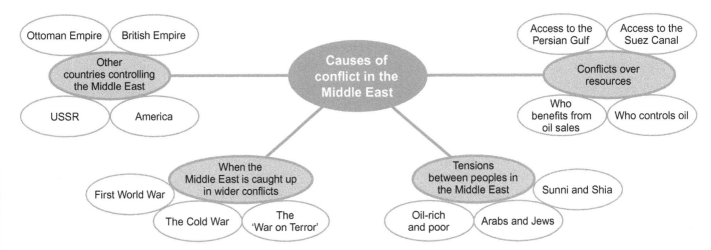

Figure 5.17: Causes of conflict in the Middle East – a review.

Timeline

Middle East conflicts

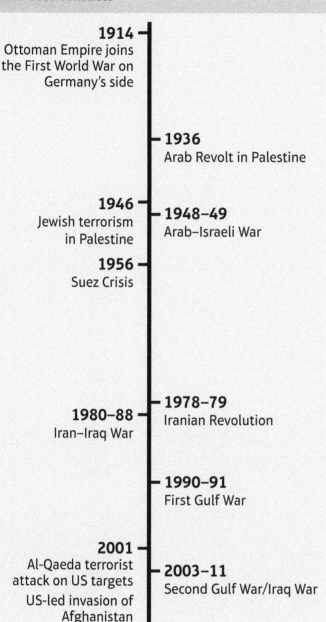

1914 — Ottoman Empire joins the First World War on Germany's side

1936 — Arab Revolt in Palestine

1946 — Jewish terrorism in Palestine

1948–49 — Arab–Israeli War

1956 — Suez Crisis

1978–79 — Iranian Revolution

1980–88 — Iran–Iraq War

1990–91 — First Gulf War

2001 — Al-Qaeda terrorist attack on US targets; US-led invasion of Afghanistan

2003–11 — Second Gulf War/Iraq War

Your turn!

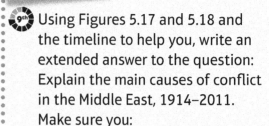

9th Using Figures 5.17 and 5.18 and the timeline to help you, write an extended answer to the question: Explain the main causes of conflict in the Middle East, 1914–2011. Make sure you:
- include at least three causes in your answer
- back up each cause with an example to support your answer
- write a conclusion that says which cause you think is the most important, and explain why.

Checkpoint

1 How many countries joined the UN force against Iraq in the First Gulf War?
2 Why did US President Bush order the invasion of **(a)** Afghanistan in 2001 and **(b)** Iraq in 2003?
3 Identify two consequences of the Second Gulf War.
4 Study Figure 5.17. Give examples of conflicts where each of the following causes were involved:
   a access to the Suez Canal
   b tensions between Arabs and Jews
   c the 'War on Terror'.

Why is the Middle East in the news so much?

- Decide why you think the Middle East is so often in the news.
- Write your answer on a sticky note. Make sure you include an explanation.
- Everyone in the class puts their notes on the board.
- Review other people's reasons. Vote for the best three reasons you see (you can't vote for yourself) by putting a 1, 2 or 3 on your top three choices.

What have you learned?

In this chapter, you have learned:

- that foreign intervention continues to be part of the story of conflict in the Middle East
- that conflict in the Middle East today has long-term causes as well as short-term causes.

Change/causation questions

Interventions by Western countries in the Middle East have led to changes in conflict in the Middle East, some of them unexpected. For example, Western intervention in the Middle East has increased terrorism aimed at Western countries, inspired by Middle Eastern issues.

Changes do not always have the same consequences for different groups of people. Figure 5.18 looks at three key events for the Middle East, and outlines consequences that followed for three different groups.

The First World War	Arabs	Jews	Westerners
	Despite fighting for the British, Arabs outside Arabia do not get the independence they were promised.	The Balfour Declaration encourages Jewish migration to Palestine.	Britain and France take on mandates in the Middle East following the collapse of the Ottoman Empire.
The Cold War	**Arabs**	**Israelis**	**Westerners**
	Opportunities to use the Cold War rivalry to their own advantage. For example, Nasser gets the British to leave Egypt by threats of links with the USSR.	US support for Israel is very important for Israel's survival. The USSR stops supporting Israel when it sees how close Israel is to the USA.	The USA is concerned about Soviet support for countries like Egypt. In turn, the USA supports oil-rich states such as Kuwait and Saudi Arabia.
The 'War on Terror'	**Iraqis**	**Other Arab countries**	**Westerners**
	Hundreds of thousands die due to the fighting after the Second Gulf War. ISIS takes control in Sunni areas.	The USA's war in Iraq fuels Arab resentment against the USA. The USA is already resented for supporting Israel.	The threat of terrorism in the West is not reduced. Public opinion turns against more military interventions in the Middle East.

Figure 5.18: What changes did these three conflicts bring for different groups of people in the Middle East?

Quick Quiz

1 Name three countries that are in the Middle East today.

2 What was 'Lawrence of Arabia' famous for?

3 What happened at the King David Hotel in Jerusalem in 1946?

4 What did President Nasser want to build at Aswan, to help the Egyptian people?

5 Name three Arab countries that joined the UN coalition against Iraq in the First Gulf War.

6 As well as the 'twin towers' of the World Trade Center, what other US building was targeted in the 11 September 2001 terrorist attacks on the USA?

Writing historically

Change/causation questions

Questions about explaining changes ask you to explain why one period was different from another. A key skill is to link the points you make together into a joined-together explanation. This is called a 'line of reasoning' (reasoning is to do with giving reasons for something).

Consider the following question:

Explain why there were changes in Western intervention in the Middle East during the 20th century. You may use the following in your answer:

- mandates

- the Cold War.

You must also use information of your own.

Structuring your answer

- This answer needs at least three points. Two can be the two stimulus points (the bullet points) in the question, plus one of your own, or some other combination.

- Back up each point with relevant detail.

- Link your points into a line of reasoning.

The table below gives three main points of argument for answering the question above. The table includes relevant detail to back up the first point. Can you fill other details for the other two points in the table?

Point	Relevant detail to back up this point
Mandates changed Western intervention because, instead of taking resources out of a colony country, Western powers were supposed to be helping the country get ready for independence.	Britain had the mandates for Palestine and Iraq. Both Jews and Arabs in Palestine did not want British control over Palestine. There were attacks against British forces.
Link to the next point: After the Second World War, Britain no longer had enough money or motivation to deal with its mandates in the Middle East.	
The Cold War changed Western intervention because colonial powers like Turkey, Britain and France were replaced by the superpowers – the USA and the USSR.	
Link to the next point: After the Cold War ended, the USA no longer needed to worry about Soviet reactions to it intervening in the Middle East.	
After 1991, the USA felt it could intervene militarily in the Middle East.	

Your turn!

Try answering the question at the top of the page, using the information in your completed table.

What's the best way to bring about change?

Change can be brought about in many ways. Violent and peaceful methods have been used throughout history to spark change. For example, the violence of war brings about change, and so, to some extent, does the violence brought about by terrorism. Peaceful methods drive change, too. People can inspire others to make changes by showing a good example. Other people may take a moral stand against something they believe to be wrong, bringing about change by their outrage and anger. But which way is best?

This section of the book will look at:

- the different ways in which change has been brought about

- the significance of individuals, groups and governments in bringing about change.

Can change come by stirring up moral outrage?

Learning objectives

- Learn about the ways in which Elizabeth Fry and Josephine Butler brought about change.
- Understand the strength of moral outrage* in bringing about change.

What do you think?

What is the most important change you would like to see and how would you bring it about?

Key term

Moral outrage*: Anger that other people have been mistreated.

Quaker*: A member of the 'Society of Friends', a faith group who reject violence as a means to bring about change.

Elizabeth Fry (1780–1845): prison reformer

Elizabeth Fry, a Quaker*, was appalled when she learned from a family friend about conditions in Newgate prison. In 1813, Fry decided to go and see for herself, in particular to find out how women prisoners were treated. Newgate prison was the most notorious prison in London, where men and women prisoners were kept in crowded, filthy conditions, and where violence and abuse were common. By deciding to visit the prison, Elizabeth was putting herself in considerable danger. What she found horrified her, as you can see from Source A.

Source A: From a report on conditions in Newgate prison, written by Elizabeth Fry in 1813.

Nearly 300 women, sent there for every grade of crime, some untried [waiting for their trial] and some under sentence of death, were crowded together in two wards and two cells. Here they saw their friends and kept a multitude of children, and they had no other place for cooking, washing, eating and sleeping.

They all slept on the floor. At times 120 in one ward without so much as a mat for bedding and many of them were very nearly naked. They openly drink spirits and swearing is common. Everything is filthy and the smell quite disgusting.

Fry immediately organised some Quaker women to make clothing for the babies and supplied clean straw for bedding. In 1817, she founded the 'Ladies' Association for the Reform of the Female Prisoners in Newgate'. These 'Ladies':

- organised a prison school for the children

- provided materials so that the female prisoners could sew and knit and make things to sell

- visited them regularly and read the Bible to them.

Source B: Elizabeth Fry visiting women in prison, an etching made in 1817.

What did Elizabeth Fry do next?

Spoke to parliamentary committees about prisons in 1818, 1826, 1832 and 1835, the first woman invited to do so.

In 1821 set up the 'British Ladies' Society for Promoting the Reformation of Female Prisoners', the first national all-women's organisation. It was supported by many important people.

Campaigned for better treatment of women prisoners and their rehabilitation rather than punishment. This changed the way many prisons were run.

Her recommendations influenced the 1823 Gaols Act, which said that female prison guards were to guard female prisoners, gaolers were to be paid, and there would be regular visits from priests and prison inspectors.

In 1827 published *Observations on the Visiting, Superintendence and Government of Female Prisoners*, which sold widely and influenced many prison governors.

Travelled to Scotland, Ireland, the Channel Islands and Europe, changing people's views about prisons and prisoners.

Figure 6.1: Elizabeth Fry's impact on prisons.

Did you know?

Before she went into the cells, Elizabeth Fry was told by the prison governor to take her watch off and leave it in his office, otherwise it would be torn off by the prisoners.

Your turn!

 1 What questions would a historian have to ask about Source B before being sure it gave reliable evidence about the improvements made by Elizabeth Fry to the treatment of women prisoners in Newgate prison?

 2 Does Source B prove that the conditions described in Source A no longer existed in Newgate prison by 1817? Explain your answer.

Key terms

Repeal*: Withdrawing an Act of Parliament.

Prostitute*: A person who has sex in exchange for money.

Dual standards*: Where different rules are applied to two groups, such as men and women, in the same situation.

Josephine Butler (1828–1906): repeal of the Contagious Diseases Acts

In 1869, Josephine Butler formed the 'Ladies National Association' (LNA), with the aim of forcing parliament to repeal* the Contagious Diseases Acts. On 1 January 1870, 140 respectable, middle-class members of the LNA, signed a public document protesting against the Acts. This was sensational. Not only were women organising a protest movement, but they were campaigning about something that they were not supposed to talk about – sex.

What were the Contagious Diseases Acts?

The Contagious Diseases Acts were designed to protect sailors and soldiers from sexually transmitted diseases (STDs). Prostitutes*, and women suspected of being prostitutes, were subjected to unpleasant medical examinations to find out whether they were infected. If they did have an STD, they were put into a locked hospital until they were cured. If they were 'clean', they were given a certificate and allowed to continue as sex workers. Many innocent women were arrested and examined in this way. Some lost their jobs and their marriages as a result, and some even committed suicide. Soldiers and sailors were not examined.

Josephine Butler and her supporters saw this as dual standards* and were determined to get the Acts repealed.

The Ladies National Association's campaign

The strategy and tactics used by Josephine Butler and her supporters set the pattern for many future protest groups. There were letters and petitions, mass meetings and protest marches. The idea that the Contagious Diseases Acts were barbaric and humiliating quickly attracted popular support. Repeal committees were set up in every major city.

> **Source C:** From *Personal Reminiscences of a Great Crusade* by Josephine Butler, published in 1896.
>
> One MP said to me, 'We know how to manage any other opposition in the House [of Commons] or in the country, but this is very awkward for us – this revolt of the women. It is quite a new thing; what are we to do with such an opposition as this?'

Repeal!

Finally, the campaign was successful. Parliament suspended the Contagious Diseases Acts in 1883 and repealed them three years later. This was largely due to the work of Josephine Butler and the women of the LNA. Women did not have the right to vote in 1883, but they had managed to influence parliament.

Did you know?

One tactic used by the LNA was to target specific parliamentary candidates. Henry Storks, a strong supporter of the Contagious Diseases Acts, stood as a candidate for Newark in 1870. However, a fierce poster campaign was mounted against him and he withdrew from the election.

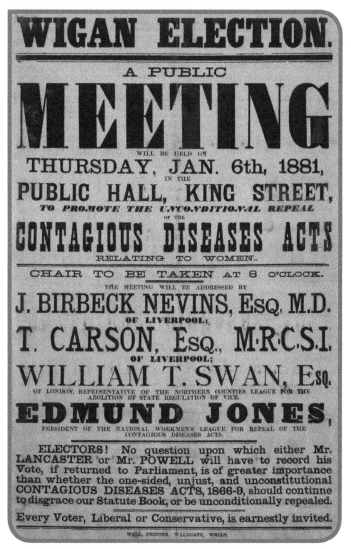

Source D: A Wigan election poster, 1881.

Your turn!

 1 How far does the election poster (Source D) explain the concerns of the MP reported by Josephine Butler in Source C?

2 Draw a large grid with five columns and six rows, with the title 'Bringing about change'. Head the columns: 'Name', 'Public support', 'Violence involved', 'Government support' and 'Success'. On each row in the 'Name' column, write the name of each weekly enquiry from this book, as you come to it (e.g. 'Stirring up moral outrage' for this week). Then, working across the grid, put up to five ticks in each column according to its strength in that particular enquiry.

3 Research William Wilberforce and the campaign to abolish the slave trade. What similarities can you find between that campaign and those of Fry and Butler?

Checkpoint

1 Name the prison where Elizabeth Fry first introduced her reforms.

2 Give two ways in which Elizabeth Fry campaigned for prison reform.

3 What was unusual about Josephine Butler's campaign?

4 Give two ways in which Josephine Butler campaigned for the repeal of the Contagious Diseases Acts.

Is war the best way to bring about change?

Learning objectives

- Learn about the causes and consequences of two civil wars*: American and English.
- Understand that the consequences of conflict are not always what was being fought for.

Key term

Civil war*: A war between people of the same country.

Did you know?

Harriet Tubman was born a slave but escaped from her master's plantation in 1849. Between 1850 and 1860, she helped about 300 slaves, including her parents, escape to freedom in the North. Rewards were offered for her capture, but she was never caught.

Source A: Part of a letter from American president Abraham Lincoln, published in the *New York Tribune* on 24 August 1862, where he set out his war aims.

My paramount object in this struggle is to save the Union, and it is not either to save or destroy slavery. If I could save the Union without freeing any slave, I would do it, and if I could save it by freeing all the slaves, I would do it, and if I could save it by freeing some and leaving others alone, I would also do that.

The American Civil War (1861–65)

Less than 80 years after gaining independence from Britain, the USA was torn apart by a terrible civil war in which over half a million people died. How had that happened?

What caused the American Civil War?

There were many differences between the Northern and Southern states in America. These differences became so bad that, by the end of 1860, the Southern and Northern states were on a collision course for war.

1. The USA is organised so that a federal government is responsible for national issues and states are responsible for their own matters.

2. Southern states were mainly agricultural, and depended on cotton and sugar plantations worked by black slave labour.

3. Northern states were mainly industrial and prosperous. They did not approve of slavery.

American Civil War

4. Slave rebellions led the Southern states to tighten laws against their slaves. Many fled to the North, where they were given their freedom.

8. December 1860: South Carolina, a slave-owning state, broke away from the USA and formed its own union of Confederate States.

7. November 1860: Abraham Lincoln was elected president of the USA. He wanted to abolish slavery.

6. When new areas were settled and asked to join the USA as states, there were debates as to whether they could have slaves or not.

5. In 1850, the US federal government passed the Fugitive Slave Act, which said that runaway slaves had to be returned to their owners.

Figure 6.2: Why was there a civil war in the USA?

Civil war!

The Northern (Union) states in America did not want the Southern (Confederate) states to break away and make their own country. On 12 April 1861, the first shots in the civil war were fired when Confederate forces attacked Fort Sumter in South Carolina. Most of the fighting of the war took place in the Southern, Confederate, states. In the end, the superior firepower and resources of the Union meant a victory for the North.

How did things turn out?

Wars usually achieve what the victors want, but there are often unexpected consequences, too.

- The victory of the Northern states meant that the Southern states were forced to join with them in the United States of America. Many Southerners resented this, believing that their states' rights had been trampled on.

- Slavery was abolished throughout the USA and former slaves were given equal rights as citizens. This was written into the American constitution.

- The war destroyed the sugar and cotton plantations in the Southern states. This made the South a lot poorer than before. Because slavery was abolished, plantations also couldn't be run in the same way. The way of life in the South was changed forever, leading to further resentment.

- A period of reconstruction (1865–77) began for the Southern states, aimed at rebuilding them. However, state after state passed laws that made former slaves 'separate but equal' to white Americans. This meant African Americans were treated as inferior to white Americans.

- The Ku Klux Klan was founded in Tennessee in 1865. It was, and still is, an extremist, violent organisation, whose members believe that white people are superior to all other races. Membership spread through all the Southern states.

- Five days after the South surrendered, Abraham Lincoln was assassinated by a Confederate spy.

Source B: The Battle of Franklin, Tennessee, on 30 November 1864.

Your turn!

1 a Use the information in Figure 6.2 to create a flow chart showing the connections between the events and situations leading to the American Civil War.

  b Research the following and add them to your flow chart: Nat Turner's Rebellion (1831), the Kansas-Nebraska Act (1854) and John Brown's raid on Harper's Ferry (1859).

  7th 8th c Draw a blue box around any event that is to do with keeping the USA together as one country. Draw a red box around any that are to do with slavery. You may find that some events will have both red and blue boxes!

8th 9th 2 'The American Civil War was all about slavery.' Write a paragraph to explain how far you agree with this statement. Use Source A in your answer.

9th 3 Imagine you are a plantation owner from South Carolina. Write a letter to the *New York Times*, explaining what you feel about the outcomes of the civil war.

Key term

Royal standard*:
The monarch's flag.

The English Civil War (1642–49)

On 22 August 1642, King Charles I raised the royal standard* at Nottingham. This was the signal for all loyal supporters to rally to his side. Many did not and so the king was at war with his own people.

What caused the English Civil War?

For years there had been struggles between king and parliament as to who ran the country, but how did these quarrels end up in civil war?

1. Charles I was a stubborn and arrogant man. He believed that he had been chosen by God to rule. He believed he could ignore parliament.

2. Charles ruled without parliament for 11 years (1629–40). MPs began to regard him as a tyrant.

3. Charles married a French Princess, Henrietta Maria, who was a Catholic. She went openly to Catholic Mass.

7. In November 1641, parliament presented a Grand Remonstrance complaining about Charles' behaviour. Charles went to parliament with 400 soldiers to arrest five MPs.

English Civil War

4. Archbishop Laud introduced changes to the Protestant Church. MPs were afraid Charles wanted to turn England into a Catholic country.

6. In 1641, Catholics in Ireland rebelled and killed nearly 3,000 Protestant settlers. Parliament refused to grant Charles money for an army to end the rebellion.

5. There was a rebellion in Scotland, starting in 1637, against Archbishop Laud's changes. Parliament refused to grant Charles money for an army to end the rebellion.

Figure 6.3: Why was there a civil war in England?

Source C: James I, speaking about kingship in 1603. His son, Charles I, shared his father's belief in the Divine Right of Kings. This means that they believed God had given them the right to rule.

It is not lawful to argue with the king's power. It is contempt in a subject to say that a king cannot do this or that. Kings are the makers of laws… and as the king is overlord of the whole land so he has the power of life and death over every person that lives in the same.

Civil war!

As in all civil wars, people were forced to take sides. Royalists, or cavaliers, fought for the king and roundheads, or parliamentarians, fought for parliament. The choice of who to fight for wasn't always an easy one. The war split families, with fathers, sons and brothers fighting on opposite sides. Finally, the parliamentarians won. This was largely due to the skill and efficiency of their army, the New Model Army.

Source D: A contemporary painting of the execution of Charles I in 1649.

How did things turn out?

At the end of the war, the parliamentarians put the king on trial, found him guilty and had him beheaded. Things were never going to be the same again.

- England was a republic, without a monarch, bishops or House of Lords. It was called a Commonwealth.

- There was a another Civil War, where Charles I's son, also called Charles, joined up with the Scots and fought the New Model Army at Dunbar (1650) and Worcester (1651). Charles was defeated and fled.

- Oliver Cromwell, a parliamentarian, did not work well with parliament and often ran the country without one. He tried out different sorts of government, none of which were successful.

- In 1653, Cromwell became Lord Protector of the Commonwealth. When parliament was not meeting, he passed laws called ordinances. Some were very strict – for example, banning Christmas celebrations. Not everyone liked this.

- Cromwell was a leading member of the army and relied on it to back him up.

- Cromwell died in 1658. He was succeeded by his son, Richard, who was a weak ruler.

In 1660, parliament invited Charles II to come back and reign as king. He was crowned in April 1661.

Your turn!

1 **a** Use the information in Figure 6.3 to create a flow chart of events and situations leading to the civil war.
   b Research the part played by William Prynne, the Earl of Strafford and John Pym. Add these to your flow chart.

2 'The civil war broke out in 1642 because of Charles I's belief in the Divine Right of Kings.' Explain how far you agree with this statement. Use Source C in your answer.

3 Do you agree that both the American and English civil wars failed to achieve their aims? Explain your thinking.

4 Now update your grid 'Bringing about Change' (from page 167).

Checkpoint

1 Give two reasons why civil war broke out in the USA in 1861.
2 List three things that happened as a result of the American Civil War.
3 Give two reasons why civil war broke out in England in 1642.
4 Why was the monarchy restored in England in 1660? Give two reasons.
5 Find two points of similarity between the reasons for the civil wars in England and the USA.

Can people bring about change by peaceful protest?

Learning objectives

- Find out about the peaceful protests of Gandhi in India and the civil rights campaign in the USA.
- Understand the significance of these protests in bringing about change.

Key terms

Passive resistance*: Non-violent opposition to authority.

Civil disobedience*: Refusal to obey certain laws as a peaceful protest against authority.

One way of protesting against authority is by passive resistance*, a peaceful way of protesting against authority. It is sometimes called civil disobedience*. This section looks at two peaceful protests, one in India and one in the USA.

The Salt March, 1930

India was part of the British Empire from 1858 to 1947. Many Indians wanted freedom from Britain's rule and, by 1930, this had developed into an independence movement. In January 1930, the Indian National Congress* issued a declaration that India should be an independent nation, governing itself. The leader of Congress, Mohandas (or Mahatma) Gandhi, and his followers were committed to non-violence and they found a way of confronting the British government without violence.

Source A: Gandhi at the head of the Salt March.

The salt tax

In India, the British government had a monopoly* on making salt. Indian's were banned from making their own salt. When buying British salt, they paid part of its price in tax to the British government. The tax was small, but the emotional impact was great: all Indians needed salt and yet the British controlled its production and sale. Gandhi decided to make salt the symbol of British oppression of the Indian people. He planned a march to the sea at Dandi, on the west coast of India, where he would make salt himself.

Key terms

Indian National Congress*: An Indian political party, usually called 'Congress'.

Monopoly*: Total control of something (usually a trade) without any competition.

Spreading the word and breaking the law

The Salt March attracted tremendous publicity. Thousands of people greeted the marchers and Gandhi addressed the crowds about the oppression by the British government and the need for non-violent protest. Thousands joined the march, too, and, by the time it reached Dandi, the procession of marchers was 3 km long. The world's press were there, too, and news of the march, and the motives behind it spread throughout the world.

When the march reached the beach at Dandi, Gandhi picked up some salty mud from the seashore. He then issued a public statement confessing he had broken the law and urged Indians to do the same. Thousands of Indians broke the law by making their own salt. The authorities made hundreds of arrests and, in May 1930, Gandhi himself was arrested and imprisoned.

Source B: Women illegally making salt by boiling sea water.

Source C: From an interview with Kamaladevi Chattopadhyay, who took part in the protests.

Bravely, they [the women] stood at street corners with little packets of salt, crying out: 'We have broken the Salt Laws and we are free! Who will buy the salt of freedom?' Their cries never went unheeded. Every passer-by stopped, slipped a coin into their hands and held out proudly a tiny pinch of salt.

Was the Salt March a success?

The Salt March had the following consequences.

- The British government had organised a series of conferences in London to discuss India's future. Gandhi was invited to represent India at the second one, in the autumn of 1931.

- A nationwide wave of civil disobedience spread throughout India.

- The independence movement in India was given a boost.

- Worldwide attention was focused on the situation in India and on the independence movement.

However, India did not become independent until 1947.

Your turn!

 1 How useful is Source A as evidence of the importance of the Salt March?

 2 Why would historians have to be careful before using Sources B and C in an enquiry into the effects of the Salt March?

Key terms

Segregation*: Separating people based on their race, for example, making black people attend different schools to white people.

Boycott*: When people refuse to buy or use something to make a point.

Sit-in*: Occupying a place and refusing to leave as a protest.

Civil Rights in the USA, 1955–64

The American constitution was amended after the Civil War so that all citizens of the USA were given equal rights. However, the Southern states passed laws that enforced segregation*, claiming they were creating a 'separate but equal' status for Americans of African descent. These racist laws were challenged in the law courts (sometimes successfully) by a tiny number of well-educated people. However, thousands of people wanted to get involved in challenging segregation.

The Montgomery Bus Boycott, 1955–56

Bus travel was segregated in Montgomery, Alabama. White and black people had to sit in separate parts of the buses. If the buses were crowded, a black person had to give up their seat so that a white person didn't have to stand. In December 1955, Rosa Parks refused to give up her seat to a white man. She was thrown off the bus and arrested. This was the start of something big. A young Baptist minister, Martin Luther King, organised a boycott* of the bus company. Black people refused to use the company's buses and walked instead.

Source D: Black people walking to work in Montgomery, February 1956.

The USA and the rest of the world followed the boycott on television, radio and in the newspapers. Finally, after 381 days, the bus company gave in and the US supreme court declared that segregation on buses was against the constitution.

It was a tremendous victory for black people, but it was only the beginning of a whole series of peaceful protests across the USA.

Source E: Spoken at a news conference by US President Eisenhower on 16 March 1960.

[I am] deeply sympathetic with the efforts of any group to enjoy the rights of equality that they are guaranteed by the Constitution.

Lunch counter sit-ins

Cafeteria lunch counters in the Southern states were segregated. In February 1960, four African-American students sat down at the all-white lunch counter in the Woolworth department store in Greensboro, North Carolina. They asked to be served and were refused. So, they staged a sit-in* until closing time. This was repeated by growing numbers of students, day after day, and the idea spread across the Southern states. It began to include art galleries, beaches, parks and swimming pools – any segregated public space. Within 18 months, about 70,000 people had taken part in similar sit-ins and 3,000 had been arrested.

Source F: Three protesters staging a sit-in at the Woolworth store in Jackson, Mississippi, in May 1963. They were smeared with sauce and mustard and sprayed with paint. Later, the two men were beaten up.

Source G: A civil rights demonstrator being attacked by a police dog in Birmingham, Alabama, on 3 May 1963.

What was gained?

- Many towns quietly desegregated their lunch bars.

- Martin Luther King emerged as the leader of the non-violent civil rights movement.

- The media made sure that the world was aware of the civil rights issues in the USA.

- In July 1964, the US Congress passed the Civil Rights Act. This outlawed discrimination on the basis of race, colour, religion, sex or national origin. Segregation was banned in schools, employment and public places.

Your turn!

8th 1 How reliable is Source D as evidence of the success of the Montgomery bus boycott? Explain your answer.

8th 9th 2 Sources F and G are photographs. What questions would historians have to ask about them before using them to illustrate reactions to civil rights demonstrations in 1963?

9th 3 The media was important in publicising the civil rights issue in the USA. Choose one source from this section that you think would have had the greatest impact on public opinion, and explain why.

4 Now add to your grid 'Bringing about Change' (from page 167).

Checkpoint

1 Who led the Salt March in India and what was the aim of the march?
2 Give two results of the Salt March.
3 What did Rosa Parks do in 1955 that helped the civil rights movement?
4 Give two ways in which civil rights protests spread in the USA after 1955.
5 What was the importance of the media in both the Salt March (1930) and the civil rights movement (1955–63)?

Using the media to change how people think

Learning objectives

- Learn about the ways in which governments can use propaganda to persuade people to follow their policies.
- Understand how political and public information campaigns try to change behaviour.

Governments and other organisations can use the media to persuade people to change their behaviour or adopt a point of view. Sometimes this propaganda is misleading or untruthful, but the aim is always the same – to persuade people to think in a certain way.

Source A: The London milkman, 1940.

Government-approved propaganda in wartime: the London Blitz

In September 1940, a year into the Second World War, German bombers began bombing British cities heavily – with particularly heavy raids on London. For 57 days, London was bombed night and day and fires raged through the city. This was the Blitz. When the Blitz ended in May 1941, over 30,000 Londoners were dead and thousands more injured and homeless. The aim was to frighten the British people and so force British politicians to negotiate a peace. The British government had to make sure the British people stayed focused on the war effort, on the need to win and to keep their morale high. This is the aim of Source A: to show everyone that life was carrying on as usual, when, for thousands, the opposite was true.

How did this photograph come about?

- The British government censors* banned the publication of photographs of bombed buildings and dead civilians.

- Photographer Fred Morley wanted to get around this. On 9 October 1940, he borrowed a milkman's outfit and a crate of milk bottles. His assistant then dressed up as a milkman and Fred photographed him amongst the ruins of a city street, with firefighters in the background.

- The censors allowed the photograph to be published in British newspapers the next day.

Key term

Censor*: A person who examines books, films, photographs and plays to remove anything believed to be unsuitable.

Government propaganda in wartime: German youth

Hitler believed that the future of Nazi Germany was its children. The Hitler Youth movement (the *Hitlerjugend*) for boys aged 10–18 started in the 1920s. When Hitler came to power in 1933, its membership was around 100,000. Three years later, membership reached four million. However, teachers complained that boys were so tired from attending evening meetings that they fell asleep during lessons. By 1938, attendance at meetings had fallen by 25 per cent and membership was made compulsory. However, this did not seem to be working. In 1940, the Nazi Ministry of Propaganda issued the poster shown in Source B. It aimed to persuade parents and their sons that, by attending the *Hitlerjugend*, they would become Nazi army officers. This was not necessarily the case.

Government propaganda in a communist state: Stalin's Russia

Soviet Russia, controlled by Stalin, introduced 'collective farming' in 1929. Peasants in each village were ordered to unite their small farms into one collective farm to be run by the village. In this way, it was argued, more food would be produced. The peasants hated it. They believed their land was being taken away. They burned their crops and killed their animals rather than hand them over to the collective farms. There was famine in the countryside and millions died from starvation. Even so, the government pressed on with its policy of compulsory collectivisation. Source C shows the image of collectivisation that the government wanted people to believe, even though it was far from reality.

Source B: A Hitler Youth recruitment poster published in 1940. The German words read: 'Officers of tomorrow'.

Source C: A Soviet government poster produced in 1930. The Russian words read: 'Day of harvest and collectivisation'.

Your turn!

1 Why do you think the government approved the publication of Source A?

2 a What is the message of Source B?

   b What can you learn from Source B about German society at that time?

3 By 1939, 99 per cent of farmland in Russia was collectivised. Does this mean that Source C was a success?

4 Explain which source is most effective for propaganda purposes.

Source D: A Labour Party poster for the general election of 1945.

Key term

Illegitimate*: A child born to parents who are not married to each other.

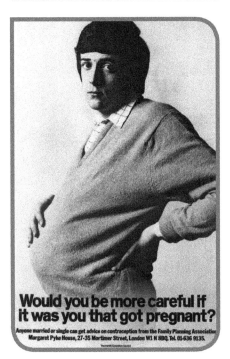

Source F: The 'Pregnant Man' poster produced for the Family Planning Association in 1970. Many people found it shocking.

Using the media after 1945

In the years after the end of the Second World War, a growing number of organisations used the media to try to influence the public. Ways to get a message across developed rapidly, from radio and television, cinema, magazines, newspapers and posters to electronic media, which now allows organisations to deliver tailored propaganda to individual devices. While the images shown here are all posters, they were delivered to the public in a variety of ways.

Political organisations: the Labour Party

The first post-war election was held in the UK in July 1945. Source D tells voters nothing about the policies of the Labour Party and how they would improve people's lives after the war. It appealed to voters' emotions. The general election resulted in a landslide victory for the Labour Party, who won 393 seats to the Conservative Party's 213 seats.

Political organisations: the Conservative Party

The Conservative Party won the 1979 election with a majority of 43 seats. Margaret Thatcher became the first woman prime minister. The image in Source E was faked to try to persuade people to vote Conservative. There was no queue outside an unemployment office. Twenty people were photographed again and again and put together to make it looks as though there was a queue.

Source E: A Conservative Party poster for the general election of 1979.

A public health campaign: family planning

Before 1970, to be an unmarried mother was considered by most people to be shameful. There was no state support for single mothers, and often they had no choice but to give their babies up for adoption. In the 1950s, for every thousand children born, around 50 were illegitimate*. By 1968, there were 85 illegitimate births in every thousand. The government believed that young people had to be persuaded to have safe sex. Source F is an example of a poster from the government-backed campaign. But, by 1979, for every thousand babies born, 110 were illegitimate.

A public health campaign: HIV (AIDS)

In the 1980s, the virus HIV (AIDS) was sweeping the world. Millions of people were becoming infected and there was no known cure or effective treatment. Wild rumours circulated about how it was spread and people were beginning to panic. In the UK, the Department of Health and Social Security started a hard-hitting campaign: information leaflets were sent to every home, posters were placed on advertising boards and television adverts were broadcast. The slogan 'AIDS Don't Die of Ignorance' was seen everywhere.

Source G: The HIV (AIDS) poster, 1986.

Source H: From an interview in 2017 with Norman Fowler, the Health Secretary 1981–87, about the public health campaign targeting HIV (AIDS).

We did follow-up research that said 90% of the public recognised the advert and a vast number changed their behaviour because of it. Reporters at the time said we were going over the top, but the public didn't agree. It was a life and death situation. There was no time to think about whether it might offend one or two people. And history shows we were right – people took care and HIV cases went down.

Your turn!

1 Look at Sources D–G. Which sources are giving positive messages, which negative and which information? Explain your thinking.

2 How useful would sources D and E be to historians researching the way people vote in general elections?

3 How far does Source H prove that Source G did bring about change?

4 Remember to update your 'Bringing about Change' grid (from page 167).

Checkpoint

1 Give two reasons why governments used propaganda in wartime.

2 How did the Nazis try to persuade boys to attend the Hitler Youth?

3 Why did totalitarian states like Soviet Russia use propaganda?

4 Why is it difficult to work out whether propaganda campaigns have been successful?

What have you learned?

In this section you have learned:

- about some of the factors that drive change
- how sources can be used in different ways.

Source utility questions

What is utility?

By 'utility', historians mean 'usefulness'. Before using a source, historians will ask themselves how useful it is and this is what you must do, too.

Useful for what?

It isn't enough to ask about usefulness in a general way. You must ask what it's useful for.

For example, look at Source B, the German recruitment poster, on page 177. It's very useful for understanding how boys were recruited into the German youth movement, but it's less useful for knowing what uniforms were worn at the time by soldiers and boys in the youth movement – and it's not useful at all for knowing about the size of the German army.

Deciding on utility

As well as the relevance of the content of the source, you will need to consider three things:

- the nature of the source
- the origin of the source
- the purpose of the source.

One way of remembering this is by the three initials: N, O and P. Let's unpack these a bit further:

Your turn!

1 Look at Source C, the Soviet government poster, on page 177. Think about the information you have about Russia at that time.
   a For what is the source very useful?
   b For what is the source partly useful?
   c For what is the source not useful at all?

2 Now answer the same questions for Source E on page 173, part of what President Eisenhower said about civil disobedience.

Nature → What is it?

Origin → Who made it?
When was it made?
Where does it come from?

Purpose → Why was it made?

Figure 6.4: Unpacking 'nature', 'origin' and 'purpose'.

Writing historically

Source utility questions

We're now going to consider how to use ideas about the nature, origin and purpose of a source to answer the question: 'How useful would historians find Source A on page 176 for an investigation into conditions during the London Blitz?'

Before you begin planning an answer to the question, look back to page 176 and the information you have about the source. Make notes under the headings 'Nature', 'Origin' and 'Purpose'.

Now read these student answers to the question.

Student 1

The photograph would be very useful because it is a photograph taken at the time by someone who was there when the Blitz had just happened. It must be remembered that photographs don't lie. The source shows exactly what London was like in the Blitz. In the background are bombed-out buildings and you can see firefighters trying to put out fires in the buildings that are still partly standing. This shows that the emergency services were still operating. It wasn't just the emergency services that were operating. The milkman is clearly still trying to deliver milk, making sure that people still had their supplies.

This student has looked at the **nature** of the source – that it is a photograph – but has asserted that photographs don't lie. This is clearly wrong, and not just in this case – photographs can often be staged. With the use of computers, photographic images can be changed in many different ways to suit the photographer's **purpose**. This is what the student has missed. The student has only considered the origin of the source by noting that the photographer was there at the time. This should have been developed further and linked to the **purpose** of the source – why had the photographer bothered to take the photograph at all?

Student 2

This is a photograph and so would be partly useful because it does show bombed buildings and firefighters in the background. But, apart from this, the photograph wouldn't be useful at all. This is because it is a fake. The milkman is wearing clean overalls and carrying a crate of milk bottles that are undamaged. This is not likely during, or just after, a raid. The milkman would, too, be very silly trying to deliver milk to bombed-out buildings. There wouldn't be any people left alive to want the milk.

This student has looked at the **nature** of the source – that it is a photograph and does give an idea of what the Blitz must have been like. The student, too, has picked up on the idea that the origin of the photograph is suspect. It is unlikely to be showing reality and in this the student is correct. The student needs to go further and ask about the **purpose** of the source. Does the fact that the photographer decided to stage this scene suggest anything about conditions during the Blitz?

Student 3 – you!

Write an answer to the question that is better than the answers written by these two students.

Plan your answer under the headings 'Nature', 'Origin' and 'Purpose'. Use the comments made on the two answers above to help you avoid making the same mistakes and build on the good parts of their answers.

What's the best way to bring about change? (continued)

Groups can try to bring about change both legally and illegally.

This section of the book will look at:

- how the changes in the law can be brought about legally

- whether it's ever justified to use illegal and sometimes violent methods to try to bring about change.

What do you think?

How far would you go to bring about a change you really believed in?

How can we change the law?

Learning objectives

- Learn about the abolition of the death penalty and abortion law reform.
- Understand the impact of changing 20th-century attitudes on parliament.

Timeline

Events leading to the end of the death penalty in Britain

1908
People under the age of 16 no longer hanged.

1933
People under the age of 18 no longer hanged.

1950
Timothy Evans wrongly hanged for the murder of his baby daughter.

1953
Derek Bentley wrongly hanged for the murder of a police officer.

1955
Ruth Ellis hanged for the murder of her boyfriend.

1956
Bill to abolish capital punishment* passed by the Commons, but rejected by the Lords.

1964
Peter Anthony Allen and Gwynne Owen Evans hanged for killing a friend for money.

1965
Parliament suspends capital punishment for murder for a period of five years.

1969
Abolition of the death penalty for murder.

During the 1960s, British parliament passed laws on a number of social issues. Why were these changes made to the law?

- Sometimes pressure groups outside parliament changed public opinion. This in turn influenced MPs to vote to reform a particular law, for example, abolishing the death penalty*.

- Sometimes reforms were brought about by MPs themselves. People would bring their problems to their MP. If the MP felt the problem was serious, they would raise it in the House of Commons. This could result in a change in the law, for example, abortion law reform.

The abolition of the death penalty, 1969

Throughout the 20th century there was a gradual change in attitudes in Britain towards using the death penalty for murderers. People began to question whether it was right for the state to kill in this way. Many prison officers who had to supervise executions began to change their views. Pressure groups such as Amnesty International campaigned against the death penalty and started petitions. Even so, there were people who wanted it to stay.

Key term

Death penalty (capital punishment)*: Legally killing someone as punishment for a crime.

Three high-profile cases

The hanging of Timothy Evans, Derek Bentley and Ruth Ellis led to more and more people being critical of capital punishment.

- **Timothy Evans** was hanged at Pentonville prison, London, on 9 March 1950 for the murder of his daughter. He was suspected of murdering his wife, too. The murderer was later discovered to be Evans' neighbour, John Reginald Christie, who turned out to be a serial killer. Evans was pardoned in 1966, 16 years after his death.

- **Derek Bentley** was hanged at Wandsworth prison, London, on 28 January 1953, for the murder of a policeman during a robbery. The policeman had been killed by Bentley's accomplice, but both were found guilty of murder. Thousands of people, including 200 MPs, campaigned unsuccessfully to stop the execution. Bentley was pardoned in 1998, 45 years after his death.

- **Ruth Ellis** was hanged in Holloway prison, London, in 1955 for the murder of her violent boyfriend. On one occasion, he had attacked her when she was pregnant and caused a miscarriage. She was the mother of a young child. A petition containing 50,000 signatures asking for leniency was ignored by the Home Secretary*.

Finally, in 1965, parliament agreed to abolish the death penalty for an experimental five years. In December 1969, parliament abolished capital punishment for murder.

Source A: People demonstrating outside Wandsworth prison, London, against the hanging of Derek Bentley. The prison officer is trying to post the notice of execution on the prison door. It was later torn down and smashed as the crowd chanted, 'It's murder!'

Source B: From the autobiography of Albert Pierrepoint, *Executioner: Pierrepoint*, published in 1974. He was Britain's hangman for 25 years. During this time, he executed over 400 people, some of whom had been convicted of war crimes.

```
It [the death penalty] is said
to be a deterrent. I cannot
agree... All the men and women
whom I have faced at that final
moment convince me that in
what I have done I have not
prevented a single murder.
```

Your turn!

 1 Draw a mind map showing the connections between events leading to the abolition of the death penalty.

 2 'The hanging of Derek Bentley was the most important factor in bringing about the abolition of the death penalty.' How far do you agree with this statement? Use the information in this section and the diagram you drew in answer to question 1 in your planning.

Did you know?

After December 1969, people could still be hanged for treason, piracy with violence and arson in the royal dockyards. In 1999 the death penalty was abolished altogether in the UK.

Key term

Home Secretary*: An important government minister in charge of law and order, among other things.

Source C: Betty Brown lived in a poor area of Grimsby and worked in a local jam factory in the early 1930s. Here she remembers some of the horrific methods used to cause a miscarriage.

```
If you got pregnant you was told by
some old woman to go to the chemist
and get one shilling's worth of
Penny Royal or Bitter Apple and
take it with gin. It used to make
you very sick. They used to say
keep taking it and you will have a
miscarriage … One dreadful method
we was told by the old midwives was
to put a mattress at the bottom
of the stairs and jump from top to
bottom. My friend died doing this.
Also there was this surgical shop
in town and the man who owned it
sold us boxes of pills. They was
like big black bombs and cost 30
shillings a box. If you didn't have
a miscarriage after three boxes,
he would tell us to go to the back
door after tea. And he would use
an instrument on you … This was all
done in secret.
```

Source D: There were some demonstrations in favour of abortion, but because of the very private, secret and illegal nature of the topic, these were very limited.

Abortion Law Reform, 1967

In 1861, the Offences Against the Person Act stated that abortion was illegal in all circumstances. Just over 100 years later, in 1967, another Act of Parliament allowed abortion in Britain if two doctors agreed the woman had a good reason for needing one, and if she was less than 28 weeks pregnant.

How had this change come about?

- In 1929, a woman could have an abortion if the pregnancy threatened her own life.

- Thousands of women, faced with unwanted pregnancies, used home remedies or backstreet illegal abortions. These often had disastrous effects, and many ended up in hospital (see Source C). It has been estimated that, in 1935 alone, there were 68,000 illegal abortions.

- The Abortion Law Reform Association (ALRA) was formed in 1936. It campaigned for abortions to be allowed if women suffered from economic, social or psychological problems, as well as medical ones.

- In 1938, Dr Aleck Bourne, supported by the ALRA, tested the legal situation by carrying out an abortion on a 14-year-old girl who had been raped. Bourne was arrested. In court he argued that the girl's mental health would have been seriously affected if she had been forced to have the baby. He was acquitted.

- A hard-hitting television play, *Up the Junction*, was watched by a wide audience in November 1965. It featured a botched abortion with a horrific miscarriage. This created sympathy for legal, safe abortions.

Acts of Parliament

MP David Steel introduced the Abortion Act into the Commons in 1967. Steel was deeply influenced by the ALRA and by the suffering of the women who had undergone illegal abortions. In 1966 alone, 40 women died as a result of illegal abortions. After an intense debate, there were 262 votes in favour and 181 votes against. On 27 October, the bill became law in England, Wales and Scotland, but not in Northern Ireland.

Poll Tax reform, 1992

In 1990, the Conservative government introduced the Community Charge – popularly called the Poll Tax – to finance local government in England and Wales. It replaced a system where people paid according to the value of their property with a system where all adults paid the same amount. There were immediate protests; by March 1991, over 18 million people were refusing to pay the Poll Tax. Thousands of people took to the streets.

On 21 March 1991, the government announced that the Poll Tax would be abolished. Margaret Thatcher had been closely associated with the tax and its failure was one of the reasons she resigned as prime minister in November 1990. Her successor, John Major, replaced the Poll Tax with the council tax that is still in place today.

Source E: Peaceful Poll Tax protests, London, 31 March 1990.

Source F: Mounted police charge poll tax rioters in Trafalgar Square, London.

Checkpoint

1 Name the three cases that helped people make up their minds about the death penalty.
2 When was the death penalty abolished **(a)** temporarily and **(b)** permanently?
3 Give two factors that helped get abortion law reform agreed by MPs.
4 Under what circumstances did the 1967 Abortion Act allow a woman to have an abortion?
5 Why was the Poll Tax hated so much?

Your turn!

 1 Draw a flow chart showing how abortion law reform came about.

 2 Explain why it took so long to introduce abortion law reform, but the Poll Tax was abolished quickly.

Is terrorism ever justified?

- Understand how to apply the definition of terrorism to different events to determine whether or not they can be called acts of terrorism.
- Learn about the ways in which Nelson Mandela and the actions of the ANC have been interpreted.

The words 'terrorism' and 'terrorist' are often used in the media to describe violent events and the people carrying them out.
We can define 'terrorism' as 'the organised use of violence to force a government or community into agreeing to certain demands'.

Bear this definition in mind as you look at the following organisations.

Source A: The IRA bombing of the Grand Hotel, Brighton, 12 October 1984.

Source B: Protesters from the Animal Liberation Front, following a raid on a laboratory owned by Boots the Chemist in London, 4 November 1990.

The Irish Republican Army (IRA)

The aim of the IRA was to end British rule in Northern Ireland and so bring about the unification of Ireland. Between 1969 and 1998, members carried out acts of violence against civilians and the British Army in Northern Ireland and on mainland Britain. In October 1984, the IRA planted a bomb in the Grand Hotel, Brighton. Their intention was to kill the British prime minister, Margaret Thatcher, and members of her government, who were staying there. Thatcher and members of her government escaped, but five people were killed and 34 injured.

The Animal Liberation Front (ALF)

ALF is an international organisation founded in 1976, with groups operating in different countries, including the UK. It takes direct action in pursuit of animal rights. Members take animals from laboratories and factory farms, burn down facilities and harass staff. They have never killed anyone.

The Women's Social and Political Union (WSPU)

The WSPU was a militant organisation campaigning for women's suffrage, 1903–14, led by Emmeline Pankhurst (see page 27). Starting by interrupting meetings and holding marches, the movement became steadily more violent. For example, suffragettes broke shop windows, set fire to post boxes, cut telephone wires and burned down the houses of famous people who disagreed with them. Their violence was always against property, but they came close to accidentally killing people on several occasions.

Al-Qaeda

Al-Qaeda is a militant Islamist organisation, founded in 1988, aiming to reshape the Muslim world by reintroducing strict Islamic religious laws and removing all Western influences. It claims, too, to be righting the wrongs that members believe have been done to Muslims by Christians in the past. Al-Qaeda claimed responsibility for a series of attacks in western Europe and the USA, including attacking the World Trade Center in New York on 11 September 2001 (see page 156) and the 7 July 2005 London bus and tube bombings. In the London bombings, 52 people were killed (including the four suicide bombers) and hundreds injured.

Source C: Trevethan House in Englefield Green, Surrey, was burned down by suffragettes in March 1913. As always, they made sure there were no people or animals at home before they set fire to it.

Source D: The London Transport bus blown up in Tavistock Square on 7 July 2005 by Al-Qaeda.

Your turn!

1   **a**   Work in groups of four. Take each of the four groups in this section in turn and, using the definition of terrorism on page 186, discuss which of them are terrorist groups.
    b   Each person takes one of the events shown in Sources A–D and writes a short paragraph explaining whether or not it was a terrorist attack.
    c   Share your group's judgements with those of the rest of your class. Are you all agreed? If not, how do you disagree and why?

2   Do you now think the definition of terrorism needs rewriting? Rewrite it so that it matches your own views on how terrorism should be defined.

Apartheid*: A policy of segregation and discrimination on the grounds of race, giving preference to white people. This meant that black people in South Africa were condemned to poor housing, low-paid jobs, poor education and daily humiliation.

Nelson Mandela: terrorist or freedom fighter?

Nelson Mandela (1918–2013) was a controversial figure during his lifetime and even more so after his death. In 1944, he joined the African National Congress (ANC), a black liberation group in South Africa. When the white-only government established a system of apartheid* in 1948, he wanted to overthrow the government and end apartheid. He led a violent sabotage campaign and was imprisoned for 27 years. Released from prison in 1990, he headed a national reconciliation movement and was elected president of South Africa in 1994. As you work through this section, remember the work you did on the previous two pages about terrorism and terrorists.

Studied law at university and worked as a lawyer in Johannesburg.

Became involved in African nationalist politics. Joined the ANC in 1944 and became committed to overturning apartheid.

Co-founded the militant Umkhonto we Sizwe in 1961 and led a sabotage campaign against the government, including bombings.

Arrested in 1962 for plotting against the state. Imprisoned for 27 years because he refused to renounce violence.

Worked with President de Klerk to end apartheid and, in 1993, they were both awarded the Nobel Peace Prize for doing so.

Organised the first multiracial election in South Africa in 1994, led the ANC to victory and became South Africa's first black president.

In 1995, created the Truth and Reconciliation Commission to investigate human rights abuses.

Released in 1990 by President F.W. de Klerk because of international pressure and fears of a racial war in South Africa.

In 1999, stood down as president and set up the Nelson Mandela Foundation, committed to ending poverty and HIV/AIDS.

Figure 6.5: Nelson Mandela's career.

ANC*: The African National Congress, a political party in South Africa that fought against apartheid.

What have people written about Nelson Mandela?

Nelson Mandela died in Johannesburg on 5 December 2013, aged 95. These interpretations were all written in tribute to him after his death.

Interpretation 1: Matthew Graham, a lecturer in history and politics at the University of Dundee, took part in a discussion about Mandela's legacy. It was published in the BBC's *History* magazine in January 2014. This is part of what he said.

Did Mandela advocate the overthrow of the government by violence? Yes. Strictly speaking, by international law, Mandela could certainly be described as a terrorist. However, in 1966 the UN General Assembly stated that apartheid was a 'crime against humanity'. I wouldn't describe Mandela as a terrorist – he regarded himself as a freedom fighter.

Interpretation 2: Written by Jesse Jackson, a campaigner for civil rights in the USA and a friend of Nelson Mandela. It was printed in the *Guardian*, a British left-wing newspaper, on 5 December 2013.

Mandela was a transformational figure. To be a transformer is to plan, to have the vision to chart the course, the skills to carry it through. It is to have the courage of one's convictions, to sacrifice, to risk life and limb, to lay it all on the line. Mandela was a giant of immense and unwavering courage and moral authority. He chose reconciliation over retaliation. He changed the course of history.

Interpretation 3: Written by Andrew Bolt, a political commentator, for the *Herald Sun*, a right-wing Australian newspaper, on 8 December 2013.

Mandela was for decades a man of violence. In 1961, he broke with African National Congress colleagues who preached non-violence, creating a terrorist wing. He later pleaded guilty in court to acts of public violence. Behind bars he sanctioned more, including the 1983 Church Street car bomb that killed 19 people. Mandela claimed that the apartheid regime left him no option but to fight violence with violence, but it is too easy to claim that events proved him right.

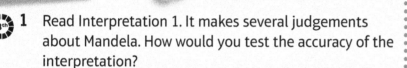

Your turn!

1 Read Interpretation 1. It makes several judgements about Mandela. How would you test the accuracy of the interpretation?

2 a What view of Nelson Mandela is given by Interpretations 2 and 3? Summarise each interpretation in a sentence.
b Explain why these interpretations are so different.

3 Write an answer to the question: 'Was Mandela a fighter for freedom or a terrorist?' Explain your answer using the interpretations in this section.

4 Now update your 'Bringing about Change' grid (from page 167).

Checkpoint

1 What happened in Brighton on 12 October 1984 and who claimed responsibility?

2 What happened in London on 7 July 2005 and who claimed responsibility?

3 What was the ANC and what were its aims?

4 When was Nelson Mandela imprisoned? For what and for how long?

5 When did Nelson Mandela become president of South Africa?

What's the best way to bring about change?

You are going to make a handbook for people and organisations that want to bring about change.

Work in small groups and use your 'Bringing about Change' grid that you've made as you worked through this enquiry to decide on the advice you will give. Remember to point out the advantages and disadvantages of each method.

Your handbook can be in the form of a written booklet, a series of cartoons, a website or whatever form of presentation you decide will be the most helpful and informative.

What have you learned?

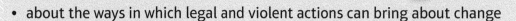

Interpretations questions

In this section you have learned:

- about the ways in which legal and violent actions can bring about change

- that an individual's actions can be interpreted in very different ways.

Quick Quiz

1 In which prison did Elizabeth Fry introduce her reforms?

2 Who led the campaign to repeal the Contagious Diseases Acts?

3 Who was president of the USA during the American Civil War?

4 When was King Charles I beheaded?

5 What was the Salt March of 1930 protesting against?

6 When was the Montgomery bus boycott?

7 What does a censor do?

8 Why did Soviet Russia use propaganda about collective farms?

9 Name one organisation that used propaganda after 1945.

10 When was the death penalty finally abolished for murder in the UK?

11 Name one terrorist organisation.

12 When was Nelson Mandela released from prison?

Interpretations

When historians evaluate different interpretations, they have to ask themselves two important questions.

1 How do these interpretations differ?

2 Why do these interpretations differ?

These two big questions can be unpacked into smaller ones, as Figure 6.6 shows:

Figure 6.6: Getting to grips with interpretations.

Writing historically

Interpretations questions

You are going to evaluate three different interpretations of the African National Congress (ANC). In order to put the interpretations into context, you need some background information.

The African National Congress (ANC)

The all-white National Party came to power in South Africa in 1948. It imposed apartheid – a system of total racial segregation and discrimination against all black people. The ANC concentrated on fighting apartheid, at first by non-violent methods. In 1960, the ANC was banned by the white South African government and forced to leave the country. For the next 30 years, the party operated in secret and a military wing used guerrilla warfare and sabotage against the South African government. The ban on the party was lifted in 1990. In 1994, in the first free elections, the ANC won and formed the government with Nelson Mandela as president.

Interpretation 1: From a textbook, *A History of South Africa*, by Martin Roberts, published in 1990.

Within the [South African] townships, the ANC remained the most powerful political organisation. Led from exile by Oliver Tambo, it sent more than 4000 guerrillas back into South Africa between 1977 and 1984. Most of them were young people who had fled after the Soweto riots. Many of their targets were buildings like oil refineries and power stations which could be damaged without loss of life. However, they also attacked buildings which housed people whom they thought to be supporters of the government, like the Air Force headquarters in Pretoria (1983) and the dockyards in Durban (1984). In both these cases, the bombs killed many innocent people, including blacks.

Interpretation 2: From an article by Chris Saunders, a history professor at the University of Cape Town, South Africa, published in 2004.

While many historians of the ANC suggest, either explicitly or implicitly, that the ANC was the leading organisation in the wider struggle, there is no doubt that this was not always the case. For much of its long history, the ANC was helped by other organisations… by the newly formed Pan Africanist Congress in late 1959 and early 1960, [and] by the Black Consciousness Movement in the 1970s… In the 1980s the bulk of the internal resistance was not the result of ANC activity.

Interpretation 3: From an article by Dan Roodt, a South African author, publisher and commentator, written in 2016.

At least since the 1950s, the ANC has really been a front for the more sinister South African Communist Party (the SACP). In 1989, the ruling Nationalist Party embraced the SACP and its front organisation, the ANC, and willingly installed it in a position of power. The fact that the ANC was ultimately successful does not change the nature of its former crimes against us all.

Your turn!

1   Look back at Figure 6.6. Apply the 'How?' questions to all three interpretations.

2   Still using Figure 6.6, apply the 'Why?' questions to all three interpretations.

3   Which interpretation did you find the most difficult to evaluate? Why?

Murder mystery: who killed Kennedy?

On 22 November 1963, American President John F. Kennedy was assassinated in Dallas, Texas. Subsequent investigations named Lee Harvey Oswald as the sole killer. However, in the decades since the event, Kennedy's assassination has become the focus of numerous conspiracy theories. Thousands of books have been written on the topic, as well as numerous documentaries and even a Hollywood film! The key question is: who really killed Kennedy? Was it Oswald, or was he framed? In this section, you will look at some of the evidence to make up your own mind.

Murder of an American president

Learning objectives

- Understand the basic facts about Kennedy's assassination.
- Look at different evidence to decide whether you think there was a conspiracy or not.

What do you think?

Why do so many people refuse to believe government explanations of events such as the Kennedy assassination and the 1969 moon landing?

It was just after midday on 22 November 1963 and the crowd at Dealey Plaza in Texas were becoming increasingly excited. In a few minutes, a procession of open-top cars would pass by, and everyone was eager to catch a glimpse of President John F. Kennedy and his glamorous wife Jackie.

Just before 12.30pm, the crowd on the plaza saw the black Lincoln convertible that contained the president and his wife, who both smiled and waved happily at the crowd. Kennedy was keen to project a positive image to the people of Dallas. A presidential election was due in 1964 and Texas would be a key state to win. However, Kennedy expected to face opposition. Only weeks earlier, the US ambassador to the UN, Adlai Stevenson, had been attacked in Dallas and had warned Kennedy about the hostile mood in the city. Kennedy decided to go ahead with the visit, hoping that his charm would win people over. Accompanying him was the Governor of California, John Connally, and his wife, who sat in front of John and Jackie.

Source A: Kennedy and his wife in Dallas, minutes before the assassination.

Kennedy's assassination

As Kennedy's car passed down Dealey Plaza, the sound of gunfire erupted, causing panic. Kennedy was hit in the throat and clutched his neck, while Jackie tried to help him. Seconds later, Kennedy was hit in the head and slumped into Jackie's lap. The president was rushed to hospital, but there was nothing doctors could do to save him. At 1pm, Kennedy was declared dead. The USA mourned while the world looked on in shock and horror.

Meanwhile, a manhunt for the assassin was underway. There was some confusion over where the shots had come from, but several people claimed they had come from the Texas School Book Depository building, on the edge of Dealey Plaza. A search of the building revealed a 'sniper's nest' on the sixth floor, made out of boxes, along with a rifle and three spent cartridges. The building was sealed off. One employee was missing – Lee Harvey Oswald. A description was issued for his arrest.

Later, a police officer called J.D. Tippit spotted Oswald waiting at a bus stop. Tippit stopped his car to try to talk to Oswald, but Oswald drew a pistol and shot Tippit dead. Oswald fled from the scene and hid in a nearby theatre, where he was arrested. At first, Oswald was charged only for the murder of Tippit, but soon he was also charged with Kennedy's murder. He denied all involvement.

On 24 November, Oswald was being escorted through a throng of reporters and policemen in the basement of Dallas Police Headquarters. A man called Jack Ruby emerged from the crowd and shot Oswald in the abdomen. Oswald was rushed to hospital, where he died a few hours later.

Oswald's death meant the trial never took place. Instead, rumours of a conspiracy began to grow.

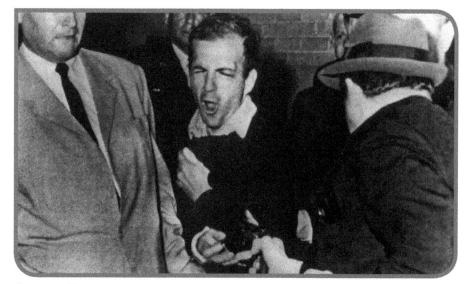

Source B: The moment Jack Ruby shot Oswald at the Texas Police Headquarters, 24 November 1963.

Your turn!

Look at the story of Kennedy's assassination so far. The events described above are mostly factual in nature. What evidence do you think there is so far that: (a) Oswald was the sole killer (b) there may be another explanation?

The Warren Commission

Kennedy's vice president, Lyndon B. Johnson, was sworn in as president shortly after Kennedy's death. On 29 November, he appointed Earl Warren, Chief Justice of the USA, to oversee an inquiry into the murder. The investigation was known as the 'Warren Commission' and, in September 1964, it delivered its findings. The findings can be summarised as follows:

- Three shots in total were fired from the Texas School Book Depository building.

- The shots were fired by Lee Harvey Oswald using his Mannlicher–Carcano rifle.

- Oswald acted alone. There were no other shooters and there was no wider conspiracy.

- Jack Ruby also acted alone.

Below is a summary of some of the evidence that the Warren Commission used to establish Oswald as the sole killer.

DEPARTMENT OF JUSTICE
The Warren Report - Summary of Evidence against Oswald
Sept 1964

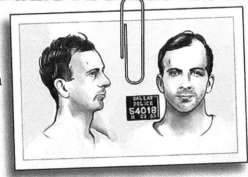

- Oswald previously attempted to assassinate US General Edwin Walker, whom he regarded as a 'fascist', in March 1963, using the same type of rifle.
- Oswald was shown in a photograph holding the same type of rifle that was found at the scene.
- Oswald's wife testified that he owned the rifle.
- The rifle, and pistol used to kill Tippit (found on Oswald), were both ordered under the alias 'A. Hiddel', which was an alias Oswald had used before.
- Oswald's palm print was found on the rifle, and on the boxes near the rifle.
- Oswald had worked at the Texas School Book Depository Building since October 1963.
- Oswald was seen carrying a long paper package into the building on the day of the assassination.
- Oswald was seen 35 minutes before the murder taking the elevator to the sixth floor.
- An eyewitness on the ground saw someone matching Oswald's description at the window carrying out the assassination. He later picked out Oswald as the person who most closely resembled the person he saw, but could not make a positive identification.
- Oswald was spotted descending the stairs after the assassination by a police officer.
- Oswald was found to be the only employee missing from the building after the murder.
- Oswald had served in the Marines and was a trained marksman capable of firing three shots in six seconds.
- Nine eyewitnesses identified Oswald as the person who shot police officer Tippit.

Figure 7.1: Evidence against Lee Harvey Oswald, presented by the Warren Commission.

OSWALD MAN STANDING ON RIGHT IN FIGURED SHIRT. PHOTOGRAPH TAKEN IN MINSK, U.S.S.R. BY AN AMERICAN TOURIST IN AUGUST, 1961. (KRAMER DEPOSITION 1)

Source C: Photo taken in the USSR, August 1961. Oswald is indicated by the arrow. Oswald attempted to defect to the USSR, after declaring himself communist. He spent over two years there, marrying a Soviet citizen. He returned to the USA in 1962.

Source D: Photo taken on or around 31 March 1963, showing Lee Harvey Oswald in the backyard of his house. He is holding an identical rifle to that which was found in the 'sniper's nest' and is holding up Marxist newspapers.

Source E: Extract from the Warren Commission's report on Kennedy's assassination, published in 1964. This section explains possible motives for the murder.

Many factors were undoubtedly involved in Oswald's motivation for the assassination... he does not appear to have been able to establish meaningful relationships with other people. He was perpetually discontented with the world around him. Long before the assassination he expressed his hatred for American society and acted in protest against it... He sought for himself a place in history... His commitment to Marxism and communism appears to have been another important factor in his motivation. He also had demonstrated a capacity to act decisively and without regard to the consequences... Out of these and... many other factors... there emerged a man capable of assassinating President Kennedy.

Your turn!

1   Look at the evidence that was presented against Oswald and jot down what evidence there is for the following points:
    a   Was Oswald on the sixth floor of the building at the time of the shooting?
    b   Did the rifle that was thought to be the murder weapon belong to Oswald?
    c   Was Oswald capable of carrying out such a difficult assassination (three shots in six seconds against a distant moving target)? Had he tried to kill people before?

2   Look at Sources C–E. Why do you think Oswald's Marxist views might have been seen as a motive? Think about what you have learned about the Cold War.

3   What other motives may he have had?

4   Based on the evidence on this spread, how far do you feel convinced that Oswald was the killer? Do you have any reasons to think he wasn't?

Did the Warren Commission get it wrong?

In 1975, film of the assassination (known as the 'Zapruder' film) was shown on US television for the first time. Many felt it suggested that there was more than one gunman and that the Warren Commission was wrong.

Source F: A photo showing President Kennedy shortly before hit by the second bullet.

Source G: Photo taken by Mary Moorman a fraction of a second after Kennedy was hit in the head. In the background is the 'grassy knoll'. Inset is a close-up of the fence in the background. Can you see a man firing a gun?

Badgeman's head

Badge

Flash from a gun going off

In the film, after Kennedy is hit in the throat by a bullet, another bullet is seen hitting him in the head, which appears to be knocked backwards. As Oswald was behind Kennedy, this led many to conclude that there must have been another gunman somewhere in front of Kennedy's car. You can see the whole film online, but be warned – it is gruesome.

In 1976, another investigation was ordered by Congress, which largely supported the findings of the Warren Commission, but also criticised the investigation. It suggested that there were probably more than three shots and that there was probably another gunman.

Some claim they can see a police officer (nicknamed 'badgeman') firing a rifle over a fence in a photo taken on the day (Source G). Others claim it is simply light and shadows. However, many did claim to have heard gunfire coming from the 'grassy knoll', including several police officers. However, their testimony was dismissed by the Warren Commission, who insisted that they had been mistaken.

In the decades since Kennedy's murder, speculation has raged about whether the full truth of the assassination has been told. What you have seen here represents only a fraction of the evidence. There are thousands of websites, books and films on the topic, and millions of documents.

There are many who believe that Oswald did not act alone or was not involved at all. Some believe there was a wider conspiracy to kill the president, involving groups including the USSR, Cuba, Cuban exiles, the Mafia and even the CIA. A significant number of people believe that there was a cover-up, in which evidence was deliberately withheld or destroyed by the government.

In American law, a jury must decide whether the evidence proves that the accused is guilty 'beyond reasonable doubt'. Look at the evidence surrounding the assassination of Kennedy. Do you believe, beyond 'reasonable doubt', that the Warren Commission was right and that Oswald acted alone?

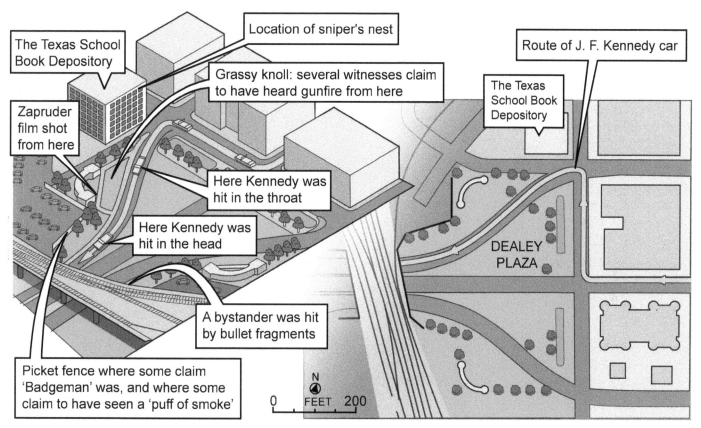

Figure 7.2: Two diagrams showing Dealey Plaza on 22 November 1963.

Your turn!

1 What evidence is there that there may have been more than one gunman? List as many points as you can.

2 Look at Sources F and G, and also think about the 'Zapruder' film. Many people argue that these are key pieces of evidence that there was another gunman. How convincing do you find them?

3 Make a summary of the arguments from both sides, presenting the key evidence. You might also want to do some wider research of your own. When finished, decide what your answer is to the key question: do you think Lee Harvey Oswald acted alone, or is there enough evidence to show that it's not that simple?

Glossary

Alliance: An agreement between countries that benefits each of them.

Allied forces: British troops and those of Britain's allies.

Allied powers: In the Second World War, the countries who joined forces to fight the Axis powers. The main allies were Britain, the USA, the USSR and China. They were helped by many groups whose countries had been occupied by the Nazis, for example French and Polish forces.

ANC: The African National Congress, a political party in South Africa that fought against apartheid.

Annex: Seizing an area of land and making it part of your country.

Anti-Semitism: Hostility or prejudice directed against Jewish people.

Apartheid: A policy of segregation and discrimination on the grounds of race, giving preference to white people. This meant that black people in South Africa were condemned to poor housing, low-paid jobs, poor education and daily humiliation.

Arabs: People originally from the Middle East or North Africa, whose language is Arabic.

Arms race: A competition between countries for the development and production of weapons.

Aryan: In the 19th and 20th centuries, some people believed that Europeans were descended from the ancient 'Aryan' race, who were racially superior to other races. There is no real evidence for an 'Aryan' race actually existing.

Aswan Dam: A dam across the River Nile in Egypt, which protects the country from flooding, provides water for irrigation and generates hydroelectricity.

Axis powers: Countries who fought on the side of Nazi Germany in the Second World War. Germany's main allies were Italy and Japan.

Balance of power: A situation where countries have roughly equal power to each other.

Battalion: Fighting unit of up to 1,000 men.

Blockade: A common tactic of war in which ships belonging to an enemy nation are prevented from reaching port, normally in order to damage the enemy's economy. Blockades were used to great effect by the British against Germany in the First World War.

Blood Libel: Libel means to make a false and damaging claim about someone or something. 'Blood Libel' refers to the lies spread about Jews committing ritualistic murders.

Bombardment: A continuous attack with shells (shelling), intended to destroy trench defences, especially barbed wire.

Boycott: When people refuse to buy or use something to make a point.

Caliphate: A state ruled by a caliph, a person considered to be a successor to the prophet Mohammed and a leader of the entire Muslim community.

Capitalist: An economic and political system in which money and property are controlled by private individuals. The USA is a capitalist country.

Censor: A person who examines books, films, photographs and plays to remove anything believed to be unsuitable.

CIA: Central Intelligence Agency, a US government agency that gathers intelligence on other nations and uses it to influence and guide US foreign policy.

Civil disobedience: Refusal to obey certain laws as a peaceful protest against authority.

Civil rights movement: Refers to groups such as the National Association for the Advancement of Colored People (NAACP) and the Congress of Racial Equality (CORE), which fought for the rights of black people from the 1950s onwards.

Civil war: A war between people of the same country.

Coalition: A group that gets together to achieve a particular aim.

Cold War: A war where the sides threaten and spy on each other, but they do not fight each other directly.

Colony: Land settled by and under the control of people from another country.

Concentration camps: A prison usually for political prisoners or members of persecuted minorities. In Nazi Germany, they were usually very overcrowded, with poor facilities and a high risk of death.

Conscription: Forcing people to join the army, rather than relying on people volunteering.

Constituency: An area represented by an MP.

Crematorium: A place where bodies are burned (cremated).

Death penalty (capital punishment): Legally killing someone as punishment for a crime.

Dictator: A single strong leader who can do what they want and has complete power.

Dual standards: Where different rules are applied to two groups, such as men and women, in the same situation.

Empire: A large group of states or colonies ruled over by a single head of state.

Encirclement: Being surrounded.

Extremist: Someone with political opinions and aims that most people would see as unacceptable. For example, Islamic extremists have opinions and aims that most Muslims would find unacceptable.

Franchise: Those who could vote in an area.

Gas chamber: In Nazi death camps like Auschwitz-Birkenau, prisoners were often killed by being put in sealed rooms, which were then filled with poisonous gas.

Great powers: Countries that have international influence and military strength.

Guerrilla: A term used to describe warfare conducted by unofficial soldiers, who fight by carrying out ambushes and hit and run attacks. Guerrillas are difficult to identify as they do not wear uniforms.

Heckle: To interrupt a public speaker with comments, questions and abuse.

Home Secretary: An important government minister in charge of law and order, among other things.

Hunger strike: To refuse to eat as a protest. This could make prisoners very weak and unwell.

Illegitimate: A child born to parents who are not married to each other.

Indian National Congress: An Indian political party, usually called 'Congress'.

Islamic fundamentalism: A movement where some Muslims want to live similarly to how the prophet Muhammad lived. They follow the teachings of the Islamic holy texts literally and want to protect religious traditions.

Kaiser: German word for emperor. Used to describe the head of unified Germany after 1871.

Khrushchev: The leader of the Soviet Union at the time of the Cuban Missile Crisis. Stalin had died in 1953.

League of Nations: An international organisation that aimed to help prevent wars between countries, set up after the First World War.

Manhattan Project: The scientific project that developed the first atomic bombs. It was led by the USA, with support from Britain and Canada.

Martyr: Someone who died fighting for their religion. It was believed they would have all their sins forgiven and were guaranteed a place in paradise.

Merchant ships: Ships carrying goods and materials, not part of a state's navy.

Militaristic: Prioritising the armed forces over other parts of society.

Militia: A group of people trained as soldiers, but not part of a regular army.

Minutes: The written notes recorded during a meeting, describing the issues discussed, as well as responses or decisions.

Mobilise: Prepare and organise troops for active service.

Monopoly: Total control of something (usually a trade) without any competition.

Moral outrage: Anger that other people have been mistreated.

Munitions: Things needed for war, including shells, bullets, guns and uniforms.

Mutiny: When soldiers or sailors rebel and refuse to follow orders.

Napalm: A type of bomb that contains flammable liquids, and which burns anything it comes into contact with.

Nationalise: To make something the property of the state.

Nationalist: Believing strongly in your own country.

Nomadic: Moving around from place to place rather than living in one place only.

Passive resistance: Non-violent opposition to authority.

Patriotism: Love for your own country.

Pogrom: Violent attacks directed against an ethnic minority, such as Jews.

Police state: A country where the government uses the police to spy on the people and stamps out any opposition.

Prolateriat: A collective noun used by Marxists to describe the class of workers.

Propaganda: Communications (for example, posters and films) designed to mislead people by giving a very biased view.

Prostitute: A person who has sex in exchange for money.

Proxy war: A war in which the 'superpowers' fight indirectly through other countries. The wars in Korea and Vietnam can be seen as examples of proxy wars.

Puppet state: A country that appears to be independent, but is actually largely controlled by another country.

Quaker: A member of the 'Society of Friends', a faith group who reject violence as a means to bringing about change.

Reichstag: The name given to the German parliament.

Repeal: Withdrawing an Act of Parliament.

Ritualistic: Set actions performed as part of a ceremony, usually with religious importance.

Royal standard: The monarch's flag.

Sanction: A type of punishment. Sanctions (such as bans on exports to other countries) are used internationally to punish countries that break international laws.

Segregation: Separating people based on their race, for example, making black people attend different schools to white people.

Shia and Sunni: Branches of Islam. Shias share many beliefs and practices with Sunni Muslims, but there are also differences that have led to conflict between Sunni and Shia.

Sit-in: Occupying a place and refusing to leave as a protest.

Sonderkommando: Jewish prisoners who were forced to help the Nazis to operate the gas chambers.

SS: Short for Schutzstaffel (protection squad), the SS were elite Nazi troops. Some operated within the army, others as police. They were heavily involved in running concentration and extermination camps during the Holocaust.

Stalemate: a situation where nobody in a conflict can win.

Stereotype: A widely held, but heavily simplified and often untrue view of someone or something – for example, that English people drink tea all day and eat fish and chips.

Suez Canal: Canal that connects the Mediterranean Sea to the Red Sea, meaning that ships going from west to east do not have to travel all the way around Africa. It opened in 1869, took ten years to construct and is 100 miles long.

Suffrage: The right to vote in elections.

Superpower: A nation that is immensely powerful and influential. Used to refer to the USA and USSR during the Cold War.

Synagogue: A Jewish place of worship.

The Balkans: An area in south-east Europe that included Albania, Bosnia, Bulgaria, Herzegovina, Greece, Kosovo, Macedonia, Montenegro, Serbia and Turkey.

The theory of evolution: Darwin theorised that evolution happens by natural selection – animals that are unable to adapt to their environment die, while those that can adapt survive and pass on their traits to subsequent generations.

Trade unions: Organisations of workers. They aimed to defend their members' interests, for example, by negotiating better pay and conditions.

United Nations (UN): An international organisation set up in 1945 to try to solve international problems and to build peace around the world.

Weapons of mass destruction: Nuclear, chemical or biological weapons that can kill very large numbers of people.

Western Front: The zone of fighting that stretched from Switzerland to the English Channel.

Answers

Chapter 1

Page 38

1 Constituencies reorganised and franchise extended to industrial towns
2 The ideal woman, from a Victorian man's point of view
3 She could control all the money and property brought with her into the marriage and everything she earned after the marriage
4 Elizabeth Garrett Anderson
5 Any two from: first woman to obtain a first-class history degree from Oxford, wrote and had published a number of books about her travels, climbed a number of mountains, spoke fluent Arabic, first female political officer in the British Armed Forces, only woman present at the Cairo Conference, helped install Faisal I as king of Iraq, set up a library and museum in Baghdad
6 Passed the Cat and Mouse Act, authorised force-feeding
7 National Union of Women's Suffrage Societies
8 1903
9 Any two from a large range: e.g. working in gas works, breweries, shipyards, as bus and tram conductors, as chimney sweeps and in munitions factories
10 1928

Chapter 2

Page 56

1 1870
2 Alsace and Lorraine
3 1871
4 Schlieffen Plan
5 (i) To defend/trade with colonies
   (ii) to challenge naval supremacy of GB
6 Dreadnought; 1906
7 Triple Entente: GB, France and Russia; Triple Alliance: Germany, Austria-Hungary, Italy
8 A secret society aimed at uniting all Serbs
9 Archduke Franz Ferdinand, heir to the throne of Austria-Hungary
10 5 August 1914

Page 69

1 1.1 million had enlisted
2 1916, compulsory enlistment
3 Western and Eastern Fronts
4 Western Front
5 Area between opposing trench lines

6 Any two from: reserve trenches, support trenches, front-line trenches, barbed wire, small post, dug-out, company command post
7 1916, General Haig
8 1919, Versailles
9 Any one from: blood transfusion and storage, x-rays, plastic surgery
10 League of Nations

Chapter 3

Page 102

1 Bolsheviks or Communists
2 *Mein Kampf*
3 Hiroshima and Nagasaki
4 Stalin
5 'Iron Curtain'
6 The Korean War
7 Cuba
8 Vietnam

Chapter 4

Page 130

1 Examples include in science (Einstein, Meitner), psychoanalysis (Freud), painting (Liebermann), literature (Kafka)
2 An anti-Semetic book, published in 1905
3 A night of violence against German Jews
4 The evacuation of German Jewish children to Britain
5 The Second World War

Chapter 5

Page 162

1 Any three from Turkey, Iraq, Iran, Syria, Israel, Saudi Arabia, Egypt, Kuwait, State of Palestine, United Arab Emirates, Qatar, Lebanon, Jordan, Yemen, Oman, Bahrain and Cyprus.
2 For fighting with the Bedouin tribes against Turkey.
3 A terrorist attack
4 The Aswan Dam
5 Saudi Arabia, Syria and Egypt
6 The Pentagon

Chapter 6

Page 190

1   Newgate prison
2   Josephine Butler
3   Abraham Lincoln
4   1649
5   British monopoly over salt production
6   December 1955-December 1956
7   Examines books, films, photographs and plays to remove anything believed to be unsuitable
8   To convince everyone they were working well.
9   One from: political parties/Family Planning Association/ Department of Health and Social Security
10 1969
11 One from: Al-Qaeda/WSPU/ALF/IRA
12 1990

Index

Acknowledgements

The authors and publisher would like to thank the following individuals and organisations for their kind permission to reproduce copyright material.

Photographs

(Key: b-bottom; c-centre; l-left ; r-right; t-top)

Alamy Stock Photo: Pictorial Press Ltd 16, 26, 58r, 71, 85, 100, 107, 178bl, 193, 195r, KGPA Ltd 19b, History collection 2016 20,167, Heritage Image Partnership Ltd 22, 27, 28br, 105, Glasshouse Images 23, Chronicle 28t,32, 43, 46, 126, 127, 165t, Amoret Tanner 28bl, 67, Hilary Morgan 30t, Hirarchivum Press 30bl, World History Archive 31, 45b, 88, 114, Classic Image 33, Peter Horree 42, akg-images 52, Historic Collection 53b,173, Hi-Story 61, John Frost Newspapers 65, James Bartholomew 75, Everett Collection Historical 80, 86, 89, 96, 195l, Prisma by Dukas Presseagentur GmbH 81l, Granger Historical Picture Archive 81r, 135, 175l, DOD Photo 87, US Army Photo 95t, Stocktrek Images, Inc. 98, A.P.S. (UK) 104, Itzhak Genut/ArkReligion.com/Art Directors & TRIP 110, INTERFOTO 113, Ruby 119, Archive PL 122t, 196b, ZUMA Press Inc 123, Military History Collection 138, Trinity Mirror/Mirrorpix 144l, Chris Hellier 145, Kaveh Kazemi/Hulton Archive 147, Bill Lyons 154, The Picture Art Collection 165b, CSU Archives/Everett Collection/Everett Collection Inc 175r, 184, Shawshots 177t, Fine Art Images/Heritage Image Partnership Ltd 177b, John Sturrock 178br, Richard Smith 185t, Trinity Mirror/Mirrorpix 185b, 186t, 187t; **BAE Systems plc:** Reproduced under licence from and courtesy of BAE SYSTEMS 66; **Bridgeman Images:** Hogarth, William (1697-1764)/Courtesy of the Trustees of Sir John Soane's Museum, London 9, English School, (19th century)/Manchester Central Library, UK 11, Universal History Archive/ UIG 15, Cauty, Horace Henry (1846-1909)/Private Collection/© Christopher Wood Gallery, London, UK 19t, Pictures from History 21, German School, (15th century)/ Private Collection 106, Weesop, John (d. c.1653)/Private Collection 171, © The Advertising Archives 178t; **Darryl Tomlin:** Darryl Tomlin 125; **Getty Images:** Matt Cardy/Getty Images News 10, Mansell/The LIFE Picture Collection 14, Hulton Archive 17, 30br, Topical Press Agency/Hulton Archive 34, Popperfoto 45t, Bettmann 51, 132l, 144r, 192, De Agostini Picture Library/DEA/A. DAGLI ORTI 53t, Paul Popper/Popperfoto 56, 62, Alfred Leete/Imperial War Museums 58l, Hulton-Deutsch Collection/Corbis Historical 115, The Jewish Museum/Getty Images News/Getty Images Europe 118, Sovfoto/Universal Images Group 122b, Keystone/Hulton Archive 140, Maher Attar/ Sygma 141, Keystone-France/Gamma-Keystone 143, NORBERT SCHILLER/AFP 148, Allan Tannenbaum/The LIFE Images Collection 152, David Handschuh/New York Daily News Archive 156, Chris Hondros/Getty Images News 158tl, Graeme Robertson/ Getty Images News 158tr, Joe Raedle/Getty Images News 158bl, 158br, JM LOPEZ/ AFP 159t, ALI AL-SAADI/AFP 159c, AHMAD AL-RUBAYE/AFP 159b, MPI/Archive Photos 169, Universal History Archive/Universal Images Group 172, Don Cravens/The LIFE Images Collection 174, Fred Morley/Hulton Archive 176, Popperfoto 183, Thomas Imo/ Photothek 188, Rolls Press/Popperfoto 196t, Three Lions/Hulton Archive 196c; **Gulf News:** Gulf News, Dubai 132r; **Jewish Museum London:** Courtesy of Jewish Museum London 111; **Mary Evans Picture Library:** © Illustrated London News Ltd/Mary Evans 64, Mary Evans Picture Library 109, Grenville Collins Postcard Collection 134; **PA Images:** PA/PA Archive 186b; **Punch Cartoons:** PUNCH Magazine Cartoon Archive, www.punch.co.uk 35; **REUTERS:** Dylan Martinez 187b; **Shutterstock:** Nick Ut/AP 95B; News (UK) Ltd 179; **United States Holocaust Memorial Museum:** United States Holocaust Memorial Museum, courtesy of Library of Congress 112, United States Holocaust Memorial Museum Collection, Gift of the Katz Family 116

All other images © Pearson Education

Acknowledgements

Text

Page 055: AJP Taylor, Guardian, The entente that ended in slaughter, 4 August 1984.

Page 062: Anthony Farrar-Hockley, History press, The Somme, 1964.

Page 097: Reprinted by arrangement with The Heirs to the Estate of Martin Luther King Jr., c/o Writers House as agent for the proprietor New York, NY.

Page 155: Contains Parliamentary information licensed under the Open Parliament Licence v3.0.

Page 179, 189: Copyright guardian news & media ltd 2018. Page 189: Andrew Bolt, HeraldSun, The dark side of Nelson Mandela, December 8, 2013, © 2018.